The Spy Who Spent the War in Bed

The Spy Who Spent the War in Bed

And Other Bizarre Tales
from World War II

William B. Breuer

John Wiley & Sons, Inc.

Copyright © 2003 by William B. Breuer. All rights reserved

Published by John Wiley & Sons, Inc., Hoboken, New Jersey
Published simultaneously in Canada

For general information about our other products and services, please contact our Customer Care Department within the United States at (800) 762-2974, outside the United States at (317) 572-3993 or fax (317) 572-4002.

Wiley also publishes its books in a variety of electronic formats. Some content that appears in print may not be available in electronic books. For more information about Wiley products, visit our web site at www.wiley.com.

Library of Congress Cataloging-in-Publication Data:

Breuer, William B., date.
    The spy who spent the war in bed / William B. Breuer.
      p. cm.
    Includes bibliographical references and index.
    ISBN 0-471-26739-2 (pbk. : alk. paper)
    1. World War, 1939–1945—Miscellanea. 2. World War, 1939–1945—Deception. 3. World War, 1939–1945—Military intelligence. 4. World War, 1939–1945—Underground movements. I. Title. II. Title: The spy who spent the war in bed. III. The spy who spent the war in bed.

D743.B669 2003
940.54'85—dc21

                  2002009948

Printed in the United States of America

10 9 8 7 6 5 4 3 2 1

Dedicated to
HARVEY WEINSTEIN,
head of Miramax Films,
in gratitude from thousands
of World War II veterans
for his epic movie of
courage and sacrifice,
The Great Raid

*These are the kind of cases
in which the imagination
is baffled by the facts.*

—Winston Churchill (1943)

Contents

Part Three—The Tide Starts to Turn

Part Four—Beginning of the End

Part Five—Allied Road to Victory

Part Six—A Shaky World Peace

Introduction

As ROBERT RIPLEY HAS SAID many times, "Truth is stranger than fiction." That incisive observation could apply to this book, in which bizarre and "impossible" happenings during World War II are described.

Many books have been written about World War II, but largely absent has been a focus on the mysterious, baffling, and oddly coincidental inexplicable events that never made the headlines. This book helps to fill that void.

A reader's first impression after perusing an incident in these pages will be: "That couldn't have taken place. It wasn't logical." Yet the intriguing and often mind-boggling occurrences described here have been carefully researched and found to be authentic—because logic is usually a stranger in wartime.

There has never been, nor is there ever likely to be, a shortage of "scholarly experts" without personal experience in war who scoff at episodes that defy the accepted terms of logic. However, combat veterans and top commanders know that mystifying affairs often surfaced and that they were indeed "stranger than fiction."

Part One

A Rocky Road to War

Amazing Encounter at Pier 86

ICY BLASTS OF WIND rocked the port of Wilhelmshaven as Admiral Wilhelm Canaris strolled into the branch office of the Abwehr, Germany's cloak-and-dagger agency. Only a few weeks earlier, the forty-seven-year-old, five-foot-six spymaster had been ordered by the new dictator, Adolf Hitler, to "energize and rejuvenate" the Abwehr, which had been virtually decimated by the terms of the Versailles Treaty imposed on a defeated Germany at the end of the Great War, as it was known. It was now February 2, 1935.

Canaris had come to inspect the Wilhelmshaven station, and he delivered a rousing speech to the staff, describing the United States as "one of the key targets" in the Abwehr's worldwide operations.

"The USA must be regarded as the decisive factor in any future war," the admiral exclaimed. "The capacity of its industrial power is such as to assure victory, not merely for the USA itself, but also for any country with which it may be associated."

Across the Atlantic Ocean, eight months after Canaris's speech at Wilhelmshaven, Pier 86 on the Hudson River in New York City was teeming with passengers preparing to board the luxury liner *Europa*, pride of the North German Lloyd Line. Morris Josephs, a U.S. Customs agent, was mingling with the crowd when he spotted a thin, bespectacled man carrying a violin case.

"What kind of violin do you have there?" Josephs asked pleasantly.

"Oh, just an ordinary fiddle," William Lonkowski, the American correspondent for *Luftreise*, a popular aviation magazine in Germany, replied.

"Is that so," Josephs said. "Mind letting me look at it?"

The Customs agent's request was due to his personal interest in violins, not to a suspicion that this man might be trying to smuggle out merchandise without paying duty on it.

Lonkowski opened the case, and as the agent lifted out the violin, his eyes widened. Under the instrument was a collection of papers that looked like photocopies of airplane blueprints.

Josephs replaced the violin and said, "Please come with me."

In the Customs office at the pier, Josephs and John W. Roberts, who was in charge of Customs for the New York City area, searched Lonkowski and found in his pockets film negatives and several letters written in German and

FBI agent with hidden camera snapped Nazi master spy Nickolaus Ritter (left) as he left the German ocean liner Bremen *in New York harbor. FBI did not know his identity when this picture was taken, but he had come to join William Lonkowski. (FBI)*

addressed to various persons in the Third Reich, as Hitler had proclaimed the nation. The film appeared to show drawings of airplanes, and the letters contained wording that looked like aircraft specifications.

Lonkowski explained that the materials were to illustrate an article he was doing for *Luftreise*.

Not certain about what action, if any, to take, Roberts telephoned Major Stanley Grogan, the Army intelligence officer for the region, at Governor's Island in New York harbor. An hour later Grogan arrived at the Customs office, glanced at the detainee who was seated calmly in a corner, and began examining the materials Lonkowski had in his possession.

Grogan asked the magazine writer to explain several pieces. "Much of this looks curious for an article in a civilian aviation magazine," the major declared.

One letter especially aroused Grogan's interest. It indicated that secret military information was being stolen at Langley Field, an Army air base in Virginia. Portions of other letters gave evidence that defense secrets were also being pilfered at several other military facilities and defense plants.

There was much more in Lonkowski's cache: photographs of a new Curtiss fighter plane and of a Voight scout bomber. Attached to the pictures were highly technical reports on each aircraft's design and capabilities. A sheaf of papers told of a top-secret four-engined bomber to be known as a B-17, or Flying Fortress, that was being built by Glenn Martin Company in Baltimore.

After an all-night session, Major Grogan and the Customs supervisor discussed what action, if any, to take. They realized that they didn't even know the detainee's name. One called across the room, "Hey, fellow, what's your name?"

Lonkowski paused momentarily, then replied, "William Lonkowski."

"Well, Mr. Lonkowski," the Customs supervisor said evenly, "you can go now, but be back in three days. We might have a few more questions to ask."

Casually, Lonkowski put on his hat and with a pleasant "Good morning, gentlemen," strolled out the door. Flagging a Yellow Cab, he leaped inside and headed for his home on Long Island.

Lonkowski could not believe his amazing good fortune. He had been caught red-handed while loaded with stolen U.S. military secrets. But these incredibly naïve Americans had turned loose one of Nazi Germany's most dangerous and productive spies—without taking down his home address.

There had been an even more astonishing aspect to this bizarre episode. At the time Customs Agent Morris Josephs had approached him, the spy was in the act of handing the violin case to the *Europa*'s steward, who was actually the ship's Orstgruppenführer, the Nazi Party functionary who had total control of the vessel. An Orstgruppenführer could even issue orders to a ship's captain—orders that had better be obeyed. When the Nazi official saw Josephs, he dashed back into the ship.

After this close call at Pier 86, Lonkowski hid out for four days in Manhattan, and then he was driven to Canada by one of his German spies, Ulrich Haussmann, who was in the United States under the cover of being a reporter for a Berlin magazine. At a port on the broad St. Lawrence River, a German freighter had just finished unloading, and Lonkowski was smuggled abroad.

After arriving in the Fatherland, Lonkowski was hailed by the Abwehr as a conquering hero. During the past few years, he had organized a widespread spy ring, mainly in the New York City area, and collectively they had stolen about every major military secret the United States possessed. He was not only eulogized by Admiral Wilhelm Canaris, but also given a hefty cash bonus. A delighted Adolf Hitler provided him with a top job in the Air Ministry.

One of the greatest spies in history would never know that there had been no real need for his frantic escape from the United States. The incriminating espionage materials found on him at Pier 86 were pigeonholed at Governor's Island and the episode largely forgotten.[1]

A British "Mystery Plane" Vanishes

ON FEBRUARY 24, 1938, Royal Air Force Flight Lieutenant F. S. Gardiner took off from an airfield at Farnborough, England, in an experimental aircraft. It was a Vickers-Wellesley (later Wellington) two-engine monoplane featuring a novel-type wing.

Farnborough was the site of the secret Royal Aircraft Establishment (RAE), where some of Britain's top scientists and engineers conducted experiments on new aircraft and studies on foreign planes. Lieutenant Gardiner's flight was wrapped in a cocoon of secrecy.

The Vickers-Wellesley bomber, which had been designed to fly a world's nonstop record (or to strike at Germany in case of war), vanished. When no trace of the mystery plane or its pilot could be found, rumors spread about their fate.

One report being widely circulated was that fighter planes in the rapidly growing German Luftwaffe had laid in wait for the experimental aircraft and then shot it down off the coast of Scotland. Later, it was alleged, a team of German divers, operating mostly at night, salvaged the wreckage and carried it back to the Third Reich on a U-boat (submarine).

German intelligence supposedly had been tipped off about the flight of the mystery plane by a spy whose task was to keep watch on the RAE at Farnborough. But whether the Germans had indeed scored this spectacular intelligence bonanza would never be known for sure.[2]

A One-Man Espionage Apparatus

FRITZ BLOCK WAS a mild-mannered, unpretentious businessman who was German but owned and operated a ladies' dress factory in Amsterdam. Most of his stylish garments were exported, especially to England. He was married to an American woman whose parents lived in London, so he made frequent visits to that city.

On February 15, 1938, the thirty-nine-year-old Block arrived alone in London, presumably to look into his export business. But actually, he had been sent there by Erich Pheiffer, who held a doctorate in political economy and was second in command of the Wilhelmshaven branch of the Abwehr, Germany's secret service agency. Pheiffer's title was V-*Mann Leiter* (leader of agents).

Several weeks earlier Block had volunteered to be a spy for the Abwehr. After being checked out he was dispatched to London for the mandatory field test for new agents. His assignment was to take photographs of sensitive installations.

When Block returned to Wilhelmshaven, Pheiffer was astonished. The embryo spy had brought back scores of photos, including the water storage reservoirs of King George and Queen Mary, eight of the thirteen main sources of London's water supply, and relay stations of the Metropolitan Electricity Board.

Later this key information was incorporated into the special target maps that would be used by the German Luftwaffe when it hammered Britain in mid-1940.

Erich Pheiffer knew now that he had an ace agent. So in the months ahead he had Block return to London many times to visit his wife's parents. He collected more than four hundred photographs, sketches, and maps, along with some one hundred and fifty reports on British defense facilities.

His "album" contained snapshots of such strategic targets as airfields around southern England, shipyards, and gun emplacements along the White Cliffs of Dover facing France across the English Channel. His "scrapbook" of reports focused on aircraft factories.

Amazingly, although Adolf Hitler was vigorously rattling his saber, Fritz Block was never accosted a single time by law enforcement officers or security agents. Conceivably, the spy's unpretentious demeanor and professorial countenance contributed to his seeming immunity from suspicion.

Block had another attribute to deflect attention—brains.

At this time the British government was distributing secret notices to newspaper editors and radio officials, listing defense installations, fortifications, and ammunition depots. These civilian media were asked not to mention them in print or broadcast. Block gained access to these secret "D" documents through a friend on Fleet Street, the London newspaper district. This intelligence proved to be a bonanza for the Abwehr. These papers not only listed the "secret" installations, but also included a description of them and their purposes and where they were located.

Fritz Block was an enigma. Why did he risk his freedom, even his life, by spying? He expected no praise from German leaders, and got none. He was not gripped by a superpatriotism, and he may not even have belonged to the Nazi Party. Money was no factor; throughout his brilliant espionage career the Abwehr paid him the equivalent of $200 per month.

Whatever had motivated the shy, soft-spoken Block, he may have been Germany's ace spy during the war.[3]

Recruiting Crossword Puzzle Geniuses

BLETCHLEY PARK WAS a large, gloomy Victorian mansion near the London and Scottish Railway just outside the sleepy town of Bletchley, some forty-five miles north of London. Over the years, Bletchley Park sat largely unnoticed except by the succession of owners. Then in late May 1938, a strange article appeared in the *Bletchley District Gazette*, a small weekly newspaper, that set tongues to wagging in the region. The piece stated that some unknown person, presumably connected to the government, had purchased the property in great secrecy.

This Victorian mansion at Bletchley Park was home to the British crossword puzzle geniuses. (National Archives)

The mystery deepened when crews descended upon the grounds immediately and began laying telephone lines, and the foreman on the site refused to disclose anything about the cables.

Unbeknownst to anyone outside of a handful in Whitehall (the government offices in London), the mystery buyer was Admiral Hugh Sinclair, head of the cloak-and-dagger agency known as MI-6, which was responsible for collecting intelligence and conducting espionage abroad.

Within MI-6 was the supersecret Government Code and Cipher School, which was responsible for breaking foreign cryptograms. Deducing that war with Nazi Germany was inevitable, Sinclair wanted to move the GC&CS to a remote locale in anticipation of German bombings of London. Bletchley Park, he concluded, was ideal, and he petitioned the Treasury for 7,500 pounds sterling (about U.S. $35,000) to buy the property. Frustrated by the refusal of the Treasury to put up the money to buy what he was convinced were needed accommodations, Sinclair dug deep into his savings and bought Bletchley Park himself.

It was while Sinclair, an energetic, charismatic leader who had the reputation for being something of a lady's man, had been inspecting his new holdings a few days later that he bumped into a *Bletchley District Gazette* reporter who demanded to know what use was going to be made of the property. Forced to create a cover story on the spur of the moment, Sinclair said it was to be used in the air defense of England.

That offhand explanation had triggered the *Gazette* "mystery story." But the mystery grew thicker when the Air Ministry in London stated it knew nothing about Bletchley Park.

On August 1, 1939, precisely one month before Adolf Hitler would ignite what came to be known as World War II by invading neighboring Poland, Admiral Sinclair ordered the GC&CS to move immediately to Bletchley Park. Staff members were shoehorned into the mansion and other buildings on the grounds. Barely controlled chaos erupted.

When Great Britain declared war on Nazi Germany on September 3, leading British scientists, mathematicians, and cryptanalysts even more energetically plunged into the primary mission of GC&CS: break the "unbreakable" Enigma code used by the German military and government to send out hundreds of messages each day.

All the while Bletchley Park was searching for cryptanalyst (those who break codes) talent from the general population. Cracking Enigma would be a task requiring teamwork by hundreds of people. Many techniques were utilized to locate and recruit the desired talent, but perhaps the most imaginative focused on crossword puzzle addicts.

For nearly fifteen years, Leonard S. Dawe, a quiet, unassuming physics teacher, and his friend, Melville Jones, also an educator, had created each morning's *London Daily Telegraph* crossword puzzle. In that time, their tough, intricate puzzles had exasperated and enthralled countless millions.

In 1941, the *Telegraph*, amidst much hoopla, published its five thousandth puzzle. That announcement generated a blizzard of letters from addicts who claimed they had never failed to solve each day's puzzle. An avalanche of mail resulted in the *Telegraph's* holding a competition to determine the champion solver.

Twenty-five men and women were invited to compete. Each was given a puzzle to solve, and the winner's time was seven minutes and fifty-seven seconds. Others followed within only short intervals.

A few days later, each of the contestants received a letter on official government stationery inviting him or her to call on a certain army officer to discuss "a matter of national importance." Most of the curious contestants responded. Many of these crossword puzzle geniuses had accepted the invitation out of curiosity. Only after they had been interviewed at length—grilled would be a better description—the mystery colonel identified himself as being with GC&CS and the prospect was asked to join the Bletchley Park team. Most eagerly joined up.

Much of the actual work of breaking codes was not a matter of science or mathematics, but the mental habits the job required were ones that crossword puzzle solvers possessed, psychological studies had disclosed. They tend to think in ways that separate them from most men and women.

Through the diligent efforts of the brainy people and after countless thousands of hours of painstakingly scrutinizing huge masses of intercepted Enigma wireless messages, the Bletchley Park team cracked the code. The seemingly impossible feat would prove to be an intelligence bonanza of unprecedented magnitude.

German deciphered information was given the code name Ultra. Throughout most of the remainder of the long war, the British (and later the Americans) would have the enormous advantage of knowing in advance the precise plans of Adolf Hitler and his military commanders.

But could this remarkable situation have been achieved had not the frustrated Admiral Hugh Sinclair personally bought the remote estate to provide space, secrecy, and security for the clandestine experiments? Or would the "unbreakable" German code have been deciphered without the aid of a large number of faceless crossword puzzle addicts with brilliant intellects?[4]

New York's IRA Hoodwinks Spymaster

OSKAR KARL PFAUS had come to the United States from Germany in the mid-1920s, and over the years he took a stab at a wide array of jobs. An impetuous type, he was always seeking adventure. He had been a cowboy, a prospector, a forester, a newspaper columnist, and had tramped around the nation in boxcars as a hobo.

In between these endeavors, he served a short stretch in the peacetime U.S. Army and he wrangled a job as a policeman in Chicago, where he eagerly learned the tricks of undercover work on assignments against the notorious and powerful Al Capone mob.

In late 1938, Pfaus returned to Germany on a nostalgic visit and was smitten by the promise of Nazism. This outlook fit precisely the contents of a newspaper column he had penned a few years earlier in which he proposed a movement to be known as the Global Brotherhood.

While in the Fatherland, the restless Pfaus made contact with the Abwehr and offered his services in whatever capacity needed. On February 1, 1939, he was dispatched to Ireland to coordinate arrangements for the Irish Republican Army (IRA) to step up its sabotage and espionage operations in England.

On the completion of his mission, Pfaus enthusiastically told his Abwehr controller in Berlin that an anti-American IRA underground was organized in New York City. Consequently, Karl Franz Rekowski, a forty-eight-year-old Austrian businessman, was assigned the task of encouraging dissident Irishmen in New York and Boston to launch sabotage operations. Energetic, shrewd, and a devout Nazi, Rekowski was an ideal choice—he had worked for years as a paper salesman in the United States and spoke the language like a native.

Rekowski was briefed by his Abwehr controller and assigned the code name Rex. No doubt realizing the enormous potential of harnessing dissident Irishmen in the United States, Rekowski was given an enormous sum of money—$200,000 (equivalent to some U.S. $3 million in 2002).

He was told to commute between New York and the Abwehr's major station in Mexico City.

On June 6, 1940, Rekowski arrived by ship in New York City and promptly began contacting leaders of the IRA whose names and addresses had been provided the Abwehr by Oskar Pfaus. One of the first men Rekowski talked to was identified as "the roving ambassador of the Irish Republican Army in the United States." In a report to Berlin, Rekowski said that "this patriot is the organizer of sabotage in America."

In another report to Berlin, Rekowski said that "the Irish have agreed to undertake sabotage on a substantial scale . . . against British ships in New York, Boston, and elsewhere, and against warehouses filled with war supplies to be sent to England."

Rekowski listed "a few" of the sabotage operations conducted by "our Irish friends." An explosion at the Hercules Powder plant at Kenvil, New Jersey, which killed fifty-two people, injured one hundred, and left the facility a charred wreckage. One day, only minutes apart, tremendous explosions virtually destroyed war production plants at Edinboro, Pennsylvania, and Woodbridge, New Jersey. He mailed newspaper clippings to support his claims.

Rekowski realized that he had to cover his trail to his Irish agents, so he spent a good deal of time in Mexico City, where the Abwehr agents masqueraded as employees of the German Embassy. No mission was too bizarre. In one cable to Berlin, he asked for the formulae "of stink bombs to disrupt political rallies in the United States."

Rekowski explained that he could not safely leave Mexico City to supervise actual operations in the United States because he was convinced that he was being tailed, possibly by agents of the Federal Bureau of Investigation who were operating covertly with the secret blessings of the Mexican government. However, Rekowski held periodic meetings at night at a secluded locale outside of Mexico City with Irish agents coming from New York City.

A major logistics problem for Rekowski was the smuggling of the bulky explosives from Mexico to New York City. He resolved this problem by having Berlin provide his "Northern friends" with the formulae of explosive compounds that they could concoct themselves.

During the next six months, Rekowski bombarded Berlin with vivid accounts of the carnage his "Northern friends" were perpetrating: damaged ships, charred forests, wrecked factories, derailed trains.

At his headquarters in Berlin, Admiral Wilhelm Canaris, the Abwehr chief, showered his enterprising operative in Mexico City with profuse praise. Only later would Rekowski learn that he had been hoodwinked by his own IRA accomplices. Their highly successful boom-and-bang operations had been largely the product of their own vivid imaginations.

It had been a curious venture. Rekowski had shuttled most of the huge amount of money he had been receiving from Berlin to his "Northern friends," who had gotten rich and were leading the high life at his—and Adolf Hitler's—expense. His dreams of becoming wealthy from Operation Rex, as his mission was called, and using his new fortune to get into a legitimate business in Mexico City would forever remain a fantasy.[5]

Stalking a Soviet Defector

IN EARLY 1939, Admiral Wilhelm Canaris, chief of the Abwehr, Germany's far-flung cloak-and-dagger agency, launched the strangest and most mysterious operation ever mounted in the United States. Curiously, the maneuver did not directly affect America, whose antisubversive capabilities were virtually nonexistent. The target was General Walter Gregorievitch Krivitsky, a former chief of Soviet intelligence for Western Europe.

Two years earlier Krivitsky had emerged from the shadows in The Hague, Holland, and rocked the world's intelligence organizations by announcing that he had "broken with (Josef) Stalin" and would seek asylum in the West.

Every secret service was eager to make contact with this fugitive, none more so than the Abwehr. Through bribes or by brutal methods, the Germans hoped to obtain information about the large ring of Soviet spies known to be operating in the Third Reich.

Before Abwehr agents could track Krivitsky down, they learned that he had sailed for the United States. So Canaris ordered his ace operator for locating refugees, Dr. Hans Wesemann, to take up the chase in America.

Wesemann was clever and charming. He had been welcomed into the best society circles in European capitals. His specialty, one that endeared him to Adolf Hitler, was kidnapping émigrés.

Two years earlier, Wesemann had engineered the abduction of Berthold Jacob, a famous military writer, who was living in Switzerland. But Swiss police arrested Wesemann, and during his trial he confessed to being associated with the Nazis and declared that he had learned his lesson. After two years in prison, however, he secretly returned to the service of the Abwehr.

Soon he was working on a scheme to kidnap Willie Muenzenberg, a former leading Soviet propagandist, who was living in exile in Paris. Then he was suddenly taken off that operation and rushed to the United States, traveling on a phony passport that listed his occupation as "journalist."

Wesemann had been in New York City only a few days when he bumped into an old friend, Emery Kelen, at a bus stop on Lexington Avenue. Kelen had a global recognition as a political cartoonist, and he had been friendly with the German during the early thirties in Geneva, where Wesemann headed a news service.

Kelen was astonished that a notorious Nazi spy and convicted kidnapper would be running loose in America. Without a word, Wesemann spun around and fled, losing himself in the throng of pedestrians.

Kelen rushed to a nearby telephone booth and called the local Federal Bureau of Investigation office on Foley Square to give notice that the Nazi agent was in the United States. However, at that time the FBI was not responsible for investigating matters involving espionage, sabotage, and subversive activities, and apparently did not follow up on the report.

Meanwhile, Walter Krivitsky was seeking to hide out in New York City, but Wesemann quickly got on his trail, following the Russian wherever he went. The refugee, an astute man, soon became aware that not one but two agents were tailing him. The second spy was a hit man for the Soviet secret service, the GPU, who was known as "Hans the Red Judas."

Krivitsky knew that the Red Judas was in the United States to kill him. Even worse, he feared that the slick Hans Wesemann would kidnap him, sneak him aboard a German ship in New York harbor, and send him to the Gestapo in Germany.

One day Krivitsky came out of a restaurant on Times Square and literally bumped into the Red Judas, whom he had known back in Russia. Exasperated, Krivitsky asked, "Did you come to kill me, Hans?" The unexpected question seemed to shock the assassin. He blurted out, "Not me!" and he hurried away.

Presumably the Red Judas deduced that Krivitsky was being shadowed by FBI agents, and he did not want to be caught near the refugee. So the Red Judas was not seen again, and presumably had gone back to Russia.

Hans Wesemann apparently knew nothing about the Red Judas and his confrontation with the target in Times Square. So the German continued to shadow the former Soviet spy chief.

After war broke out in Europe on September 1, Wesemann became extremely nervous. He advised the Abwehr in Berlin that "the American authorities obviously suspect that my presence here is connected with activities for you."

Wesemann was ordered to remain on the job, which was to kidnap Krivitsky. But a few weeks later, when the secret agent pleaded that "the authorities are closing in on me," the Abwehr permitted him to take a Japanese ship to Tokyo.

Shortly after the German reached his destination, a cable from Berlin advised him to return to the United States by way of Brazil and resume the Krivitsky chase. He had to spend many months getting out of Japan and more weeks in South America, but by December 1940, Wesemann was back in New York City.

By now, Krivitsky was beginning to find the strain of his exile and being hunted like a beast for eighteen months to be unbearable. On February 9, 1941, he was in Washington, D.C., and checked in at the Hotel Bellevue. It was 6:00 P.M. and the capital was gripped by cold and snow.

The next morning a maid knocked on Krivitsky's locked door, and when there was no reply, she entered with a passkey. The woman stifled a scream. Sprawled across the bed was the guest, a pistol near one hand. Police ruled the death a suicide.

Reading about Krivitsky's death in the *Washington Star*, the devious-minded Wesemann decided to take full advantage of the situation to embellish his own reputation as a cagey operative. Through the German Embassy, he sent a coded cable to the Abwehr in Berlin, taking full credit for the demise of General Walter Krivitsky.[6]

Two Spies Roam British Ports

By NEW YEAR'S DAY 1939, Adolf Hitler had decided to launch war in Europe by invading neighboring Poland with his powerful Wehrmacht.

England would most certainly come to the aid of Poland, the führer knew, so he instructed his Oberkommando der Wehrmacht (German High Command) to collect intelligence to pave the way for an eventual invasion of the British Isles.

The burden of gathering information about British ports and bases belonged to "M" branch, the Abwehr's naval intelligence service headed by Captain Hermann Menzel. A man in his early fifties, Menzel had the ideal attributes for a successful spymaster: cunning, resourcefulness, and a passion for personal anonymity.

It was too late to plant German agents in British ports (Hitler planned to strike on September 1). So Menzel assigned the task to his D-K group, whose specialty was matters dealing with foreign ports and installations.

Two *Kriegsmarine* (navy) captains, Hans Kirschenlohr and Erwin Schmidt, donned civilian clothes and entered England several times under the guise of businessmen. They returned to Germany loaded with charts of the ports of Plymouth, Swansea, Barry, Greenwich, Dagenham, Gravesend, Purfleet, and all the harbors in the Thames estuary leading from the English Channel to London. The two spies' reports included detailed descriptions of the port installations and fortifications, along with current hydrographic and topographical data.

In the meantime, Captain Menzel planted his trained and experienced spies on German cargo ships skippered by men of the D-K group known as *Dampfer-Kapitaen* (merchant marine masters). These merchantmen ostensibly were involved in peaceful commercial trade, but the ships' captains were ready to launch an espionage mission on a moment's notice.

When Navy headquarters in Germany called for information on the Isle of Wight, off England's southern coast, an agent posing as a photographer on a civilian liner was assigned to the task. As the ship leisurely circled the island, the agent clicked away with his camera, returning with scores of photographs of shore fortifications.

Incredibly, with ominous war clouds gathering over Europe, a D-K ship managed to insinuate its way into the major naval base of Portsmouth to monitor the Royal Navy's wireless traffic, which provided first-rate information on the fleet's communications patterns.

When England declared war on Nazi Germany on September 3, 1939, Grossadmiral Erich Raeder, commander of the German navy, was armed with perhaps as much information about British ports and installations as was the Admiralty in London.[7]

Stealing Secrets by Mail

FREDERICK JOUBERT DUQUESNE was the brain of a German spy ring based in New York City. In his forty years as a secret agent in various countries, he had posed as a magazine writer, lecturer, newspaper reporter, botanist, and scientist. Born in South Africa, the sixty-two-year-old spy often told friends that he was motivated by his "insatiable hatred of anything British."

Now, in early 1939, Duquesne had been harvesting bountiful crops of America's military secrets. He sent to Germany the blueprints of a new bomber, drawings of range-finders, blind-flying instruments, and sketches or blueprints of other top-secret devices of the U.S. armed forces.

Duquesne obtained most of his leads by scanning the *New York Times,* which historically boasted it covered all the news that is fit to print. Among the "fit" news were items on new military weapons and devices. America was living in an Alice in Wonderland world.

One day the master spy saw an item in the *Times* that electrified him. It stated that the Chemical Warfare Service of the Army was developing a mysterious new gas mask. Not only would the design of the gas mask be of immense value to Adolf Hitler's generals, but it would also provide clues about the nature of the new poison gases the U.S. Army was developing.

Duquesne always approached an espionage task as though it were a military operation. He concluded that it would probably be impossible to sneak into the Army's top-secret Aberdeen Proving Ground in Maryland, where new devices were tested, so he would make a flanking attack instead of a frontal assault.

An FBI hidden camera took this picture of ace Nazi spy Frederick Duquesne on a New York City street. (FBI)

On stationery carrying his true home address in New York City, he wrote a letter to the chief of the Chemical Warfare Service in Washington, D.C., identifying himself as a "well-known, responsible and reputable writer and lecturer." Then he asked for information on the new gas mask.

Across the bottom of the typed letter, Duquesne wrote in longhand: "Don't be concerned if this information is confidential, because it will be in the hands of a good, patriotic citizen."

A short time later all the information the German spy had asked for arrived in the mail at his home. A week later it was being read with great interest by intelligence officers in Berlin.[8]

"Simple Simon" Trips Himself Up

EVEN BEFORE Adolf Hitler plunged Europe into war on September 1, 1939, the Abwehr was confident it could flood England with spies through her back door, neighboring Ireland. Consequently, German agents were sent to Ireland, but one after the other, they met with mishaps before they even arrived at their destination.

Soon the Abwehr branch in Hamburg responsible for subversive activities against the British Isles had exhausted its pool of potential agents and began scraping the bottom of the barrel. By now Germany was at war with England, so the Abwehr broke a time-tested rule among cloak-and-dagger agencies: never send a fallen agent to his or her old beat. So a not-too-bright Walter Simon was tapped to sneak into Ireland, then infiltrate England.

Simon was well known to British security officers from his having spent a few months in Wandsworth Prison, in late 1939. The Britons had known that he was a spy, but they couldn't prove it, so he was released.

Now the Abwehr in Hamburg provided Simon with an AFU radio and sent him to Ireland. His phony passport identified him as Karl Anderson.

At dawn on June 13, Simon waded ashore at a remote locale in southwest Ireland, then walked to a nearby railroad station. There he walked up to three Irishmen who apparently were waiting for the next train.

Speaking fluent English with an Irish accent, Simon asked, "When is the next train due for Dublin?"

The strangers eyed him suspiciously for several moments, then one replied: "The last train for Dublin left here fourteen years ago. I reckon it might be another fourteen years before the *next* train will leave."

An hour later Simon was ensconced in the local jail. His spying career was over.[9]

A Taxi Ignores Theory

IN THE LATE 1930S, even while Nazi dictator Adolf Hitler was grabbing up one country after the other in Europe, U.S. armed forces were small in number and lacked guns, tanks, and artillery. Its clandestine agencies were operating on a shoestring. One of the latter was the army's hush-hush Signal Intelligence Service (SIS), whose task was to break enemy codes.

Even now, with a woefully weak America being threatened on the east by Nazi Germany and on the west by the powerful Japanese war machine, the covert operation had to be kept under wraps so that so-called civil libertarians in the United States didn't rise up and howl because foreign radio messages were secretly being intercepted and studied by the SIS.

As a cover in the event of wide public outcries in America, the official instruction for the SIS was that the interception of foreign radio signals was for "training purposes only." The small number of cryptanalysts that the agency's budget could retain was told to deny any involvement in breaking codes. If anyone asked, they were to say they were studying War Department communications.

When Adolf Hitler invaded Poland on September 1, 1939, and Great Britain and France declared war on Nazi Germany, Americans demanded that the nation remain out of the conflict unless the United States itself were invaded by "foreign armies," according to major opinion polls.

At his office in the Munitions Building in downtown Washington, D.C., William F. Friedman, the SIS chief, was a genius, not only in breaking codes, but attracting brainy people who would work at the puny salaries the budget permitted. Because of the nature of the tedious work that demanded long hours and intricate study, most of the SIS cryptanalysts marched to their own drummer and had what outsiders would consider to be "peculiar outlooks."

One of those in that category that Friedman recruited was John B. Hurt, who joined up after the invasion of Poland. Hurt was a free spirit. He had attended several colleges, but had graduated from none of them. However, he had the type of analytical mind that Friedman was seeking. Hurt had taught himself to speak the complicated Japanese language without ever having been in Japan or ever having taken a course in that vernacular.

Like most of his SIS colleagues, Hurt had his own ideas about what living on Planet Earth should be. One of the theories he practiced was that when crossing a street he would ignore traffic. If a vehicle were bearing down on him while en route to the other side of the street, he stared at it as one would an approaching animal and it would halt.

On one occasion Hurt was crossing a busy Washington street when an oncoming taxi presumably paid no attention to his "stare." Hurt was brushed by the vehicle and knocked down. The cabbie halted the taxi, leaped out, and ran back to the man he had hit.

Hurt was still lying in the street, and the anguished cabbie repeated over and over: "Are you hurt? Are you hurt?"

The SIS analyst got to his feet, said, "Yes, John B.," and walked on across the street.[10]

The IRA Bilks the Abwehr

IN EARLY JANUARY 1940, MI-5, the British agency responsible for homeland security, received a tip that unknown saboteurs were going to blow up the Royal Gunpowder factory at Waltham Abbey. Chief Inspector William Salisbury, who had just been assigned to MI-5 from his post in Scotland Yard's famed murder squad, was handed the case.

Before Salisbury could act, three loud explosions inside the factory killed five people, injured thirty, and badly damaged the crucial plant.

No doubt in an effort to calm jitters among the people, the British government firmly denied that these explosions, and several other bombings that had occurred since war erupted four months earlier, had been caused by "enemy action."

That disclaimer was technically accurate; none of the perpetrators were *enemy* nationals. But at Abwehr headquarters in Berlin, the series of bombings were attributed to "a group of Irish patriots with whom we are in contact."

Ireland had long been in a state of undeclared war against England. Early in 1939 Jupp Hoven and Howard Clissman, two German intellectuals living in Ireland, had become deeply impressed with the "achievements" of the Irish Republican Army (IRA), the boom-and-bang arm of the anti-British movement. They took note of the fact that the IRA had blown up power stations and business places in London, Birmingham, Manchester, and Almwick, wrecked a major communications cable, and planted an infernal machine in crowded King's Cross Station that killed several Londoners.

Just after war had broken out in Europe, Hoven and Clissman went to Berlin and called on the Abwehr. Why not establish a working partnership with the 15,000-member IRA for a major sabotage campaign against England?

Colonel Erwin von Lahousen, who directed sabotage operations for the Abwehr, was enthused about the prospect of having 15,000 potential agents ready and presumably willing to mount sneak attacks across St. George's Channel and the Irish Sea, to strike clandestinely through England's "back door."

Colonel Lahousen soon sent Captain Friedrich Marwede, a career intelligence officer whose specialty was "dirty tricks," and Kurt Haller, a civilian expert in boom-and-bang operations, to Ireland to hold covert meetings with IRA leaders. Much to the delight of the two Germans, they found that the IRA already had a complex and wide-ranging plan whose goal was "the paralysis of all official activity in England and the greatest possible destruction of British defense installations."

No doubt with the approval of Adolf Hitler, the equivalent to millions of American dollars was funneled to IRA cash registers. In return, the IRA conducted only a few minor bombings, while shrewdly taking full credit and boasting about a wide array of industrial, marine, and railroad accidents with which they were in no way involved.[11]

Clash of Two Top Nazis

ENERGETIC, ASTUTE Dr. Hans Thomsen, the chargé d'affaires in the German Embassy in Washington, D.C., was deeply involved in a keep-America-neutral campaign. His boss in Berlin, Foreign Minister Joachim von Ribbentrop, had been ordered by Adolf Hitler to mastermind a pacification program to keep Uncle Sam from aiding beleaguered Great Britain.

Ribbentrop's grand strategy was to flood the United States with propaganda and for saboteurs to refrain from committing acts of violence that might arouse the sleeping giant and draw it into the shooting war.

Thomsen knew that he had been handed a tall order. The overwhelming majority of Americans were sympathetic to England and convinced that Germany was the culprit in the war in Europe. Consequently, Thomsen became highly agitated when he heard rumblings over the Nazi grapevine that professional saboteurs were being infiltrated into the United States.

On January 17, 1940, the diplomat cabled Ribbentrop: "There will be dire consequences [to German plans] if any attempt is made to carry out sabotage operations in the United States at this time."

Despite the urgent warning, the rumors of saboteurs persisted. On January 25, Thomsen again cabled Ribbentrop: "I have learned that a German-American,

A major target for Nazi boom-and-bang expert Georg Busch was the huge Triborough Bridge that connects three boroughs of New York City. (New York Port Authority)

von Hausberger, and a German citizen are planning acts of sabotage against the American arms industry by direction of the Abwehr. I gravely call attention to the danger which such activities, if discovered, would represent to German American relations during the current period of tension."

Thomsen anxiously awaited a reply. None came. His worst suspicions were confirmed. The Abwehr was not concerned with what Americans thought; it was interested in conducting boom-and-bang operations in the United States. The fact that Ribbentrop and the Abwehr chief, Admiral Wilhelm Canaris, hated each other contributed to the weird conflict in America between two of Hitler's top henchmen.

Four weeks later, on February 20, a husky man walked into the German Embassy, identified himself as Walter von Hausberger, and said that he had been sent to the United States to conduct sabotage on a massive scale. He said that he had come to the embassy for a personal reason: he was broke.

A week later a self-styled master saboteur who called himself Julius Georg Bergman also appeared at the embassy with the same problem: he was out of money.

Thomsen was horrified to be sheltering a pair of boom-and-bang desperadoes, who might well blow to smithereens Ribbentrop's strategy for keeping America neutral. He cabled Berlin, protesting the appearance in Washington of the two saboteurs. The reply came: the Foreign Office had checked with Admiral Canaris—the Abwehr had never heard of Hausberger or Bergman.

Thomsen was furious. He knew the reply was a blatant lie. So he sent another cable: "If the saboteurs were not Abwehr agents, then why had they been trained in sabotage techniques at the Abwehr's school in Hamburg?"

Ten days later Colonel Erwin von Lahousen, a covert operations officer in Abwehr headquarters in Berlin, wrote to Thomsen. The colonel had suddenly recovered his memory. Now he recalled that he had indeed sent Hausberger and Bergman to the United States, but only as "observers." The two agents had strict orders not to conduct any action remotely resembling sabotage, Lahousen explained.

Actually, for more than a year, Lahousen and his staff had been implementing a master plan for launching a series of sabotage operations in America. Through Nazi agents already in place, a long list of key targets had been drawn up. Detailed information had been obtained on power plants, factories, railroads, water works, and telephone exchanges.

Nazi agents also sent Berlin descriptions and maps of all major cities, with New York selected as the main target. One eager spy mailed to Berlin the blueprints of New York City's water supply system, and another supplied details and maps of strategic spots in the U.S. railway system, including the Horseshoe Curve of the Pennsylvania Railroad near Altoona and the Triborough Bridge over the East River in New York City.

Reports for sabotage purposes disclosed a wide variety of operations. An enterprising Nazi spy eagerly suggested to Berlin that German saboteurs sneak into the United States by private aircraft, and he provided a detailed map showing the locations of more than fifty Long Island golf courses that could be used for landing fields.

Far from being a benign "observer," as Colonel Lahousen had described him, Walter von Hausberger was an ardent boom-and-bang operative. Since arriving in the United States a year earlier, he had planted saboteurs at the Packard, Ford, Chrysler, and Hudson automobile factories in Detroit, at the Harrison Gas Works in New Jersey, in the New York Liquidometer factory, and at the four Brewster aviation plants.

Julius Bergman, the other spy the nervous Hans Thomsen had been forced to harbor in the German Embassy, was a hardened old pro in the sabotage and espionage fields. Bergman was an alias. His true name was Georg Busch, a one-time music publisher who had decided he would rather blow things up.

After reaching the United States in mid-1939, Bergman purchased a modest home in a New York City suburb (with Abwehr funds) and began collecting a large cache of explosives, caps, and fuses. His main targets would be ships in New York harbor.

Taking along a pair of genuine American stevedores he had recruited, Bergman conducted several reconnaissances of the waterfront. He was shocked by an almost total absence of security. Looking for places to hide bombs later, the three men boarded two large cargo ships and wandered around for more than thirty minutes without being challenged.

Bergman excitedly told the Abwehr in Berlin that he could blow many ships "sky high" and that all he needed were funds to begin active operations. However, no money would be sent.

Unbeknownst to Bergman, Foreign Minister Joachim von Ribbentrop had emerged victorious in his strange behind-the-scenes duel with the Abwehr. Fearful that ships being blown up in New York harbor might tilt America toward joining England in a shooting war, the boom-and-bang operations were squashed—at least for the present time.[12]

Hitler's Pipeline into Washington

DURING THE EARLY MONTHS OF 1940, while Adolf Hitler was preparing to launch an all-out offensive against France, Belgium, the Netherlands, and Luxembourg, Hans Thomsen, a Nazi master spy in Washington, was pulling off a dynamite intelligence coup. Thomsen, a shrewd practitioner of devious machinations, was masquerading as a chargé d'affaires at the dreary German Embassy on Massachusetts Avenue.

When armed violence had erupted in Europe on September 1, 1939, Thomsen had been convinced that America would eventually be drawn into the war against Germany, or at least break off diplomatic relations, actions that would expel Hitler's diplomatic corps and leave the Third Reich without eyes and ears in Washington.

So the cagey Thomsen created a pipeline directly into the inner sanctum of the U.S. State Department. The coup was scored because of the amazingly lax security in that key branch of government. Secrets in the State Department code room had long been waiting to be plucked, and the German master spy was bent on doing the picking.

State's code room was located in the old State, War and Navy Building on Pennsylvania Avenue, and had been headed for twenty-nine years by David A. Salmon. Even when ultrasecret codebooks had been stolen repeatedly over the years, the code room did not change its means for communicating with scores of embassies overseas. That method was a cryptograph system invented a hundred and fifty years earlier by Thomas Jefferson, the first secretary of state.

Even in 1939, as Hitler was igniting war in Europe, when Admiral W. H. Stanley, ambassador to the Soviet Union, cabled home that it was "a matter of common gossip" in Europe that the State Department codes were insecure, nothing was done to change Jefferson's antiquated cryptology system.

A year after Stanley's urgent warning, on April 30, 1940, Hans Thomsen cabled his boss in Berlin, Foreign Minister Joachim von Ribbentrop: "A reliable and tried confidential agent who is friendly with the director of the [State Department] code room reports as follows after having seen the relevant telegraphic reports." The chargé d'affaires then related verbatim a secret message sent from London by Joseph P. Kennedy, the U.S. ambassador to Great Britain.

A few days later Thomsen cabled Berlin messages sent by U.S. ambassadors in Spain and in Portugal, along with other top-secret materials.

This intelligence bonanza proved to be an enormous advantage to Adolf Hitler, for it permitted him to plan strategy with full knowledge of what was going on in enemy and neutral camps.

Thomsen's "reliable and tried confidential agent" was a slick German spy who had cultivated the friendship of Joseph P. Dugan, technical operating chief of the State Department code room.

Dugan had allowed himself to be trapped in an enormous indiscretion because of the almost nonexistent security measures in the code room and his deep-rooted isolationist views, ones held by millions of Americans at that time. "Keep out of other nation's quarrels!" was the slogan across the nation.

Dugan often discussed the cables arriving in the code room with his trusted friend who, he thought, shared his isolationist opinion. So when the German spy asked Dugan to bring home key cables for him to copy, Dugan complied. The "friend" had explained that the top-secret information was to be passed on to "certain [isolationist] friends in Congress" who were "entitled to know what is going on in the Roosevelt administration."

Dugan was convinced that his "friend" was a selfless American patriot who was deeply worried that his country was heading hell-bent down the road to war. So this devastating code-room espionage bonanza continued for a year and a half.[13]

A Senator Helps a German Spy

IT SEEMED TO BE a routine, insignificant act. Simon Emil Koedel, who had served in the U.S. Army as a corporal in what was known as the Great War, applied for membership in the American Ordnance Association (AOA), a semi-official, quasi-confidential organization of armament and munitions makers that was virtually a branch of the War Department's Ordnance.

In his application, Koedel stated that he was a chemical engineer and a large stockholder in such major defense industries as Sperry Gyroscope, Curtiss-Wright, and several factories producing ammunition. Enclosed was a copy of his Army discharge papers.

L. A. Codd, secretary of the AOA, was impressed. "You can be justly proud of your service to our country," Codd wrote back in granting membership to Koedel. It was late 1939.

Neither Codd nor anyone else in the AOA had even a clue that the sixty-one-year-old Koedel, who had indeed served in the U.S. Army, was a spy, holding the rank of captain in the Abwehr, Germany's cloak-and-dagger agency.

Koedel's registry number in Germany was A.2011. The prefix "A" meant that he was one of the regular secret agents, a professional. The "2" indicated that he worked for the Abwehr subbranch in Bremen, and "011" showed his place in the registry. His low number identified him as being an early secret agent.

Koedel had been born in Würzburg, Germany, and had come to the United States in 1906. Five years later he became an American citizen. On a sentimental visit back to the homeland in 1937, Koedel had become mesmerized by the vision of Führer Adolf Hitler's plan for one world under the Nazi banner. So the World War I corporal in the U.S. Army called at the Abwehr substation in Bremen, and volunteered to act as a spy in his adopted homeland. After an investigation of Koedel's background, the Abwehr accepted him into its ranks and he was commissioned as a captain in the German army.

Now, three years later, Koedel had already impressed the Abwehr with his energy and resourcefulness. He had been sending back a stream of information sought by Bremen. Unlike most spies, the gray-haired operative made no bones about his views of America. In an apparent temper tantrum, he wrote to the commanding general of the 43rd Infantry Division, the Connecticut National Guard, that the average American was a "double-crosser" and "crooked at heart."

With his acceptance into the AOA, the lean, wiry man with the hard cold eyes had fulfilled his scheme to worm his way into the innermost secrets of the American defense industry and into the War Department itself. This "patriotic" citizen now enjoyed all of the confidential privileges that belonging to the AOA entailed.

Koedel was placed on the War Department's confidential mailing list, and all releases involving ordnance, a gold mine for a spy, were delivered by mail to the Abwehr agent's apartment at 660 Riverside Drive, in New York City.

In March 1940, Adolf Hitler was preparing to launch Case Yellow, a massive invasion of France, Belgium, the Netherlands, and Luxembourg. But the Oberkommando der Wehrmacht (German High Command) in Berlin was hampered in its planning by the lack of specific information on the French ports of Nantes, La Pallice, and La Rochelle.

The German generals and admirals needed to know what size ships these ports could handle, and the Abwehr was ordered to get the facts—and soon. Along with many agents scattered about the world, Simon Koedel was contacted. But how could a man working as a chemist in New York City, three thousand miles from the French ports, acquire such detailed information?

Koedel plunged into the challenge. Through his membership in the AOA the spy had developed a friendship with Senator Robert A. Reynolds of North Carolina, who was impressed by the great amount of time and effort this patriot and war veteran had been expending in the interest of America's security. Koedel contacted Reynolds, the powerful chairman of the Senate Military Affairs Committee, and explained that he needed information on the three French ports. This data would assist him in making arrangements for shipping supplies to France.

Senator Reynolds was delighted to help his crony and at the same time benefit France. He promptly wrote a letter on his official Senate stationery to the U.S. Maritime Commission, and on April 9 Koedel received a communication from the agency in his mailbox.

Koedel promptly informed his Abwehr controller in Bremen: "According to the U.S. Maritime Commission, these [three] ports are not limited in their facilities, but are capable of handling ships loading oil and coal, as well as general cargo."

A month later, on May 10, 1940, Adolf Hitler unleashed his war juggernaut against France and the Low Countries.[14]

A Peculiar River Crossing

MAJOR GIJSBERTUS SAS, an assistant military attaché at the Dutch Embassy in Berlin, was dining with an old friend, Colonel Hans Oster, at Horcher's, a popular restaurant in the German capital. The seeming leisurely social affair was actually gripped with tension and intrigue. It was the night of May 8, 1940.

Colonel Oster was second in command of the Abwehr, the German cloak-and-dagger agency that had hundreds of agents sprinkled around the world. Oster also was a leader in the Schwarze Kapelle (Black Orchestra), a conspiracy of German military, civic, and government leaders bent on getting rid of Adolf Hitler and the Nazi regime.

For months Oster had been slipping secret information to Sas, who sent it on to Dutch and Belgian intelligence authorities. They, in turn, passed the information on to MI-6, Great Britain's intelligence branch.

Now, at Horcher's, Hans Oster had blockbuster news for Sas: Adolf Hitler had ordered a massive invasion of France and the Low Countries, to be unleashed on the morning of May 10.

Major Sas rushed to his office and telephoned the War Ministry in The Hague. There the top Dutch intelligence officer discounted the report.

At dawn on the designated day, hundreds of panzers clanked across the German border. Some 2 million foot soldiers headed for objectives. Hitler had scored a total tactical surprise.

In the path of the powerful German war juggernaut stood the Royal Dutch Army—far outnumbered, outgunned, and ill-equipped. As the invaders pushed rapidly inland, the Dutch soldiers resisted tenaciously, but soon were overwhelmed. When one SS regiment reached the town of Bornebroek, its advance was halted by a blown bridge over a river.

Officers dispatched small groups of SS men to scavenge the farms in the region. They returned with an array of large doors they had ripped off barns.

These items were used as improvised rafts. No doubt it was the only time in the war that an assault crossing of a river against an entrenched foe was made by men riding barn doors.[15]

Dame Fate Saves General Rommel

"GENERAL ROMMEL IS EVERYWHERE!" a German captain reported to a high-ranking official at headquarters.

The junior officer was referring to Erwin Eugen Rommel, who at forty-seven years of age was leading his crack 7th Panzer Division hell-bent across France after the German army invaded the country on May 10, 1940.

On the night of May 13, Rommel was with his spearheads when they were forcing a crossing of the Meuse River. By morning thirty tanks were across what the French had counted on to be a major barrier to German advances.

General Erwin Rommel was the second most popular German on the home front. Here he graces the cover of a magazine. (National Archives)

Rommel ordered his tanks to drive on. Three miles west of the Meuse he was in a tank with his face pressed against the periscope. A French shell exploded.

A fragment struck the periscope through which Rommel was peering. The splinters flew to each side of his face. Had it not been for the periscope, the man who would become one of the war's outstanding generals would have been killed instantly.[16]

Going in Style to a POW Camp

IN THE EARLY MORNING DARKNESS of May 10, 1940, a cavalcade of blacked-out vehicles rolled up to a huge concrete bunker on a mountaintop near the ancient city of Aachen, on the western border of Germany. Emerging from a limousine, Adolf Hitler strode into the thick-walled fortification, which would be his command post for directing Case Yellow, an all-out offensive on the Western Front.

In only two weeks, the spirited Wehrmacht conquered Belgium, the Netherlands, and Luxembourg and trapped some 340,000 British and French troops at Dunkirk, on the English Channel.

Incredibly, Hitler ordered his divisions to halt in place while Reichs-marschall Hermann Goering's powerful Luftwaffe would wage the remainder of the battle above the beaches. Goering, one of the most pompous of the Nazi leaders, had guaranteed the führer that not a single British or French soldier would escape from the trap.

Hurricanes and Spitfires, the newest and best British fighter planes, repeatedly challenged the German flights. In one instance, six Hurricanes pounced on a Junkers 88 bomber piloted by Captain Hajo Hermann and shot up both engines. Hermann managed to guide the stricken aircraft to a crash landing in the water just off the beach. Before the plane sank, all on board managed to get out and reach the shore.

Realizing that they were in no-man's-land, the Germans slipped back into the cold water and began wading along the shallows in search of friendly uniforms. Soon they came upon one of the Hurricane pilots responsible for their predicament. He, too, had been shot down and was trudging through the water to find British soldiers.

Outnumbered, the Royal Air Force pilot was taken in tow by the Germans, and the bedraggled group pressed onward along the shore. Luck was with Captain Hermann and his crew. They stumbled onto German positions.

Hermann commandeered a large black limousine and drove his prisoner to a POW compound in Belgium. The Briton may have been the only captive in the war to have been hauled to a POW enclosure in a limousine.[17]

Clanging Bells Rock Germany

LESS THAN ONE MONTH after Adolf Hitler had sent his powerful war juggernaut charging into France and the Low Countries, British Prime Minister
Winston S. Churchill was in his bombproof command post deep beneath the
pavement in London. Drawing on a long, black cigar and peering through eye-
glasses resting near the tip of his nose, the portly sixty-six-year-old Churchill
was studying reports on Operation Dynamo, a massive, improvised evacuation
of British and French forces that had been trapped in the English Channel
port of Dunkirk. It was June 5, 1940.

On the previous day, the last waterlogged Allied soldier had been snatched
off the fire-swept beaches. The prime minister was stunned. Although a near-
miracle had brought 338,226 men to England, the refugees arrived with only
twenty-five tanks, twelve artillery pieces, and a few machine guns.

Left behind along the French coast were 63,879 vehicles, 2,472 artillery
pieces and mortars, 8,000 Bren guns, 90,000 rifles, and 76,097 tons of shells
and ammunition. Great Britain had suffered a shocking military debacle, perhaps the worst in her history.

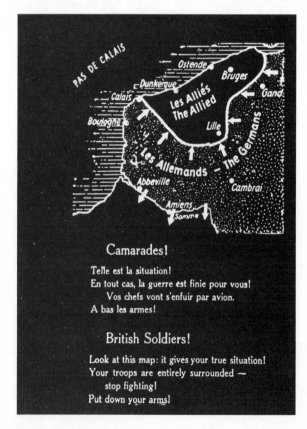

*Thousands of these accurate
maps were dropped from the
air on British and French
forces trapped at Dunkirk.
(Author's collection)*

In his ornate, high-ceiling office in the Chancellery in Berlin, Adolf Hitler was euphoric. Now the stubborn Churchill had no course but to surrender. In his unbridled glee, he failed to realize how hollow the victory would be. Despite the gargantuan loss of most of their weapons and vehicles, 338,226 veteran Allied soldiers had been saved to fight again.

In the meanwhile, Hitler was determined to stridently tell the world about his "invincible" Wehrmacht's feat. He decreed that all bells in the Third Reich should toll continuously for three days and three nights. No doubt at the conclusion of the clanging-and-banging celebration, most of the *Herrenvolk* (people) hoped they would never again hear a pealing bell.[18]

Did Prime Minister's Mistress Influence Surrender?

EVEN BEFORE the last British and French soldiers had been evacuated from Dunkirk, Adolf Hitler sent his panzer-tipped spearheads racing onward. Within two weeks, the French Army, which had been hailed as the world's best, simply came apart.

On June 10, 1940, French Prime Minister Paul Reynaud and his entourage, including his mistress Countess Hélène de Portes, fled Paris and set up the seat of government in Tours, one hundred and fifty miles southwest of the imperiled capital.

With the battle of France near an end, the sixty-two-year-old Reynaud was confronted by two choices: surrender, or salvage what remained of the French armed forces and ship it southward across the Mediterranean to continue the war against Hitler from North Africa.

Reynaud's own cabinet was deeply divided on a course of action. He was being hammered from all sides. His morale was under attack from a more intimate source: the Countess de Portes. Reynaud's mistress, a thirty-year-old chattering woman who had floated about in Parisian high society for years, was said to have nurtured fantasies of running France the way the Marquise de Pompadour, the mistress of Louis XV, had done two centuries earlier.

At times she did indeed think that she was a leader of France. A few months earlier, the journalist Pierre Lazareff called on Reynaud and found that he was in bed with the flu. But "government" was continuing to function. Surrounded by generals, high officials, and members of parliament who sat quietly like schoolboys, the Countess de Portes, seated behind a large desk, was presiding over the meeting. "She did most of the talking, speaking sharply and with a tone of authority," Lazareff would later say.

Having both wealth and title, the countess was unkempt and had a raucous voice. Circles in Paris had been unable to fathom why she had such a

*French Prime Minister
Paul Reynaud. Did his
young mistress cause
France to surrender?
(National Archives)*

fatal allure for Reynaud. Whatever may have been the case, she sustained him and goaded him in his ambitions.

This peculiar woman was highly in favor of immediate capitulation to Adolf Hitler. Her role in encouraging the defeatist elements around Reynaud was a crucial one.

H. Freeman Matthews, the First Secretary of the American Embassy, who had been in almost constant touch with Reynaud since the führer struck in the West, said, "Never once did I see him that Hélène de Portes was not just coming out of or going into his office. I think his gradual loss of nerve was in large part due to her influence on him."

By now most of France's leaders were reconciled to defeat. Hearing of this mood, the British Prime Minister, Winston Churchill, flew to Tours for a last-ditch plea to Reynaud and his generals. The Briton urged them to fight for Paris "street by street, as we are prepared to do for our cities."

Reducing Paris to ashes would make no change in the final result, the spunky Churchill was told.

Two days later, on June 14, not a shot was fired as spirited German soldiers barged into Paris. They goose-stepped under the Arc de Triomphe and down the broad Champs-Élysées, while a gigantic swastika flag was placed atop the Eiffel Tower.

Still, Winston Churchill was determined to goad the French generals into continuing the fight. Again he flew to Tours. But things were in such chaos that there was no one to greet the British leader at the airport, and he had to hitchhike a ride in a private conveyance to Reynaud's headquarters. Gloom was thick. German spearheads were only sixty miles away and advancing almost at will.

Efforts by Reynaud and his officials to reach some decision were fruitless. All the while, the Countess de Portes hovered outside the conference room.

She sent in a message: "Tell Paul that we must give up. We must make an end of it. There must be an armistice!"

On June 16, Reynaud resigned his office. No doubt the countess knew that her heavy-handed and incessant badgering of her paramour had paid off. The remainder in the rump government would seek an immediate armistice.

Reynaud and his mistress fled Bordeaux by automobile. A week later she died instantly when the car he was driving ran off the road and struck a tree.[19]

Venus de Milo Fools Germans

ON A LOVELY SUMMER DAY in Europe Adolf Hitler arrived in the woods of Compiègne outside Paris. In only six weeks, the führer's mighty legions had crushed the once vaunted French Army. Now the Nazi warlord was going to lay down his armistice terms to the defeated French generals. It was June 21, 1940.

The extravaganza would take place on the same spot where Germany had capitulated to France and her allies on November 11, 1918: a railway car that was sitting in a clearing in the Compiègne woods.

Hitler, solemn-faced, climbed into the old railway coach in which the French delegation was seated, and, according to script, seated himself in the chair that had been occupied by French Marshal Ferdinand Foch, the Allied commander, in 1918.

When the armistice was signed, the führer and his entourage departed.

In the meantime, some 25,000 German soldiers occupied Paris and promptly began enjoying the pleasures of the City of Light until duty called them elsewhere.

In the months ahead, Germans wandering around Paris may have numbered 200,000. On leave, they flocked to the city from all over France. Although wine and women were the primary attractions for the young *Feldgrau* (field gray, the average German soldier), their sojourns in Paris were not without cultural enlightment.

When the soldiers reached the fabled Louvre, France's great treasure house of art, they viewed the famous *Venus de Milo* with awe. The statue of the goddess of love had probably been sculpted in the first or second century B.C. by an unknown Greek master.

None of the tens of thousands of Germans who traipsed to the Louvre to ogle *Venus de Milo* were aware that they were the victims of a monumental hoax. When the German armies had been nearing Paris, French authorities removed the marble masterpiece and replaced it with a plaster replica. The genuine sculpture would remain hidden in France until after the war.[20]

Part Two

The Allies' Hours of Crises

Mission: "Nazify"
a Conquered Nation

LUXEMBOURG, with its rolling hills, forests, and ancient castles, is one of the smallest and oldest nations of Europe. It covers an area that is about the size of Rhode Island in the United States. In the spring of 1940, when Adolf Hitler unleashed his mighty legions to conquer much of Western Europe, Luxembourg, with an army smaller than the New York City police department, was rapidly overrun.

Luxembourg's historical links with Germany date back to the Holy Roman Empire of medieval times. Despite those roots, Hitler called the tiny nation "enemy territory" because the proud Luxembourgers refused to benignly accept their new masters and because the Grand Duchess Charlotte, the legal ruler, had fled to England.

The German warlord sent to Luxembourg a staunch Nazi, Gustav Simon, to serve as *Gauleiter*, a political appointee who was to act as head of a German civil government. Simon was charged with "recovering the former German Reichsland for the German empire."

Like other gauleiters, Simon had been selected mainly for his unswerving devotion to the Nazi cause and to Hitler, not through aptitude. On his arrival in the capital of Luxembourg City, Simon laid down his goal in a public statement: "On the day when the first grave for a German hero-soldier was dug, we made the following decision: This land was won and will be kept by German blood and therefore will remain German for all eternity."

Simon then began issuing a series of stern edicts. German would replace French as Luxembourg's official language. Nazi textbooks were introduced to the schools, and the courts were reorganized along German lines. Post offices and utilities were no longer part of Luxembourg: they were integrated into the Third Reich's systems.

All political parties in the nation were banned—except for the Nazi Party. Luxembourgers were ordered to Germanize their names, and change all place names, street signs, and building names to German.

In his zeal to "Nazify" Luxembourg, Simon even decreed that the inscriptions on tombstones were to be changed to German.[1]

Curfew for Dutch Dogs and Ducks

ALMOST FROM THE MINUTE the Dutch were forced to capitulate to the German war juggernaut in May 1940, patriots began publishing underground newspapers that uplifted the spirits of the masses and bedeviled the Nazi occupiers. These "illegal" journals exhorted the people to organize and resist, and offered advice on how to achieve that goal.

At first the underground press was mainly primitive newsletters, but soon these were replaced by sophisticated publications, written and edited by professionals and distributed by couriers at great personal risk.

The journalists did their work in churches, attics, basements, garages, factories, and laundries. One enterprising Dutch publisher even set up a printing plant in a haystack. Readership of these clandestine newspapers was heavy, and their influence was so pronounced that the Germans organized special branches to wipe out these pesky publications.

Ridicule of the Germans was the primary focus of the journalists. Almost every issue contained parodies that generated widespread glee among the subjugated Dutch people and thoroughly angered the Nazi masters.

On June 5, 1944, the issue of the *Haarlemse Courant* took a humorous swipe at the Nazis' top officer, SS General Hans Rauter, who, it was stated, had imposed a curfew for dogs and ducks for their anti-German activities.

Dutch underground members printing a clandestine newspaper. (Dutch Institute for War Documentation)

The Dutch people loved the phony decree, and Rauter and his German underlings went berserk. An immediate investigation was launched to try to uncover ties between the *Haarlemse Courant* publishers and the Allied secret service in London. These Dutch journalists had to have been informed of the date of the Allied invasion, which struck Normandy the next day, and had timed the biting parody of the dogs and ducks accordingly.

Actually, it had been simple happenstance.[2]

Wild Schemes for Saving England

GREAT BRITAIN HAD STOOD for centuries against the periodic threat of invasion. But not since the Spanish Armada sailed against the country in 1588 had the British Isles been in such grave danger. It was the summer of 1940.

After Dunkirk, the British army was in disarray and lacking weapons and supplies; the Royal Air Force, whose pilots were of high quality, was small; and the Royal Navy, although remaining one of the world's largest, was seriously extended in its operations to patrol the English Channel and to keep open the supply routes from the United States and elsewhere around the world.

Winston S. Churchill, who had succeeded Neville Chamberlain as prime minister after the Dunkirk debacle, was counting on a top-secret organization to help thwart a looming Wehrmacht invasion from across the Channel. Headed by an energetic, brainy Canadian in his late thirties, Charles F. Goodeve, the clandestine group of scientific geniuses was known as the Directorate of Miscellaneous Weapons Development (DMWD). They called themselves the Wheezers and Dodgers, and their function was to conceive offbeat accoutrements of war.

Lieutenant Commander Goodeve and his free-spirited associates would eventually develop a wide array of weapons and equipment that would play a major role in the conflict in Europe. One of the reasons for the Wheezers and Dodgers' success was that the team was willing to tackle any proposed idea that flooded the British Admiralty in this era of extreme danger.

One man came calling with plans for a death ray. It could be mounted in one of the navy's balloons, and he gave detailed specifications of what the operator in the balloon basket would need in the way of provisions and signaling devices.

"But what about the death-ray apparatus itself?" a navy officer asked.

"Oh, that's no problem," the caller declared. "The Admiralty is bound to have several death rays in its secret archives, so you can take your pick!"

Another proposal that came from the public was one intended to confuse and misdirect the Luftwaffe night bombers with searchlight beams that solidified at the appropriate moment. A targeted aircraft would be smacked by the beam until it dived to earth. There was one shortcoming in the plan for this ingenious weapon:

"What would be the actual method for solidifying the searchlight rays?"

"Oh, that's merely a matter of research and development," was the reply.

There was no shortage of fanciful means put forward by citizens to discourage German invaders. While the enemy soldiers were wading ashore, they would be electrocuted by high-tension cables laid on the Channel bed. Brushed off by the protagonists of this scheme was the enormous amount of power required, perhaps as much as was being used to provide electricity for all of England.

Ideas were submitted—and considered—for machine guns fired by centrifugal force. Unfortunately, the lightest of these weapons would have weighed several tons.

At the time of the blitz in mid-1940, when Reichsmarschall Hermann Goering's Luftwaffe was trying to pound Great Britain into submission, a plan reached DMWD that mesmerized the Wheezers and Dodgers. It called for building a gargantuan antiaircraft mountain, thousands of feet high, in Kent in southeastern England. From atop this towering elevation, the scheme's advocates argued, even high-flying German bombers could be shot down before they got to London.

Other plans reached DMWD for a unique gun to be mounted on merchant ships. The weapon was supposed to squirt columns of water at approaching aircraft, presumably with the goal of drowning Luftwaffe pilots in midair.

Sophisticated renderings of an amazing contraption, called a Rocket Guard Rail by its sponsors, could enable the Home Guard (elderly men and boys) to fire two-inch projectiles from the shoulder. The great merit of this contraption, its advocates enthused, was that it could later be used to club German paratroopers.

Not all the flaky schemes circulating in the high levels of the British government and military came from civilians. One of the Wheezers and Dodgers, Lieutenant J. H. G. Goodfellow, managed to frighten top officials when the British Isles were bracing for a cross-Channel invasion. He wrote a memorandum in which he calculated that Adolf Hitler, by using slave labor, could build two tunnels under the English Channel in only eighteen months.

Goodfellow's memo ignited a series of rumors that the German army in France was already feverishly involved in burrowing their way to England.[3]

Curious Duel in British Skies

DAWN WAS BREAKING OVER EUROPE when thousands of German airmen climbed into Junkers, Dorniers, Heinkels, Stukas, and Messershmitts at scores of airfields in France, Belgium, the Netherlands, Norway, and Denmark. Armed

Defiant British civilians kept daily score of air battles. Many tallies were exaggerated, such as this one. (National Archives)

with photographs of their targets (taken by the civilian airlines Lufthansa "weather flights" over England before the war), the Luftwaffe men were brimming with confidence. As their planes sped down runways and set courses for England, those aboard were unaware that they were being "watched"—by British radar. It was August 13, 1940.

All across southern England, Royal Air Force pilots leaped into their sleek Spitfires and Hurricanes and roared skyward to meet the challenge. These young warriors were a breed apart—brash, scrappy, and courageous. The elite. All knew the survival of the empire would be at stake during the next few weeks in what Prime Minister Winston Churchill would label the Battle of Britain.

As the days and nights wore on, German air assaults grew heavier, scores of RAF planes were destroyed, and British pilots, fighting bitter air duels almost constantly, were near exhaustion. The Luftwaffe also suffered heavy casualties in planes and men, but could more easily absorb the losses, being much larger than the RAF.

One day hundreds of pilots on both sides were swarming through the skies of southern England, tangling in a wild series of dogfights. One of the lethal duels involved the top ace of the Luftwaffe, Colonel Werner Moelders, and a leading ace of the Royal Air Force, Flight Officer Adolphus "Sailor" Malan.

Moelders shot down a Spitfire, then, by happenstance, fastened onto another Spit piloted by Malan, who would have been the German ace's twenty-seventh "kill."

Malan had other ideas. He yanked his Spit into a tight right turn and managed to get behind the foe he later would learn was Moelders. Sailor squeezed the trigger of his eight Browning machine guns and sent bullets ripping into the German plane's radiator.

The bursts wounded Moelders in the legs, but he managed to fly back to France, where he survived a crash landing.

In a million-to-one encounter, the RAF ace had won this duel with Germany's ace. But they would never clash again. Newly promoted General Moelders, only twenty-eight years of age, was soon killed as a passenger on a transport plane that crashed in the Third Reich.[4]

A German Pilot's Unlikely Captor

As THE BATTLE OF BRITAIN continued to rage, scores of airplanes on both sides were being shot down. It had become an almost common sight to British civilians to see a German airman parachuting to earth. The aliens were pounced on by the Home Guard (elderly men and boys), many armed with pitchforks and clubs, and taken into custody.

Most of the intruders surrendered peacefully, perhaps glad to have survived the lethal duels in the sky. Moreover, they were convinced that the looming Wehrmacht invasion of England was a matter of days or weeks at the most, so they expected to be liberated soon.

One Luftwaffe flier who didn't subscribe to that line of thought was tall, blond Lieutenant Joseph Markl, who bailed out of a Heinkel bomber at midnight. His parachute caught on a tall pine tree outside the town of Newbury, forty-five miles west of London.

Markl cut himself loose, then hid in thick underbrush alongside a road. Three days later, a hunter and his dog approached, and the German climbed onto a large branch of a tree. The canine spotted him and barked angrily. But the hunter strolled beneath the branch without seeing the fugitive.

After eight days without food—his only sustenance was tree bark—Markl decided the invasion was not imminent, so he decided to surrender. This goal turned out to be exceedingly difficult.

Hungry, haggard, and unshaven, he began walking along a country road. Soon two bicyclists came by, and he tried to surrender to them. Their reply was to speed off as rapidly as their legs could pump.

Next a lone motorist approached, and Markl waved him down. The driver slowed, then stepped hard on the fuel pedal and raced away, leaving the German standing in a cloud of thick dust.

Perhaps a half hour later, a chauffeur-driven Bentley limousine halted beside the German. An elderly, aristocratic British woman motioned for the stranger to climb onto the seat beside her. Displaying not the least surprise nor concern, the dowager accepted the pistol and sixteen rounds of ammunition Markl handed her, then ordered the chauffeur to drive to a police station where the Luftwaffe officer was handed over to the constables.

Perhaps the owner of the limousine was the eldest British woman to "capture" an armed German during the war.[5]

The Royal Navy's Invisible Ship

ROYAL NAVY LIEUTENANT DONALD CURRIE was a retread from World War I. Between the two global conflicts, he had lived in the pastoral countryside, where he painted watercolors and did his best to avoid the daily routines he detested. Currie had left the Royal Navy after the first war because he told friends, "the regulations were so boring."

When Adolf Hitler triggered what would become known as World War II with the invasion of Poland on September 1, 1939, Currie applied for reinstatement to active duty. However, the Admiralty was unsure what the navy could do with a man who had spent the past twenty years painting watercolors in the countryside.

Then Currie learned that there was a call out for "elderly yachtsmen," and again he offered his services. This time he was accepted, and soon found himself assigned to the supersecret Directorate of Miscellaneous Weapons Development (DMWD).

Currie was assigned to a project all of his own. In an organization cloaked in mystery, he quickly became the focus of much office conjecture about the nature of his project. Some thought he was "slightly goofy, you know."

Before departing early in the day, he would tell the desk officer, "If anyone wants me I shall be in the swimming pool at Wembley." That remark in itself got tongues to wagging, especially since his arms would be loaded with paint pots, brushes, and strips of colored fabric.

On other occasions Currie would visit various museums and public libraries. After these jaunts, obscure telephone messages that made no sense to others were left for him at the DMWD office. One gave a terse description of coral formations in the Bay of Bengal.

Currie, in fact, was deeply engrossed in one-man research into methods of camouflaging ships and small craft, either in harbor or at sea. His research was based largely on a bold experiment conducted earlier by Royal Navy Lieutenant Peter Scott of HMS *Broke*.

During the First World War, the accepted camouflage technique was to dazzle-paint ships in a mosaic of colors and designs. Little effort was made to blend a ship into its background. Drawing on experience gained in his youth when stalking birds from a duck blind, Scott advanced a revolutionary new theory.

Scott noticed that on starlit or moonlit nights, a ship on the horizon was a black blob jutting up from a darker sea against a lighter sky. To counter this effect, the navy officer conducted tests that produced an off-white paint with which to camouflage the *Broke*.

Painting a ship white went against the Admiralty's hidebound view that stemmed from World War I. But the navy brass soon changed its collective mind: the white-painted *Broke* was rammed by a trawler while at anchor in an estuary. Afterward, the trawler's skipper protested that the *Broke* had been invisible. It was a spectacular triumph for Donald Currie and Peter Scott.[6]

Hitler's Plot to Murder Franco

ADOLF HITLER'S SPECIAL TRAIN was racing across Europe and halted at Hendaye in the foothills of the Pyrenees Mountains that ran along the border of France and Spain. The führer, who was the absolute master of most of Western Europe, had traveled the long distance for a face-to-face meeting with Generalissimo Francisco Franco, the El Caudillo (leader) of Spain. It was October 23, 1940.

Only a year earlier, the bloody three-year Spanish Civil War had concluded and Franco emerged as undisputed dictator. Thereafter he concentrated on consolidating his personal power and keeping Spain out of another savage conflict.

Adolf Hitler had other ideas. He was bent on using his considerable powers of persuasion to coerce Franco to declare war on Great Britain and join the Nazi camp. He had seriously underestimated the Spanish leader's guile and tenacity.

Franco, in fact, took the lead in the gamesmanship: he kept the powerful German cooling his heels for two hours before showing up at the führer's private railroad coach.

Hitler chose to ignore the affront. Instead, he launched into nine hours of almost incessant oratory intended to "overbear Franco," as a German aide would describe it. As Franco listened without change of expression, Hitler rambled on about the awesome power of his Wehrmacht, the enormous amount of shipping his U-boats were sinking, the horrendous damage being done to London by his Luftwaffe's blitz, and how England was in a hopeless predicament and could not hold out much longer.

When Hitler finally came up for air, Franco remained uncowed. In an affable tone, he explained that Spain would have "serious problems" were she to get into another conflict so soon after the civil war. Nothing was settled. The

Francisco Franco (right) outfoxed Adolf Hitler (left) at a meeting along the Spanish border. (National Archives)

two dictators parted. For the first time since Hitler had seized power in early 1933, he had been outmaneuvered on the diplomatic front.

In Germany, two powerful figures, Foreign Minister Joachim von Ribbentrop and SS Gruppenführer (three-star general) Walter Schellenberg, director of foreign intelligence, began plotting to get rid of Generalissimo Franco. His replacement might take Spain into the German camp.

Both Ribbentrop and Schellenberg were ambitious and ruthless. They had even picked out the man to become El Caudillo: General Agustin Muñoz Grandes, who was highly respected in Spain. By the time the Nazi plot was about ready to be hatched, Muñoz Grandes was leader of the Blue Division (Spanish volunteers) fighting the Russians. Franco had not been as interested in aiding the Germans as he was in evening the score against the hated Soviet Communists, who had opposed his side in the Spanish Civil War.

Schellenberg, who was only thirty years of age despite his exalted SS rank, secretly made contact with General Muñoz Grandes, who became a willing accomplice. As the German already knew, the Spaniard hated England, which, he said, had oppressed Spain for centuries.

The machination called for Muñoz Grandes to return to Spain, where he no doubt would be eulogized for his exploits against the Soviets. Then, before the world's press, he would demand that Spain join Germany and Italy in the war.

If Franco stonewalled, Hitler would bolster Muñoz Grandes's demand by having the Luftwaffe heavily bomb Madrid and target Franco's headquarters.

Then, if El Caudillo continued to stall, Muñoz Grandes was to "neutralize" Franco and organize a coup to form a new government that would get Spain into the German and Italian camp.

As with most powerful dictators, Franco had spies everywhere—including in the Oberkommando der Wehrmacht (German High Command) in Berlin. So he soon got wind of the plot against him. Typically, El Caudillo moved in a calculating manner. In due course, he ordered General Muñoz Grandes to return to Madrid, and he put on a rousing hero's welcome for the conspirator.

Franco summoned the general to the palace, pinned a high decoration on his tunic, praised him for his actions on the Eastern Front—and immediately shunted him off to the ceremonial post of Commander of the Military Household.

Again, El Caudillo had "outplotted" Adolf Hitler. When General Muñoz Grandes had been put on the sidelines with a meaningless job and no troops to support him, the Nazi scheme to murder Generalissimo Franco evaporated.[7]

A Cleaning Woman Foils Hitler

FEW PEOPLE IF ANYONE paid attention to the man in work clothes who was going about his job inspecting apartment buildings in the Bronx, a borough of New York City. This ordinary-looking inspector was actually an investigator for the Radio Intelligence Division (RID) of the Federal Communications Commission.

In the palm of his hand the sleuth carried a "snifter," a tiny meter that could tell if electronic signals were coming from inside a certain building. America was not officially at war, so it was RID's responsibility to use its portable and stationary monitors to detect illegal transmitters.

In January 1941, RID detected an unauthorized radio set at an apartment building in the Bronx. George E. Sterling, chief of RID, informed J. Edgar Hoover, director of the Federal Bureau of Investigation, about the discovery. Convinced that this clandestine transmitter was a German espionage operation, Hoover ordered his New York City office in Foley Square to track it down.

G-men, as Hoover's agents were called, began canvassing stores selling parts that might be used for constructing a shortwave radio station. They quickly hit pay dirt. At a shop in Manhattan, a salesman recalled having sold radio parts to a man who had drawn the clerk's suspicions. The reason he recalled this particular transaction, the salesman explained, was that the customer was highly nervous and kept looking back over his shoulder toward the front door. It occurred to the clerk that this furtive individual might be planning to use this equipment for some sinister purpose.

A radio transmitter built by espionage agents Felix Jahnke and Alex Wheeler-Hill for use in their New York City apartment. (FBI)

At the request of the G-men, the clerk thumbed through records and came up with the customer's name—Joseph Klein. He gave his address as a rooming house on East 126th Street.

Hoover's men questioned residents in that area and found that Joseph August Klein, a German American who scratched out a livelihood as a part-time commercial photographer, had been the subject of considerable neighborhood gossip: he lived with two other men, a Mr. Frederick and a Mr. Hill— and a large German shepherd dog.

As the sleuths continued to probe into Klein's activities, other revealing facts surfaced. He was a longtime radio ham, and his two roommates had close ties to Nazi Germany. Mr. Frederick was an alias of thirty-eight-year-old Felix Jahnke, who had been an officer in the German army and became an American citizen in 1930. Mr. Hill was pegged as Alex Wheeler-Hill, a forty-year-old native of Russia who had come to the United States in 1923, was naturalized, and worked for a decade as a motorman for the Third Avenue El.

Jahnke had been called to the Third Reich in 1939 to be trained as a radio operator by the Abwehr, the secret service. Then he was sent back to the United States as a "sleeper," awaiting a specific assignment from Berlin.

At about the same time, a restless Wheeler-Hill had given up what he considered to be his humdrum life on the Third Avenue El and went to Germany. There he volunteered his services to the Abwehr, which trained him in sending and receiving coded messages by radio.

In January 1940, his Abwehr controller sent him back to New York City to team up with Felix Jahnke. The Jahnke–Wheeler-Hill radio center (call letters REN) was code-named Operation Jimmy.

Jahnke and Wheeler-Hill had been having trouble finding a location that would provide clear broadcasting, so they had moved their portable set to another site before reassembling it a third time in a rooming house on East 126th Street, the address Joseph Klein had given to the radio-store clerk.

Apparently that base was also unsatisfactory for broadcasting, for FBI agents who had staked out the rooming house observed Jahnke and Wheeler-Hill laboriously lugging the dismantled radio set to the top floor of a rooming house on Caldwell Avenue. The two spies were apparently satisfied with results obtained in their new *Meldkopf* (communications center).

Through electronic monitors, the FBI eavesdroppers were recording each message sent to Germany from the sixth floor on Caldwell Avenue. But the G-men were frustrated. They knew from secret sources the basic principle of an Abwehr code, that transmissions at each clandestine radio were based on popular novels of the time.

Until the FBI agents could identify the book on which the Jahnke–Wheeler-Hill messages were pegged, the intercepted communications made no sense. But how could the key volume be identified?

The G-men focused their attention on a bookstore in Yorkville, a Manhattan district largely populated by people of German ancestry. While masquerading as customers browsing the shelves, the sleuths observed Paul Scholz, owner of the firm, remove a volume from a shelf, wrap it in brown paper, and hand it over to a customer—Felix Jahnke. The sleuths felt that this book could be the key to unlocking the Jahnke–Wheeler-Hill code, but they had been unable to see the book's title.

Hoover's men learned that the targeted store had a policy of stamping its name on the flyleaf of each of its books. But when its tenants were absent, the sleuths were prohibited by law from sneaking into the Caldwell Avenue flat to hunt for the book without first obtaining a search warrant. Such an action would tip the FBI's hand.

Now a bizarre aspect of the case unfolded. The G-men were stymied, but Congress had passed no law that prevented a cleaning woman from cautiously snooping around an apartment in which she did her daily chores. So the sleuths covertly called on Hilda McIntosh (not her real name), who performed housework at the Caldwell Avenue building, and asked for her help. With all the power of the FBI and its sophisticated electronic devices, the success of the highly important investigation depended on a middle-aged cleaning woman.

Hilda could hardly mask her emotions. On one hand, she was excited over being singled out by the FBI for such a crucial task. On the other, she might pay with her life if the two spies returned home and found her examining their books.

A few days later Hilda contacted the FBI men. There were a large number of books in the apartment, she said, but only one of them had the Yorkville store's name stamped on the flyleaf.

That book, *Halfway to Horror,* proved to be the key to solving the Jahnke–Wheeler-Hill code. Now Operation Jimmy's messages to Germany made sense—and their contents stunned the FBI. They disclosed that the two spies, along with subagents they had recruited, were sending to their masters in the Third Reich a bonanza of intelligence about ship convoys and American military secrets.

However, the FBI eavesdroppers were privy to the same messages. So Operation Jimmy was permitted to continue for the time being because ship convoys' departures and courses were altered, and defense plants from which they were being pilfered tightened their security.

Hilda McIntosh had played a crucial role in foiling Adolf Hitler's espionage invasion of the United States.[8]

The Battle of the Birds

IN APRIL 1941, President Franklin D. Roosevelt gave the green light for the new U.S. Air Transport Command (ATC) to establish a base of great strategic importance on Ascension Island, a barren flyspeck in the mid-Atlantic Ocean. This base made it possible for medium bombers and some fighter planes to land for refueling and make a transatlantic trip between America and Great Britain in two stages.

For nearly a year, after Adolf Hitler had conquered much of Western Europe, the United States had been shipping supplies and other materials to beleaguered Great Britain by slow-moving ocean convoys. But on occasion there would crop up an urgent need for spare parts, radar equipment, or other high-technology gear. Consequently, the ATC had been created to fill a crucial need for the rapid delivery of the accoutrements of war.

Ascension Island contained only thirty-four square miles. Pilots who flew the route had an appropriate ditty: "If I don't hit Ascension; my wife will get a pension."

The remote base was named Wideawake Field after the large colony of wideawake terns (sea gulls) that are smaller and more slender in body and bill and have narrower wings than most other sea gulls.

These terns—thousands of them—had a favorite roosting place: the rocky area at one end of the runway that had been blasted out of solid rock when the

A bomber runs the gauntlet of thousands of sea gulls that nearly caused
the shutdown of a key American air base on a tiny Atlantic island.
(U.S. Air Force)

ATC moved in. These feathered creatures posed a serious threat to airplanes
landing or lifting off.

On the approach of an aircraft, the terns grew panicky, and they rose en
masse from their nesting place. Suddenly, a pilot was confronted by a dense
feathery cloud in front of his aircraft. The cloud threatened to break the plane's
windshield, clog its engines and air scoops, or dent the leading edges of the
wings or tail. This situation resulted in the pilots being in danger of crashing
into the runway or into the ocean.

ATC officers on the base launched a precision offensive against this threat.
Without success, the terns were assaulted with dynamite and then smoke can-
isters. Presumably the gulls felt that it was their turf, that they had been on the
island far longer than had the Americans.

The "tactical strategists" at Wideawake Field were on the brink of admit-
ting defeat in their war against the terns. Then a young lieutenant came up with
an idea: call in an ornithologist from the American Museum of Natural History.

The consultant came up with a new approach: move the terns' eggs to a
new location on the island and the birds would not return to their nesting
place at the end of the runway.

This scheme required an enormous logistics challenge. But somehow
perhaps fifty thousand eggs were laboriously taken to a site more than a mile
away. The ornithologist had solved the vexing problem, for the birds never
returned.[9]

Roosevelt in a Shouting Match

DAVID GRAY, the U.S. ambassador to neutral Ireland, was determined to draw that island nation into the war on the British side. Eamon de Valera, the *taoiseach* (prime minister), had incessantly rejected Prime Minister Winston Churchill's demands that British warships be permitted to use Irish ports to fight German U-boat operations in the Atlantic.

When the Irish government inquired about the United States providing rifles, vehicles, and artillery pieces to equip its army, Ambassador Gray hatched a plot. He slyly suggested to de Valera that a top Irish official be sent to America to call on President Franklin Roosevelt to discuss the arms request.

As Gray had intended, de Valera interpreted that proposal to mean that the ambassador would recommend filling the order to equip the 40,000-man Irish army and its 200,000 reserves. Actually, Gray regarded the mission to Washington to be a golden opportunity to put heavy pressure on the Irish to abandon neutrality and get in the war on the side of the British.

De Valera's choice to go to the United States was Frank Aiken, his minister for the Coordination of Defensive Measures, a designation intended to convey that Ireland was interested only in defending itself. As matters developed, the choice could hardly have been worse. Even those in his own government regarded Aiken as a liability as a cabinet minister and diplomat. One privately described de Valera's long-time friend as "rather stupid."

Ambassador Gray informed de Valera that he had arranged for Aiken to call on President Roosevelt on April 7, 1941.

Gray had informed the White House that he felt Aiken was pro-German, and he urgently recommended that Roosevelt should mince no words in telling the Irish official that the United States would support Great Britain by every means short of a shooting war.

After Aiken had been escorted into the Oval Office, Roosevelt wasted no time on idle chitchat. He immediately took the minister to task for having stated that "the Irish have nothing to fear from a German victory," a charge Aiken vigorously denied. No doubt Roosevelt had hurled this initial broadside to put the visitor on the defensive.

Aiken had expected an in-depth discussion about Ireland's defense needs, but what he received was a presidential monologue on why Ireland should support Great Britain in the war against Germany.

Roosevelt never ceased talking until an aide came into the office to escort Aiken out. His allotted time was up. But the Irishman refused to budge. Not until a waiter came in and laid a cloth and luncheon service on the chief executive's desk did Aiken get a chance to speak. He explained that Ireland needed arms to repel aggression.

Anxious to begin his lunch, Roosevelt replied curtly, "Yes, against German aggression!"

*President Franklin D. Roosevelt
outshouted Ireland's emissary.
(National Archives)*

Aiken snapped back: "British aggression!"

That blunt remark set Roosevelt off again. He lost interest in his lunch. It was "preposterous to suspect that the British had any such intention," he bellowed.

Roosevelt knew full well that Prime Minister Winston Churchill had discussed with his military leaders the possibility that Britain might have to invade the neighboring country of 3 million people to "keep the Germans out."

Aiken's voice rose. "If the British have no such intentions, why can't they say so?" he exclaimed. "We've asked them often."

Now Roosevelt was shouting: "What you have to fear is German aggression!"

"Or British aggression!" the minister yelled back.

Roosevelt was so angry that he inadvertently tugged the tablecloth, and cutlery and dishes were flying around the customarily circumspect Oval Office, causing great banging and clanging.

Hearing the racket, aides barged in. Still Aiken refused to depart until the grumpy Roosevelt promised that he would try to secure a guarantee from Churchill that Britain would not invade Ireland. That guarantee apparently would never be sought.

Ireland's official relations with the United States would never be the same after the shouting match in the White House.[10]

Democracy in a Battlefield Hospital

CRETE, AN ISLAND sixty miles south of the Greek mainland, at the southern extremity of the Aegean Sea, had long held the attention of the world powers. In fact, the land mass one hundred and sixty miles long and thirty-five miles at its widest had been the cradle of one of the earliest civilizations, the Minoan, fifteen hundred years before the birth of Christ.

Now, in the spring of 1941, Adolf Hitler turned his gaze on the seemingly inconsequential island. In June the German warlord planned to launch Operation Barbarossa, a massive invasion of the Soviet Union. So he told his generals Crete would have to be captured before that time to protect the Wehrmacht's southern flank.

General Kurt Student, the fifty-one-year-old commander of German airborne operations, came up with a bold and novel plan for capturing Crete from the 40,000-man British Empire force. The scheme had no precedent in history. The island was to be conquered from the air by Student's *Fallschirmjaeger* (paratroopers).

In late April Student met with Hitler, who was intrigued with the idea of astonishing the world by using fallschirmjaeger on a grand scale. Operation Mercury, as the sky invasion was code-named, would hit early in the morning of May 20.

Many British, Australian, and New Zealand troops were still eating breakfast when the mighty German sky armada of 493 Junkers transport planes roared in from the north. Minutes later the sky was filled with blossoming white parachutes.

Not all the transports reached the drop zones. Antiaircraft gunners had a field day. Fifteen of the planes filled with paratroopers were shot down in flames.

The carnage continued on the ground. One German battalion lost 312 officers in just an hour. At the end of the first day, General Student's sky assault, which was to have swept up everything before it, was in jeopardy all along the northern coast of Crete.

Some ten thousand Germans had descended on the bleak island by parachute and glider. About 40 percent of the assault force was dead, wounded, or captured.

At his headquarters in the Hotel Grande Bretagne in Athens, more than a hundred miles to the north, Student was shocked by the casualty reports. However, Operation Mercury was his plan, so the next afternoon he sent to Crete the 5th Mountain Division to, in essence, rescue his paratroopers and glider soldiers.

As the British Empire forces and the Germans tangled, a massive bloodletting evolved. Thousands of men on both sides were wounded, many seriously.

The tactical situation was so confusing that the combatants on both sides often did not know where to take their wounded comrades.

As ferocious and unforgiving as was the fighting on Crete, the opposing British Empire and German forces often displayed an amazing chivalrous compassion for each other. Wounded German airborne men were cared for in the already overcrowded British 7th General Hospital. At the same time, German medical personnel were tending to British casualties at an aide station in a gully only twenty miles away.

In what may have been the most bizarre instance of its kind during the war, the British had constructed a hospital and a radio station near the town of Knossos. Soon the Germans began blasting away at the radio station, a legitimate target because it was used for communicating with scattered units.

However, a battlefield truce was called, and the British protested because the hospital was so close to the station. Then tear down the station and they'd cease firing, the Germans replied. The British rapidly carried out the request.

Then the hospital began functioning as a joint facility, staffed by both German and British doctors and nurses. There was no effort to segregate wounded men on each side. German doctors treated the British soldiers on occasion, British doctors tended to German airborne men. It was unprecedented battlefield democracy.[11]

Strange Means for Urgent Warning

EARLY ON THE CRISP, bleak morning of December 7, 1941, General George C. Marshall, the U.S. Army chief of staff, climbed onto King Story, his horse, and with Fleet, his Dalmatian, at his heels galloped off from his Fort Myer, Virginia, home for his customary Sunday ride. Lately Marshall had been spending some long days and nights because of a Japanese war threat in the Pacific, so he was thankful to get away from telephones and appointments for a couple of hours.

At the same time at the Munitions Building on Independence Avenue in Washington, D.C., Colonel Rufus Bratton was mulling over an intercepted and decoded wireless message that had been sent by Tokyo to the Japanese ambassador, retired Admiral Kichisaburo Nomura. Bratton interpreted the text as having ominous implications. It did not declare war, but it stated firmly that continuing negotiations with Washington officials would be useless.

Bratton was especially concerned over the fact that Nomura was ordered to deliver the text to Secretary of State Cordell Hull at one o'clock on that Sunday afternoon, unprecedented timing. Business in Washington simply wasn't done on a Sunday.

Convinced that some American installation in the Pacific had been targeted for attack—and only a few hours away—Bratton frantically telephoned

*Pearl Harbor warning by
General George C. Marshall
arrived too late. (U.S. Army)*

General Marshall's home in suburban Fort Myer. Told that the chief of staff was horseback riding, the colonel asked that his orderly try to find him and ask him to get to the nearest telephone immediately.

Marshall returned home at 10:15 A.M. and took note of the Bratton message. But he took a shower before telephoning the colonel, who said he had "a most important document" that the general should see at once. Sensing the urgency in Bratton's voice, Marshall did not want to wait for his official car to arrive. So he climbed into a fire-engine-red sports roadster belonging to his stepson, Clifton Brown, and raced off for the Munitions Building.

A half hour later Marshall was in his office and reading through the long text of the Japanese statement. Finally, he took off his glasses and asked Bratton and Major General Sherman Miles, chief of Army intelligence, their opinions on the significance of the unusual one o'clock Sunday delivery to the secretary of state.

Perhaps it was timed to coincide with an early morning attack somewhere in the Pacific, the two officers agreed. It was already past five o'clock in the afternoon in Hawaii, and dawn would be only fourteen hours away.

Marshall held the same view. So he wrote an updated warning to all commands in the Pacific:

> Japanese are presenting at 1 P.M. eastern standard time today what amounts to an ultimatum. Also they are under orders to destroy their code machine immediately. Just what significance the hour set may have we do not know, but be on alert.

Colonel Bratton rushed to the Signals Center to send the crucial message. Marshall had told him to ask how long it would take to reach all the persons addressed. Lieutenant Colonel Edward F. French, who was in charge of the Signals Center, said that it would require thirty to forty minutes, and that everyone would have been alerted by one o'clock that afternoon Washington time.

Amazingly, this momentous warning was sent by commercial services. There was a direct Teletype from the Signals Room to the Western Union in Washington. Western Union wired to San Francisco, and RCA Radio shuttled the text along to Hawaii. It reached Honolulu at 6:47 A.M.—at a time a Japanese bomber force was winging toward Pearl Harbor.

At 7:30 A.M. Tadao Fuchikami reported for work at the RCA cable office in Honolulu and began assembling the telegrams that he would take on his bicycle to the addressees. There were no priority markings on any of the messages, so Fuchikami put all of them into his bag for routine delivery. One of these telegrams was General Marshall's urgent warning to Lieutenant General Walter C. Short, who was responsible for the defense of Pearl Harbor.

By the time Short received the warning, Japanese bombs were raining on the U.S. Pacific Fleet.[12]

A Dedicated Blood-Bank Volunteer

ON DECEMBER 8, 1941, the morning after the Japanese sneak attack had almost destroyed the U.S. Pacific Fleet, Dr. John Devereux, head of the Honolulu blood bank, put out an urgent appeal for blood donors. Hundreds of civilians and military men had been wounded in the bombings, and the bank had run out of containers. Sterilized Coca Cola bottles were used in their place.

Within hours of the appeal, five hundred donors swamped Devereux and his three volunteer assistants at the blood bank, and they worked for seventy-two hours straight until near exhaustion. Even then, one of the female assistants refused to quit. She continued to clean bottles and tubes and arrange the donors for extracting blood. This extremely dedicated volunteer was one of Honolulu's best-known prostitutes.[13]

The Spymaster's Peculiar Scheme

EARLY IN JANUARY 1942, William J. "Wild Bill" Donovan, a wealthy Wall Street lawyer and holder of the Congressional Medal of Honor from World War I, called on President Franklin D. Roosevelt at the White House. The two men had been longtime friends, and it was the president who had coerced Donovan to come to Washington and organize America's first cloak-and-dagger agency, known as the Coordinator of Information (soon to be designated the Office of Strategic Services—OSS).

Donovan eagerly briefed Roosevelt on a bizarre scheme for subversive warfare in the Far East. The spymaster's idea was to announce to the world that the Japanese, who were running wild in the Pacific, planned to attack Singapore, a British bastion at the southern tip of the Malay Peninsula.

When the Japanese failed to launch an assault, Donovan declared, the Allies could proclaim that this "failure" was the "turning point" in the war in the Pacific.

Roosevelt shuttled the bizarre scheme to Army Chief of Staff George C. Marshall, who replied in diplomatic wording that this was about the silliest suggestion that he had ever encountered. "It would be best not to openly invite Tokyo to strike at any certain locale," he declared.

The Japanese needed no invitation. A week later, a powerful force struck Singapore. In a lightning operation that lasted only a little more than two weeks, the "impregnable fortress" fell. Nine thousand British servicemen had been killed.[14]

A Pursuit of Bugs and Lice

AMONG THE 130,000 BRITONS captured by the Japanese in the monumental disaster at Singapore was Stanley Pavillard, a young physician from the Canary Islands, who had only recently arrived in the Far East. Along with hundreds of other captives, Pavillard was shipped to Siam (now Thailand) to help build a railroad from Bangkok to Rangoon for the Japanese war juggernaut.

Pavillard was the medical officer for the fifteen hundred prisoners at a clearing in the jungle known as Camp Wampo. Almost at once large numbers of the slave laborers were stricken with tropical diseases such as dysentery and malaria. As best as he could, the doctor treated them with medicine stolen from the Japanese at the risk of his life.

Pavillard knew that once a man lost the will to live, the drugs and treatment were useless. He used a wide array of ingenious means to keep the men from depression. If a man was past caring, use was made on occasion of the soldier's deeply ingrained habit of military discipline: he would be *ordered* to recover. As absurd as this approach seemed to be, in the brutal conditions of a Thai prison camp it sometimes worked.

Dr. Pavillard had been well schooled in the principles of occupational therapy, so he constantly endeavored to improve the captives' morale by giving them something to do. Toward this goal, much time and effort was devoted to the pursuit and capture of bugs and lice.

One man was an expert at lice catching, for he had had much experience at the practice while a POW in World War I. This "expert" gave lectures to Pavillard and others on lice-trapping techniques. The best means was for each man to place a small piece of cotton wool on his navel when retiring for the night. The "students" thought this approach was nonsensical, but when they tried it, each man discovered a large group of fat, juicy parasites.

Once a few hundred lice had been "captured," they were covertly slipped into the huts where the Japanese guards slept. Early the next morning, the POWs looked on with delight as their tormentors emerged from the huts and launched impromptu gyrations, scratching and clawing to get rid of the tiny parasites that had descended upon them as they slept.[15]

A Cantankerous Torpedo

THESE WERE THE BLACKEST of days for America. Seven weeks after a woefully unprepared Uncle Sam had been bombed into global war at Pearl Harbor, Hawaii, powerful Japanese forces had invaded the main Philippine island of Luzon and had General MacArthur's small army trapped on the Bataan peninsula, southwest of Manila. It was early February 1942.

Deep inside Malinta Tunnel on Corregidor, a tadpole-shaped rock island three and a half miles long in the mouth of Manila Bay, Lieutenant Rudolph Fabian, commander of Station Cast, a top-secret Navy cryptanalytic unit, had grown deeply concerned that the surging Japanese army might capture Corregidor and seize the cryptanalysts, whose function was to use sophisticated electronic equipment to intercept and crack Japanese codes. Such an eventuality could result in the invaders' gaining information on one of America's most secret operations.

Fabian recognized that the tactical situation was hopeless. MacArthur's force of 25,000 U.S. soldiers and 45,000 Filipino troops was starving, nearly out of ammunition, wracked by tropical disease, and fighting with obsolete weapons and firing ancient shells that failed to explode.

Lieutenant Fabian decided to radio superiors for permission to evacuate the Station Cast team and its secret equipment to Australia. Admiral Ernest J. King, the chief of naval operations in Washington, sent a strict order: "Take all steps possible to prevent loss of radio intelligence unit."

On the dark night of February 4, an American submarine stole into Manila Bay, tied up at Corregidor, and Lieutenant Fabian, four other officers, and thirteen enlisted men climbed down the submarine's open hatch, lugging fifteen pieces of heavy electronic equipment. The underwater vessel shoved off.

Six weeks later, just before Bataan fell, the second group of Station Cast personnel, four officers and thirty-two enlisted men, embarked on the submarine USS *Permit*. A few days later, the submarine's skipper, a gung-ho type, spotted a Japanese cargo ship and decided to give chase. All afternoon the *Permit* tried to get up close to the target, but failed.

Just before dusk, the skipper, no doubt through frustration, ordered two torpedoes to be fired at long range, with little if any hope of hitting the moving ship. Perhaps twenty seconds later, the sub's intercom raucously called out: "Crash-dive! Crash-dive!"

One of the torpedoes, a cantankerous type, had decided to make a wide circle about halfway to the Japanese ship, and now it was heading back—straight for the *Permit*. Those on board held their breaths when they heard the torpedo's screws turning as the missile passed only a few feet overhead.[16]

Curious Death of a German Bigwig

FRITZ TODT, head of the huge, paramilitary German public works outfit that bore his name, had been a loyal party member in the early years, but his ardor for Nazism cooled by the late 1930s. However, the engineer, who had earned the Iron Cross and been wounded in the First World War, was held almost in reverence by Adolf Hitler, who was awed by his construction achievements for the Third Reich.

Born to a wealthy family, Todt first gained Hitler's admiration when he constructed the Reichsautobahn, a national highway system that the German military planners had laid out. The network, decades ahead of roadways in even the United States, was nearing completion before an alarmed world realized that this system of high-speed roads was suited primarily for military use.

Fritz Todt was as close to being a genius as anyone else in the Nazi hierarchy. Over the years he not only centralized efforts of major technical facilities under his organization, but he also drew engineers and managers of the German construction industry into a single, gigantic effort.

The head of the OT (as the Organization Todt was popularly known) introduced innovative features to get the most out of the available manpower. He created separate units of physically handicapped men and assigned them special projects within their capabilities.

Todt had built the vaunted West Wall (Siegfried Line), the barrier against invasion from the west that stretched for hundreds of miles along the Reich's border with France. He began building concrete-encased U-boat berths in various French ports after the German war juggernaut had conquered that nation, in order to have easier access to Allied convoys.

OT also built several coastal batteries along the Strait of Dover, the narrow waist of water that connects the North Sea with the English Channel. These mammoth big guns, which were capable of shelling the British coast twenty miles to the north, had been intended to provide artillery support for Operation Sea Lion, the proposed invasion of England.

Even though Sea Lion had been called off, these big guns served as a highly effective propaganda means for the Germans. The batteries became

Adolf Hitler and his production minister, Albert Speer, at Wolfschanze (Wolf's Lair), the führer's field headquarters. (National Archives)

showpieces when they were incorporated into the Atlantic Wall, a concrete-and-steel barrier that would eventually extend for twenty-four-hundred miles along the northern coasts of Belgium, France, the Netherlands, Denmark, and Norway.

Pictures of the huge guns at the Strait of Dover were used repeatedly by Nazi propaganda minister Paul Josef Goebbels to give the Western Allies and the people of those nations the view that these weapons were studded all along the Atlantic Wall.

While Todt was supervising huge construction projects around Europe, he had developed a rival, young Albert Speer. Many were convinced that these two ambitious, strong-willed men would eventually clash.

After the führer had seized total power in Germany in early 1933, he had become deeply impressed with the architectural work done for various Nazi leaders by Speer. Subsequently, Hitler assigned a large number of construction projects to Speer, whose organization grew to 65,000 German workers.

Toward the end of 1941, with German legions bogged down in the bitter snow and cold of Russia, Hitler assigned to Speer's organization the task of repairing the enormous amount of damage the Red army had caused to the Soviet railroad system during its withdrawal.

Meanwhile, Fritz Todt's popularity with the führer had not gone unnoticed by other jealous and ambitious leaders atop the Nazi totem pole. Two of these powerful Todt enemies were rotund Hermann Goering, who held the exclusive rank of Reichsmarschall, and thirty-nine-year-old Martin Bormann, who had clawed his way up the chain of command from anonymity to being Hitler's executive secretary.

Goering, Bormann, and Speer—Fritz Todt had three of the most potent figures in the Third Reich as enemies.

Early in February 1942, Todt was summoned for a conference by the führer. Curiously, perhaps, Todt's private plane had just been sent for repairs, and he flew to the führerhauptquartier, at Rastenberg, behind the Soviet front, in a borrowed bomber.

Early the next morning, February 9, the bomber was preparing to take off with Todt and Albert Speer for Munich. Speer had also been ordered to meet with the führer. At almost the last minute, Speer canceled out, explaining he had further important business to discuss with Hitler.

A few minutes after liftoff the Heinkel bomber exploded, killing Todt and the others on board.

A short and cursory investigation into the cause of the midair disaster was conducted. A panel ruled that there had been no evidence of sabotage, although an aircraft suddenly exploding in midair was quite unique.

Two days later Hitler announced that Albert Speer would succeed Todt as head of the mammoth construction organization.[17]

Ernest Hemingway Stalks U-Boats

A MONTH AFTER Uncle Sam had been drawn into the global conflict, Grand Admiral Karl Doenitz, Befehlshaber der Unterseeboote (commander of German submarines), launched Operation Paukenschlag (Bang the Drums). The strategy was to knock America out of the war by sinking her ships loaded with troops and supplies that were bound for Europe.

Doenitz had selected eleven of his ace U-boat skippers, a resolute breed, to strangle the American east coast shipping lanes. Their craft were tough, mobile, and had excellent endurance, with a range of eleven thousand miles, sufficient to allow them to maraud the U.S. eastern shore for several weeks before returning to their base in Saint-Nazaire, France.

The U-boats were wreaking havoc in the weeks ahead. Admiral Doenitz wrote Adolf Hitler: "Our submarines are operating close inshore along the coast of the United States, so that bathers and sometimes entire coastal cities are witnesses of that drama of war whose visual climates are constituted by the red glorioles of blazing [Allied] tankers."

In the White House in Washington, D.C., President Franklin D. Roosevelt, already beset with a mountain of seemingly unsolvable problems of preparing a militarily weak America for global war, still found time to study reports on the carnage being inflicted on shipping along the eastern seaboard.

The tanker Byron T. Benson *explodes after being hit by a torpedo within sight of the Virginia shore. (National Archives)*

Roosevelt, who had been crippled at age thirty-nine by polio, had spent a lifetime as an amateur yachtsman. In the First World War he had been the assistant secretary of the Navy. So he no doubt felt qualified to bombard his Navy commanders with schemes for thwarting the U-boat onslaught on what Doenitz called "the American Front."

The president ordered the Navy to rapidly establish a large group of volunteer civilians who would use their private yachts, powerboats, and fishing vessels to patrol the shores. It was not clear what these unarmed and relatively fragile vessels were to do if they encountered a U-boat.

One of the most enthusiastic volunteers was Ernest Hemingway, the widely known author, who was a celebrity in a class with baseball superstars and Hollywood silver-screen luminaries. Hard-driving, hard-drinking "Papa" Hemingway not only wrote of adventure but he eagerly grasped every exciting, dangerous challenge that came along.

In his own yacht, Hemingway began patrolling the eastern seaboard. Armed with a Tommy gun, he prowled up and down the decks hoping for a chance to drop a hand grenade down the open hatch of a U-boat's conning tower.

The forty-two-year-old bearded novelist was destined for disappointment. He never as much as spotted a U-boat in the distance. Roosevelt's "Hooligan Navy," as the armada was dubbed by the media, may have raised civilian morale, but all it produced were large numbers of false sightings which kept genuine Navy warships hopping up and down the eastern seaboard.[18]

Fluke Saves a British Fleet

WHILE JAPANESE ARMIES were conquering vast swaths of Southeast Asia after the outbreak of general war in the Pacific, General Hideki Tojo, the master warlord in Tokyo, ordered a full-blooded attack on Ceylon (now Sri Lanka), an island 270 miles long that became a Crown Colony of Great Britain in 1802. It was now March 1942.

Making the assault on Ceylon would be the First Air Fleet commanded by Vice Admiral Chuichi Nagumo. Despite his lack of experience in naval aviation, the diminutive officer led the principal body of Japanese aircraft carriers. His air fleet had performed with distinction in the sneak attack on Pearl Harbor, so the admiral was held in great esteem in Tokyo.

Through spies and air surveillance, Nagumo knew that Britain's Eastern Fleet of twenty-nine aging warships was based at the ports of Colombo and Trincomalee in Ceylon, about a hundred miles off the southern tip of India.

Knowing the weak condition of the British naval force, Nagumo envisioned an easy victory. That triumph would give Japan control of the Indian Ocean and cut Allied access to Australia.

Following the successful pattern used at Pearl Harbor, Nagumo planned an early morning raid on Ceylon's airfields, docks, and anchorages. This time, however, the scenario would unfold in a different mode: British code breakers learned that the Japanese attack was in the works but at some unknown date.

Admiral James Somerville, a large, congenial man who, those close to him asserted, had an urge to be in the center of the stage and was regarded as an unorthodox tactician, was commander of the Eastern Fleet. He was highly regarded by the Admiralty in London, after outstanding service in the Dunkirk evacuation and in the Mediterranean.

In Ceylon and armed with the knowledge that the Japanese were about ready to strike him, Somerville may have been influenced by his alleged need to be regarded as unorthodox. In a move that other admirals would say later required more courage than sense, he ordered his twenty-nine ships to sail forth and intercept Admiral Nagumo's far superior carrier force.

Now Dame Fate got into the act to compensate Somerville for his major error in judgment. After the British warships searched for the Japanese fleet for many hours, they began to run low on fuel. All but four of the British vessels had to divert to a secret haven in the Maldive Islands, six hundred miles south of Ceylon.

At 7:40 A.M. on April 5, Admiral Nagumo introduced himself to Ceylon. One hundred and twenty-seven of his bombers flew over the island and were pounced on by British Royal Air Force fighter planes near Colombo. Perhaps to the frustration of the Japanese flight commander, the harbor was bare of Eastern Fleet ships.

In the battle that lasted for more than an hour, the British lost twenty-seven planes and shot down nineteen Japanese aircraft.

No doubt angry to learn that the chicken had flown the coop, Nagumo had his task force search over large areas of the Indian Ocean for the British fleet. However, Somerville, now aware that his armada was in peril, kept most of his warships hidden in the Maldive Islands. A few vessels that were sent out on short scouting missions had orders not to engage in combat with the Japanese.

Nagumo's pilots did locate and sink seven British ships, including the cruisers *Dorsetshire* and *Cornwall*. But the remainder of the Eastern Fleet was spared, and Nagumo eventually pulled back his task force. Had not the British ships run low on fuel, Somerville's entire fleet may have been wiped out.[19]

The War's Craziest Wedding Scenario

AFTER AMERICA WAS BOMBED into global war, the U.S. Navy, armed with wartime powers to take over any civilian property it chose, sent patrols to scour Washington, D.C., for choice spots. The rapidly expanding OP-20-G, the Navy's supersecret code-busting bureau, found the ideal home for its operation, the Mount Vernon Seminary.

A finishing school for females from wealthy families, Mount Vernon was described by its administration as "a place where young girls should continually be inspired and aided to grow towards noble, helpful, gracious, Christian womanhood."

Navy officials could care less about inspiring young girls. What they wanted was the real estate. Located in an upscale neighborhood, the seminary had a beautiful campus of green lawns and redbrick buildings, a gymnasium, a tennis court, and a lovely chapel.

What the Navy wanted, the Navy got. In November 1942, the seminary was advised that the property was being taken over in the interest of the war effort. The 170 girls were sent elsewhere to be "inspired," and the OP-20-G moved into its sumptuous quarters, which was given the "cover" designation, Naval Communications Annex.

Like a plague of locusts, workmen descended on the premises. A strong barbed-wire fence was built around the perimeter; walkways were ripped up to make way for new structures. Stern-faced Marines, with orders to shoot any intruder, patrolled the barbed-wire fence. Security was crucial at the highly sensitive and important facility.

Later the Marine officer in charge of the security detail was hit by an unexpected headache—from on high. The assistant secretary of the Navy informed the Marine that his daughter, who had been enrolled at Mount Vernon Seminary, was going to be married and wanted her wedding to be in the former school chapel, now the Navy Chapel.

Making the request more dangerous from a security point of view was the fact that perhaps a few hundred guests milling about the chapel would be only twenty-five yards from the building in which the Navy's supersecret decoding equipment was kept.

The Marine commander sent word to the assistant secretary of the Navy that he regretted that the request would have to be rejected for security reasons. The Marine was overruled; the elaborate wedding would take place as planned.

On the appointed day, guests began arriving at the Navy Communications Annex. One by one, they entered the grounds through a hole that had been cut in the perimeter fence, after having their names checked off a list and their identifications closely examined. Inside the main building, a squad of Marines armed with submachine guns ringed the chapel.

When the two hundred guests began leaving the grounds, again through the hole in the fence, no doubt they were convinced that this had been the most bizarre wedding they had ever attended.[20]

Two WACs on a Secret Mission

EARLY IN THE MORNING of June 10, 1942, curious doings emerged at Arlington Hall Junior College on the southwestern outskirts of Washington, D.C. An army lieutenant and fourteen soldiers armed with sawed-off broom handles descended on the campus and took possession of the large, modern building and grounds of more than one hundred acres.

The "armed occupation" had taken place so suddenly that a number of the junior college's young women were in showers in their dormitories when Uncle Sam's army showed up.

Although many students were confused, even frightened, by the military takeover, it was all very proper and legal. Invoking the War Powers Act, the property had been acquired by the U.S. Army to provide room for the rapidly expanding code-busting agency, the top-secret Signals Intelligence Service (SIS).

In the weeks ahead, all the trappings of a military post sprung up: guardhouses, drill fields, barracks, and other facilities. Less than a year after Arlington Hall was taken over by the army, some thirty-one hundred civilian and military personnel were assigned there.

Earlier, after Adolf Hitler declared war on the United States in the wake of the Japanese sneak attack on Pearl Harbor, intelligence agencies of America and Great Britain began exchanging top-secret information.

In Berlin, General Hiroshi Oshima, the Japanese ambassador and pal of most top Nazi leaders, transmitted the intelligence he had acquired from the

Germans to Tokyo over a high-speed radioteleprinter link in a code the Japanese considered to be unbreakable.

When U.S. intelligence learned of Oshima's steady flow of high-grade information to Tokyo, it built a top-secret intercept station at Asmara, Ethiopia, and staffed it with more than three hundred technicians. Ethiopia was violently anti-Nazi and anti-Italian.

The covert listening post in Asmara acquired the raw intercepts from General Oshima in Berlin, hundreds of miles to the north, and sent them by an on-line radioteleprinter to Arlington Hall.

After Oshima's intercepts had been decoded at Arlington Hall, they were sent on by radio across the Atlantic to the American signals center a hundred feet below ground in London. Then these intelligence reports were hand-carried to fewer than twenty top officials, in keeping with a strict technique for ensuring security.

Because of the ultra-secret nature of the code-busting operation, Arlington Hall had a special detachment to keep out spies and to assure tight security throughout the compound. There were numerous guard posts, barbed-wire fences, identity badges, armed patrols, and bright lights at night.

Near the close of work each day there was a routine procedure in which trash cans were emptied into large canvas bags. Then special teams would collect the bags and poke through the litter to make certain classified materials had not accidentally been pitched away. Officers were convinced that security at Arlington Hall was airtight.

One day two young women showed up at the main gate and told the guards that they wanted to visit a certain official. After they displayed their driver's licenses they were handed visitor's badges and given directions to the official's office.

These two women were not casual visitors. They were WACs in civilian clothes who had been sent on the mission by a secret Washington agency charged with safeguarding military installations.

Strolling unchallenged through the "airtight security" in various buildings, the WACs stole identity badges that staff members had left on desks and departed through the main gate carrying the load of top-secret documents they had collected.[21]

Strange Place for Royal Jewels

WHEN ADOLF HITLER sent his booted legions to occupy Yugoslavia in March 1941, seventeen-year-old King Peter II and the royal family fled the country before the Nazis reached Belgrade. The boy monarch established a government-in-exile in England, and then he and his family began living in luxury at the prestigious London hotel, Claridges.

Actually, the government-in-exile consisted of King Peter and his family, six of them, who occupied a large suite. Princess Aspasia was the dominant figure, and she seemed to rule the rulers.

After the United States was bombed into global war, Captain Robert H. Alcorn, an OSS operative, was assigned as contact man to the Yugoslav government-in-exile. After being invited to dinner one night in the Claridges suite, Princess Aspasia asked, "Captain, have you even seen the Yugoslav crown jewels?"

His unspoken reaction was: "Where would a man from rural Connecticut have ever encountered the Yugoslav crown jewels?" Finally, he said he didn't believe he had ever had that privilege.

"Peter, go get them," the princess ordered the king as though he were one of the servants. The boy left the room and returned pushing a casket. Fumbling with a bunch of keys from his pocket, he opened the lid.

It was a dazzling sight. Jewels of every size and description: diamonds, emeralds, sapphires, and rubies; bracelets, necklaces, earrings, and tiaras. They were to be worn on state occasions.[22]

Part Three

The Tide Starts
to Turn

Navajo Code-Talkers Ignite Panic

IN THE EARLY HOURS of darkness on the morning of August 7, 1942, an American fleet carrying some 20,000 men of the 1st Marine Division and attached units were nearing primitive Guadalcanal, a ninety-mile-long island in the Solomons chain in the South Pacific. Code-named Operation Watchtower, the invasion of Guadalcanal would be the first American offensive action of the war and the largest amphibious assault ever undertaken by U.S. forces to that time.

Among the nervous young marines aboard a troop transport was a tiny contingent known as Navajo code-talkers. Along with a few hundred others, these Indians had volunteered to leave their reservations and contribute their unique talent to Marine outfits in combat. Given crash courses on operating a communications radio, these Marines would pass along messages in a code that the Japanese would never be able to break—the Navajo language.

That tribal language could not be understood or mimicked by the Japanese. The verb forms were so complex that they could be understood and spoken only by those who had grown up with the language.

After volunteering for the Marines, the Navajos had gathered to assign Navajo words to the items of war. A dive-bomber became *ginitsob* (hawk), an observation plane became *ne-as-jay* (owl), and bombs became *a-ye-shi* (eggs), among scores of other words that would be used in combat situations.

The Navajo code-talkers were fully aware that their mission would be a highly dangerous one. They would be at or in front of friendly lines—and sometimes behind Japanese positions.

After naval gunfire and carrier-based aircraft pounded the landing beaches on Guadalcanal, the first assault wave of Marines stormed ashore and others followed.

The Navajo code-talkers were split among various spearhead patrols that pushed inland through the thick jungles and murky swamps. It was the precise combat situation for which the group had been formed. Only radio messages could keep the operation from bogging down into chaos.

Invading Marines were always in close contact with the Japanese, who often were only yards away in the dense foliage. On the first night inland, a Navajo radioed a message to another code-talker. While the two Indians were talking back and forth, their curious language touched off near panic among

Navajo code-talkers sending messages from front lines. (National Archives)

other Marine outfits, whose members had known nothing about the Navajo program. People were speaking in a foreign language on U.S. radios—and the language must have been Japanese.

Lacking combat experience, most of the young Marines were convinced that the Japanese had acquired American radios and were in the Marines' midst. Because the strange voices were being heard over several radios, the Marines conjectured that an entire American unit must have been overrun somewhere in the forbidding jungle. Perhaps the invaders were being surrounded, or cut off from the landing beaches.

Finally, officers restored order among the flustered units after sleuthing the reason for the uproar. Although the Navajo code-talkers would achieve great accomplishments during the war, for now they were ordered to cease sending messages before the entire 1st Marine Division was engulfed by hysteria.[1]

Adolf Hitler Plays Santa Claus

ON THE AFTERNOON of August 19, 1942, the bewildered and frightened citizens of Dieppe, France, slowly emerged from their homes and gawked in astonishment about them. Dieppe was an old pirate lair on what was known as

A German soldier inspects scene of carnage and dead invaders after disastrous Dieppe raid. (National Archives)

the Iron Coast, along the English Channel. Their city was a shambles. Buildings had been gutted by shellfire, and the streets were littered with broken glass and fallen telephone wires.

On the once nearly spotless beach were strewn an array of burned-out and damaged tanks and wrecked landing craft. Dead bodies were everywhere.

What the shaken 25,000 French men, women, and children saw was the aftermath of one of the boldest, largest, most intricate, and perhaps, most ill-advised commando raids of the war.

At dawn that day, 6,058 troops, mainly Canadian, along with a contingent of British Commandos and 50 U.S. Rangers, had stormed ashore in what would be called a "reconnaissance in force." Code-named Jubilee, the operation had been cloaked in mystery from the onset of planning. There were no rehearsals. Most incredible, there was no *deception plan.*

After eight hours of savage fighting, the invaders withdrew, having suffered a bloody disaster. Sixty-two percent of the assault troops (3,632 men) had been killed, wounded, and captured. For nearly two weeks bodies from the Jubilee force would be washed ashore along twenty miles of the Iron Coast.

At 5:38 P.M. on the day of the raid, Field Marshal Gerd von Rundstedt, the Oberbefehlshaber Westen (supreme commander in the West), from his headquarters in a chateau outside Paris, radioed Adolf Hitler a terse report: "No armed Englishman remains on the Continent."

Throughout the fighting the Dieppe civilians had remained under cover. In truth, there was little else they could have done. But Hitler cloaked himself in a Santa Claus garb and announced that he was going to reward the people for not helping the "Anglo-Saxons," as he always called the British. In a strange action, he sent the citizens of Dieppe 10 million francs, a presumably benevolent act that he had never performed before, and never would again.[2]

Purple Heart Stripped from Sailor

WHILE U.S. MARINES were engaged in savage battles in the thick jungles of Guadalcanal, in the waters surrounding the primitive island American and Japanese warships were slugging it out night after night. It was late August 1942.

On board the USS *South Dakota* was Seaman 1st Class Calvin L. Graham, who had volunteered to fight only a few months earlier. Now, on one dark night, he was manning a deck gun when he was seriously wounded by shrapnel.

At the hospital where Graham had been taken, he was awarded the Purple Heart. A few weeks later, after he had been sent to the United States for rehabilitation, the Navy stripped him of his Purple Heart medal. It had been discovered that Graham had lied about his age to enlist—he was only twelve years old when he had been wounded.

Much later the Navy gave the Purple Heart back to Graham—plus a Bronze Star medal for valor.[3]

Saga of Top-Secret Maps

OPERATION TORCH—the first major American offensive since the bloody Argonne Forest of World War I—was beginning to take shape. On September 20, 1942, the final piece of the massive, highly complicated plan was put into place. Complex factors of the moon, tide, and logistics dictated that D Day would be Sunday, November 8.

Americans would storm ashore at three locales along a thousand miles of coastline in Northwest Africa, a region held by the puppet government in Vichy, France.

While German intelligence agencies labored to unlock the secrets of Allied intentions, American security leaks began to multiply, as D Day grew closer.

One security flap erupted when the London bureau manager of the United Press sent a message to his New York office alerting it that the invasion would take place in Casablanca and elsewhere in French Morocco. Investigators could not confront the UP man; to do so would have confirmed that his prediction had been accurate. Worse, it could not be determined whether the dangerous message had been sent by cable or by radio. A cable would have been reasonably secure, while there was an excellent chance that German monitors across the Channel would have picked up a radio message. It was one more worry for Torch commanders and planners.

A confidential secretary in a London military office broke regulations and took home a top-secret memorandum from Churchill to his chiefs of staff suggesting that a *fourth* landing be made, this one at Bône, two hundred miles east of Algiers. While boarding a bus to go home, the memo, one of several he had carried with him, fell out of his pocket. A housemaid found the secret document, looked at it curiously, and took it home, where she turned it over to a soldier who was billeted there. Seeing the words MOST SECRET stamped on the memorandum, he rushed it directly to the Air Ministry and turned it over to the chief of staff. Had this critical document been seen—or photographed—by hostile parties? Intelligence officers had no way of knowing.

Keeping secret the printing and distribution to units of thousands of military maps was a monumental task for the British. They had the maps printed in a small shop in a country town a distance from London, away from the prying eyes of German agents. But while a large batch of maps was being trucked to various military commands, the covering on one container flew open and maps of Algeria and French Morocco were scattered for hundreds of yards along the road. Gusts of wind blew countless copies into the fields. The driver kept going, unaware that he was leaving a stream of top-secret maps in his wake.

A short time later, two local policemen on routine patrol discovered and examined the maps. Noting locales in French Northwest Africa, they gathered up as many maps as they could find and took them to their station. From there they telephoned the headquarters of General Charles de Gaulle's Free French in London: "Are you folks missing a large bunch of maps of Algeria and French Morocco?"

From the security point of view, it would have been difficult to pick a worse place to contact—short of the Oberkommando der Wehrmacht (German High Command) in Berlin. A decision had been reached earlier by President Franklin D. Roosevelt and Prime Minister Winston S. Churchill to keep General de Gaulle in the dark about Torch, fearing leaks.

De Gaulle was furious about being excluded by his "allies." Colonel André Dewavrin, the chief of de Gaulle's intelligence branch, the Bureau Central de Renseignements et d'Action (BCRA), had his men probing deeply into the corners of the Allied high command in London, seeking clues about the locale and time of the looming invasion about which many were talking.

Now the entire plan could have been in de Gaulle's hands. But strangely, the French officer on the telephone to the two policemen showed no interest in the top-secret materials the Britons had found along the road and in the fields. So General de Gaulle would learn about Torch when he heard about the invasion on the radio in London.[4]

Eisenhower Aide Helps Trick Germans

IN MID-OCTOBER 1942, German intelligence agencies were beginning to get wind of a huge Allied amphibious operation that was in the making. As D Day for Torch neared, it was impossible for the Allies to keep the world from knowing that hundreds of ships were massing in the British Isles.

Consequently, British deception agencies launched a global machination to hoodwink Adolf Hitler and his generals as to the destination of this fleet. Should the scheme fail, U-boat wolfpacks would lurk along the sea-lanes to French Northwest Africa to ambush and wreak havoc upon the Allied convoys.

As speculation grew that the Anglo-Americans were about ready to strike a heavy blow at some unidentified locale, the British secret service had scores of its agents in Paris, Madrid, Lisbon, Ankara, Cairo, and as far away as Rio de Janeiro to spread rumors in a clever campaign of sibs (taken from the Latin *sibilare*, meaning to hiss).

These sibs were whispered confidentially in the embassies known to be sympathetic to Nazi Germany. To account for the greatly increased activity in the British Isles and adjacent sea-lanes, the Anglo-Americans were preparing to unleash Operation Jupiter, an invasion of German-held Norway. Or so went the "cover" stratagem.

A major component of this disinformation campaign was the use of "turned" Nazi spies who had been captured in England. These agents had been given the choice between being hanged or radioing back to their former Abwehr controllers in Germany false information cleverly conceived by British intelligence agents. None of the spies chose to be hanged.

Americans at all levels became involved in the duel of wits to mask Torch. One of these was Lieutenant Commander Harry C. Butcher, who had been friends with General Dwight Eisenhower for many years prior to the war and most recently had been a top executive with CBS radio in New York City.

When Eisenhower had arrived in London in June 1942 to command U.S. forces in Europe, he asked for Butcher to be assigned to his staff as a "sort of naval symbol." Butcher became far more than that intangible designation: he was the general's closest personal confidant.

American media correspondents covering the European Theater of Operations knew that Butcher was close to Eisenhower. So the reporters kept a sharp eye on what the unofficial "naval aide" was doing or preparing to do. Consequently, British disinformation artists utilized Butcher's position as the centerpiece for a scheme to further confuse German intelligence.

It was a simple, yet highly effective, ruse. A pair of Arctic boots and a heavily lined parka were carefully placed in a corner of Butcher's office. The cold-weather gear was quickly detected by sharp-eyed correspondents alert for some clue to Allied plans.

Butcher played his role to the hilt. When the correspondents began eyeing the parka and boots, the naval aide quickly picked up the items, in a nonchalant manner, and put them in a closet.

There was no law against reporters creating speculative stories. So within days after the "security lapse" in Commander Butcher's office, articles began appearing in American newspapers that the Western Allies might invade an arctic locale. This could only mean Norway to German intelligence.[5]

The General's Pants Go AWOL

OPERATION TORCH WAS rife with haunting imponderables. Among the foremost of these conceivable eventualities was what one exasperated American general called "the goddamned French political mess."

When the Germans had crushed France's army in only six weeks in mid-1940, the armistice specified that Germany would occupy roughly the northern half of France, while the French could establish their own government for the nation at Vichy, in unoccupied France.

Adolf Hitler had no intention of allowing a potentially hostile, if defeated, France to govern itself. So he installed a revered French hero of World War I, eighty-four-year-old Marshal Henri Pétain, as the puppet ruler of France.

In what he projected as a benevolent concession, Hitler permitted the Vichy government to maintain control of Algeria and Morocco, two French colonies in Northwest Africa. Pétain's armed forces in those territories were limited by the armistice to 120,000 men.

The "French political mess" involved bitter quarrels between French factions, French national pride, conflicting definitions of "honor" as perceived by members of the French military corps, and a bitter dispute over which of two French governments—the one in Vichy or the one established in exile in London by General Charles de Gaulle—was the legally constituted one.

Through clandestine contacts, Allied leaders in London had learned that there was considerable pro-American sentiment among French military officers in Algeria and Morocco. At the same time, disturbing bits of information trickled into Eisenhower's headquarters to the effect that the French in Northwest Africa would resist an invasion "with all the means at their disposal."

At 9:55 A.M. on Sunday, October 18, 1942, the red telephone, a direct "scrambled-line" connecting Norfolk House in London with 20 Grosvenor Square, two miles away, jangled impatiently. U.S. Major General Mark W. Clark, the chief planner for Torch, picked up the instrument.

"Come right away!" General Dwight D. Eisenhower barked on the other end of the line.

The bleak coast of North Africa (left), where General Mark W. Clark landed by submarine. The house atop the bluff (right), where Clark met secretly with French officers. (Author's collection)

Clark, called the American Eagle by British Prime Minister Winston Churchill, rushed to 20 Grosvenor Square. Walking briskly into Eisenhower's office, he said, "When do I go?"

"Probably right away," Eisenhower replied.

Thus was launched one of the strangest secret missions of the war.

Eisenhower had received word from Robert Murphy, an American who ostensibly held a middle-level diplomatic post in French Northwest Africa but was actually a high-grade espionage agent, that London should immediately sneak a high-ranking military officer into Algeria.

Murphy said that he had been contacted by General Emmanuel Mast, French commander in Algiers, and that Mast wanted to confer with the London emissary about Allied plans for Torch. Mast had indicated that it could be arranged for the French Army to cooperate with the invaders instead of fighting them.

Mast had specifically recommended that the "senior general officer" should come by submarine. An isolated house along the Mediterranean coastline had been selected for the rendezvous site. The secret session was to be held the night of October 21, only four days away.

Mark Clark had volunteered for the covert mission. Going with him would be Brigadier General Lyman L. Lemnitzer, chief of the Allied Force Plans Section; U.S. Navy Captain Jerauld Wright; and Colonel Julius C. Holmes, who spoke French fluently.

At 6:30 A.M. on October 20, Mark Clark and his party lifted off in two B-17 Flying Fortresses for the first leg of the trip. Clark had replaced the two stars on his uniform with the silver leaves of a lieutenant colonel. If captured, he theorized, he would have a better chance of escaping if the hostiles did not immediately know that they had bagged a top general.

After the party landed at Gibraltar, the British rock fort in the opening of the Mediterranean Sea, the officers climbed into the submarine HMS *Seraph*. Shortly after dark on October 21, the undersea craft surfaced off the rendezvous point, the isolated villa owned by a Frenchman, Henri Tessier.

General Clark and others in the party scrambled into rubber boats and paddled ashore, where they were met by the superspy Robert Murphy. He took them to the Tessier home where General Emmanuel Mast and other French officers were waiting.

During a conversation lasting for about two hours, Mast and his colleagues provided the Americans with a bonanza of intelligence about troop dispositions, gun batteries, headquarters, and installations. But Clark had received strict orders not to provide the Frenchmen with the precise time and places of the invasion, only that it would strike soon.

At about 4:00 A.M. the telephone jangled. Tessier answered, then whirled around and shouted: "Get out! The police will be here in a few minutes!" A confederate in Algiers had made the call.

Mark Clark and the other Americans hid in a cold, damp wine cellar only minutes before the French police burst into the house. For an hour Clark gripped his carbine as the police moved around above him. Finally, they left but told Tessier that they would be back, that something suspicious was afoot.

Only much later would Clark learn what had triggered the raid. Tessier's five Arab servants had been sent away by him, and they believed that something illegal was to take place at the villa. So to collect the generous rewards to informers about illegal activities, the Arabs had contacted the police about the "smugglers" who had come ashore.

After the police had driven away, Robert Murphy opened the trap door leading to the wine cellar and called out, "They'll be back. You'd better get the hell out of here!"

Clark and the others needed no further urging. They hurried down to the beach where the rubber boats had been concealed. A radio carried by one of the party alerted the *Seraph* skipper to surface offshore.

The sea was angry. Gigantic waves were up. But Clark realized that the party would have to get to the submarine before daylight, because the French police would arrive back at the Tessier villa.

Knowing that he would get soaked to the skin paddling out to the *Seraph*, Clark removed his pants and rolled up his clothing to keep it as dry as possible.

Clark and the others got into the rubber boats and began paddling. Halfway to the *Seraph*, a huge wave overturned the boats, and they had to swim in the bitterly cold water back to shore.

Reaching the beach and shivering violently, the Americans hid in nearby woods to await a calmer sea. Clark and his team were chilled, soaked, exhausted, and hungry. The general, with no pants, was the coldest of them all. Somehow Tessier knew of the predicament, and he brought several sweaters—and a pair of pants for Mark Clark.

With daylight approaching and French police searching the area, the general decided another effort would have to be made to reach the *Seraph* three-quarters of a mile offshore. Clark felt that he had been paddling for hours when he reached the submarine.

As the *Seraph* headed for Gibraltar, the shivering landing party put a considerable dent in one of His Majesty's rum kegs, which the Royal Navy submarines carried for emergencies. But not before General Clark had affixed his signature to a formal document declaring that this situation was, indeed, "a serious emergency."

Mark Clark would establish a distinguished record as a combat commander during the war. But he would also forever be known as possibly the only general who had ever carried out a secret mission without his pants.[6]

Mystery of the Vanishing Report

AS D DAY FOR OPERATION TORCH, set for November 8, 1942, drew closer, Ultra, the supersecret British interception and decoding of German messages, disclosed that the Oberkommando der Wehrmacht (German High Command) was totally ignorant about the looming invasion of French Northwest Africa. However, German intelligence had been desperately seeking to learn the ultimate destination of the Allied force that had been building up in the British Isles.

One day Navy Captain Herbert Wichmann, the Abwehr's station chief of Hamburg, received a blockbuster report from what was described as "an A-1 source." Hamburg was responsible for collecting information from Great Britain and the United States.

The timely and accurate report identified, "without question," that the Allied invasion target was the French colonies of Algeria and Morocco.

Elated over this intelligence bonanza, Wichmann sent the report to the Oberkommando der Wehrmacht in Berlin under the speediest priority and highest security classification. This procedure should have assured that it would be read by Adolf Hitler.

Only years later would Wichmann learn that this report had amazingly vanished somewhere along the chain of command and never reached the Oberkommando der Wehrmacht.

The entire scenario was shrouded in mystery. Who in the Allied camp would have access to such a top-secret report and the means to slip it to the Abwehr in Hamburg? A logical "A-1 source" could have been one of the most notorious traitors of the war, Harold "Kim" Philby, a Briton.

Philby was a top official in MI-6, the British cloak-and-dagger agency responsible for collecting intelligence abroad. His desk at MI-6 headquarters was a short distance down the hall from that of Stewart Menzies, a wealthy Scot who headed the clandestine organization.

Philby, in fact, was a protégé of Menzies, who would learn only years later that the young man was a particularly intelligent and devious spy for Josef Stalin and the Soviet Union. In his undercover role, Philby maintained covert contacts with Nazi agents, and could easily have slipped the Torch report to Captain Wichmann in Hamburg. A disaster inflicted on the Torch invasion fleet by U-boats and submarines could have been a coveted goal of Stalin.

In this bizarre chain of events, there later would be much conjecture about who, in the German camp, was in such a high-level position that he could sidetrack the Torch report before it reached Hitler and the Oberkommando der Wehrmacht. That furtive figure could well have been Admiral Wilhelm Canaris, the cagey head of the Abwehr.

Even before war in Europe had erupted in September 1939, Canaris had been in secret contact with British undercover agents. Now he was a key figure in the Schwarze Kapelle (Black Orchestra), a group of prominent German military officers, government officials, and civic leaders who sought to get rid of the führer.

Whoever may have been the furtive figures—the one who sneaked the Torch intelligence bonanza to the Abwehr in Hamburg and the one who confiscated the document before it reached Adolf Hitler—would never be known for sure.

However, one factor would be certain: When the Allies invaded French Northwest Africa, the führer and his generals would be taken by total surprise.[7]

Hostile Horsemen Chase Airplane

IT WAS COLD AND DAMP in a bleak locale known as Land's End, a cape in the westernmost point of England. In the darkness, 556 men of the U.S. 509th Parachute Infantry Battalion were preparing to climb into forty-four C-47 transport planes to launch the first mass airborne operation in American history. It was November 8, 1942—D Day minus 1 for Operation Torch, the invasion of Northwest Africa.

At 9:05 P.M. the first C-47 sped down the runway and lifted off, followed by other aircraft. Forming up over Land's End, the sky train set a course for the Mediterranean coast. The paratroopers were to jump ten miles inland in support of amphibious forces storming the shore at Oran, Algeria.

On board one of the planes was Major William P. Yarborough, who had planned the daunting parachute mission, which was fraught with potential disaster. All participants were green: paratroopers, pilots, and navigators. The sky armada would fly sixteen hundred miles—four times the maximum distance German paratroop missions had traveled earlier in the war—and hit a pinpoint target, an airfield. What if the plodding, unarmed, unescorted flight were pounced on by speedy German fighter planes? It would be a turkey shoot.

For two hours the sky train kept on course and in precise formation. But over the Bay of Biscay, strong easterly winds, heavy rains, darkness, and navigators' inexperience conspired to scatter the aircraft.

Daylight brought a surge of alarm to the awakening paratroopers. Peering through the small windows, they saw that their C-47s were alone or with only two or three other aircraft. One of the C-47s lumbering along by itself in the early morning haze carried Major Bill Yarborough, who had no way of knowing that his plane was two hundred miles off-course.

Yarborough's C-47 soon reached the North African coastline, and the pilot swung eastward and began following the water's edge. Like a lost sheep the plane winged onward as the major continued to scour the terrain for a recognizable landmark.

Some fifteen minutes later Yarborough spotted a C-47 parked on the desert. Only later would he learn that the plane had landed by mistake in Spanish Morocco, which was pro-German. As Yarborough's plane drew closer, he could see many soldiers surrounding the grounded C-47. He ordered the pilot to land nearby so he could orient himself from the other plane's crew.

While the pilot was gliding into a landing, Yarborough suddenly shouted: "Pull up! Don't land! Those are hostiles down there!"

Yarborough's plane gained altitude and began circling. Only now did the major see a second C-47 on the ground and it was rolling along.

Yarborough looked on in amazement at the scenario that was unfolding. Perhaps ten men on horseback, wearing white flowing robes, were furiously waving their rifles and shaking their fists as they chased the C-47 that was in the process of lifting off. The hostiles were blanketed by thick clouds of dust.

No doubt this had been the first time in history that men on horseback were galloping along in mad pursuit of an airplane.[8]

A Dead Sergeant Walks Away

As THE OPERATION TORCH paratroop flight had been winging through the rainy night, the Oran battle convoy edged silently into position six to ten miles offshore. Oran's harbor facilities would be essential to future Allied campaigns, so a daring plan, code-named Operation Reservist, had been designed to knock out covering French forts and capture the docks before they could be blown up.

At 3:00 A.M. on November 8, 1942, two British vessels, the *Walney* and the *Hartland*, former U.S. Coast Guard cutters transferred to the Royal Navy in

1941, now crammed with assault troops, were to dash boldly into Oran harbor and carry out the mission.

Commanding both cutters was Royal Navy Captain Frederick T. Peters, who had been chiefly responsible for planning Reservist and would be in charge of the daring operation.

A retired officer who had volunteered for this crucial task, Peters was optimistic about the venture. He not only contemplated seizing the big French guns on the heights peering down on the city, but looked forward to receiving the surrender of Oran itself. Peters would be aboard the *Walney*, which would be the first vessel charging into the harbor.

Other officers on the *Walney* and *Hartland* were not noticeably enthused about chances for success. The two cutters were not only relics but were unarmored and carried only one five-inch gun apiece.

Surprise would be crucial. The plan was for the *Walney*, cloaked by darkness, to ram through the floating boom forming the Oran harbor gate. With two hundred American troops aboard, *Walney* was to dash into the harbor, lay alongside the Môle du Ravin Blanc, and the troops were to claw their way up the steep cliff directly behind the pier and knock out the Ravin Blanc gun battery.

An almost breathless hush hovered over Oran. Suddenly, the tranquility was shattered; the sound of air-raid sirens pierced the blackness. Clearly, the invaders had been discovered.

Now the *Walney* and the *Hartland* were knifing through the dark waters toward the floating boom that stretched for two hundred yards across the harbor's mouth to guard against hostile assaults. Then a brilliant searchlight on the cliff bathed the *Walney* in iridescence. The *Hartland* remained undetected. Moments later the big guns of the Ravin Blanc battery opened fire. Shells began sending up geysers to either side of the *Walney*.

Brightly illuminated, the little vessel charged onward and crashed into the boom at full speed with an ear-splitting crunch. Now inside the harbor, the *Walney* headed for its objective, the Môle du Ravin Blanc.

At point-blank range, the guns atop the cliff continued to pour shells at the cutter. Unknown to Captain Peters, two French submarines and a destroyer were moored near the pier, and they blasted away at the *Walney* with machine-gun fire and 75-millimeter rounds from only two hundred yards away.

A broadside from the destroyer's guns riddled *Walney*'s bridge, killing several officers, wounding others, and blowing Captain Peters into the night.

Down in the inky blackness of a compartment of the *Walney*, thirty-seven-year-old U.S. Sergeant Ralph Gower was huddled fearfully with comrades he could only sense were around him. A shell had ripped into the compartment, and to Gower, it seemed to explode right in his face.

The blast knocked Gower cold, and when he regained consciousness he could hardly breathe and thought he was going to choke to death. The compartment reeked with ammonia, cordite fumes, and thick smoke.

In his mind, the sergeant was puzzled. All was quiet—even tomblike. Only later would he realize that the shell's blast had left him deaf. He struggled over to a steel ladder and somehow pulled his way up to the deck. He could discern the streams of tracer bullets hissing through the blackness and countless orange bursts from exploding shells. Yet he could hear nothing.

Groggy and weak, Gower saw what he thought were stacks of rumpled barracks bags on the deck. However, these were the dead bodies of American soldiers and British sailors. Gower again lost consciousness.

Revived once more, he found himself lying on the deck by the railing. He became even more frightened, because he was unable to move. Then he realized that dead bodies had been stacked on him and were the cause of his immobility.

Apparently in an effort to clear a path on the *Walney*'s body-littered deck, someone had thought the unconscious Gower was dead and had put him to one side and stacked the corpses on top of him.

Laboriously pulling himself out from under the pile of dead men, Gower could see, by the light of exploding shells and tracer streams, the astonished look on the face of a young British sailor as he happened by and saw the "dead man" get up and stagger away.

Sergeant Gower would miraculously survive the tornado of explosives that ripped into the *Walney*, which, smoking and a tangled mass of steel, sank into Oran harbor.[9]

A Tank Commander's Close Call

DARKNESS WAS STARTING TO GATHER over Northwest Africa on D Day for Operation Torch as U.S. Lieutenant Colonel Harry H. Semmes was standing in the turret hatch of his tank that was rolling along a blacktop road. Behind him were seven tanks of his 2nd Armored Division task force that had landed that morning near Port Lyautey, sixty miles northeast of Casablanca in French Morocco.

Less than an hour earlier, Semmes had been ordered to head for the southern portion of the beachhead and block the Rabat–Lyautey road along which a French armored column was approaching.

Arriving at his destination, Semmes deployed his tanks in a blocking position and waited. The young armored commander, new to battle, was worried. It was too dark to issue orders to his tankers by arm signals, nor could he communicate with them by radio—his equipment had been ruined by salt spray while at sea. If the French struck before dawn, each tank leader would be on his own.

As the black sky began to lighten, Harry Semmes was scanning the Rabat–Lyautey road through his binoculars. Suddenly, he tensed. Approaching his tiny armored force were an estimated two battalions of French infantry supported by about sixteen Renault tanks.

Clearly, the French commander had spotted the American armored vehicles. The World War I vintage Renaults deployed in clusters of twos and threes to get into position to fire their 37-millimeter guns.

Semmes shouted "commence firing," and within ten minutes four of the ancient Renaults were smoking, blackened hulks. French tankers, in turn, began blasting away at the American force.

Soon two Cub spotter planes began hovering over the site of the shoot-out and sent instructions to the destroyer *Savannah* lying offshore. Within minutes the warship's big shells began exploding around and on the French force. Surviving infantrymen and tankers pulled back rapidly and disappeared over a ridge.

A hush fell over the battleground. Colonel Semmes was proud of his men in their first combat. His tank itself had picked off two of the Renaults. He hopped down from his tank, removed his helmet, and lit a cigarette.

Semmes began inspecting his tanks, and was amazed that none had been hit by the French shells. Returning to his own tank, he gawked and swallowed hard. Two armor-piercing shells that had failed to explode were embedded in the tank.[10]

Espionage in the Vatican

LATE IN 1942, after Allied forces had invaded Northwest Africa, the Office of Strategic Services (OSS) in Washington, D.C., received a blockbuster proposal from Vatican City, the Catholic enclave in the middle of fascist Rome. A high official of the Papal Secretariat offered to provide the Americans with firsthand information on bombing targets in Japan. This information was being collected by representatives of the Pope in Tokyo.

The OSS leaped to accept this offer, and a complicated espionage network was created. The intelligence gathered in Tokyo was sent to a certain contact in the Vatican. Some said that the unidentified cleric was Monsignor Giovanni Battista Montini (who later would become Pope Paul VI).

With the secret approval of Irish Prime Minister Eamon de Valera, who had been born in New York City of a Spanish father and an Irish mother, a Vatican courier took the top-secret data to the Irish Embassy in Rome. Then the information was taken by sacrosanct diplomatic pouch to Dublin.

There Ricardo Mazzerini, who represented the OSS, slipped into the embassy at night and left with the intelligence from Tokyo. He took the thick sheaf of paper to London, where the data was transmitted in a special code to OSS headquarters in Washington, D.C. There the information was analyzed by a former colonel in the Italian air force, who had been air attaché at the Italian Embassy in Tokyo before he "defected" to the United States. Either he had been bribed or strong-armed into switching sides.

Despite the complexity of this conduit, it required less than a week for the high-grade intelligence on bombing targets in Japan to get from Tokyo to Rome to Dublin to Washington and to air commanders in the field.[11]

OSS Agent's Hidden Bribes

THE OFFICE OF STRATEGIC SERVICES, America's cloak-and-dagger agency founded just before the nation had been dragged into the war, scored countless major intelligence and sabotage coups despite its newness to the field. But not all of its schemes proved to be effective.

In London in early 1943, an eager-beaver OSS officer sold his superiors on providing each agent infiltrating into German-occupied Western Europe with unmounted diamonds to be used as bribes to escape in case of capture. An agent could carry two or three of these small but highly valuable pieces secreted in his rectum.

It was pointed out to this OSS officer that the first thing the Germans would search on a captured spy was his rectum for just such contraband. But the officer insisted that this scheme was highly worthwhile, so perhaps a million dollars was invested in diamonds for his agents leaving for France.

In the months ahead, almost all of the returning spies reported that the stones had been "lost." OSS cynics in London agreed that the jewels no doubt had been lost—in French whorehouses.[12]

An Unlikely Spy Scores Coup

RENÉ DUCHEZ, a wiry, unimpressive-looking housepainter in his mid-forties, was well known to the Geheime Staatzpolizei (Gestapo) in Caen, the ancient capital of Normandy known for its magnificent cathedral. These secret police agents had been involved for many months in trying to crack an underground ring called Centurie that was known to be operating in the region.

Although hundreds of men and women among the forty thousand residents of Caen had been grilled by the Germans, Duchez was left alone because he was thought to be retarded, and therefore no threat to the Third Reich.

Actually, Duchez had been a courier for Centurie since it had been organized in mid-1942. His task was a perilous one; a sudden personal search by the Gestapo would catch him red-handed with the incriminating messages.

Duchez, a free spirit, worried his resistance comrades. He loved to taunt the Gestapo and had a unique talent for putting on a convincing portrayal of an idiot seized by epileptic fits. If he spotted Gestapo agents in a café when he was imbibing late at night (which was often), he strolled casually toward their table, fell on the floor at their feet, jerking and twitching and uttering gurgling noises. While the Germans looked on in disgust, Duchez drooled large amounts of saliva, and his eyes would bulge until they promised to burst from their sockets. After the "fit" continued for a minute, the Germans could endure no more and stalked out of the bistro.

Meanwhile, forty-two-year-old Marcel Girard, a cement salesman who lived in Caen and was the leader of Centurie, had grown depressed in early 1943. During recent days he had become aware that the Germans had thrown up barriers and established a Zone Interdite (Forbidden Zone) that ran several miles inland along the entire English Channel coast. What were the occupiers doing along the waterfront that required such drastic and secret actions? Allied intelligence in London wanted the answer.

Unbeknownst to Girard (or anyone else in the Allied camp), Adolf Hitler had envisioned an eventual Anglo-American assault across the English Channel against his stolen empire. So in mid-March 1942 he had decreed that an Atlantikwall stretching for fifteen hundred miles from Norway to the Spanish frontier be constructed with "fantastic speed."

Centurie's spies had been unable to penetrate the Zone Interdite, so they had been able to report only on secondary German defenses far behind the beaches.

On the night of May 13, 1943, Girard met René Duchez at the popular Café des Touristes. Glancing casually around the crowded room, the network leader spotted two men he believed to be Gestapo agents, and the bar was crowded with German soldiers.

Duchez handed a large envelope to Girard, who asked what it contained. Putting on his idiot face, the painter replied nonchalantly, "Oh, it's nothing but a blueprint of the entire Atlantic Wall in Normandy!"

Girard felt a chill race up his spine. René was a great joker; was this one of his skits for antagonizing the Germans?

"Where did you get it?" Girard finally asked in a whisper.

"Stole it from the Todt Organization," the grinning painter replied airily, referring to the huge construction bureau charged with building Wehrmacht defenses in Europe.

Girard stashed the envelope under his topcoat, shook hands with Duchez, and strolled as casually as possible out of the bar. He pledged to himself that if this was another of René's jokes, he would strangle the courier.

Only when the network chief reached home and hastily pulled down the shades did he dare to open the envelope and stare at a six-foot-long blueprint. It was stamped in several places with the German equivalent to Top Secret. Across the top of the blueprint in large letters was the word: Atlantikwall.

Clearly Duchez had pulled off a gargantuan espionage bonanza. What Girard was looking at was a map of 125 miles of Channel coast, showing all planned fortification: bunkers, machine-gun and flame-thrower positions, gun batteries, ammunition dumps, and command posts. No one in Centurie would know until a year later that this map covered the Normandy region where the Allies would storm ashore.

Within a week, the blueprint reached London by way of the underground network in France. But Girard and his resistance leaders remained mystified: How had René pulled off the intelligence coup? Later, Duchez, giggling like a mischievous schoolboy, let Girard in on the secret.

The Todt Organization office in Caen had advertised for bids to repaper its offices. Sensing a chance to get inside this heavily guarded place, Duchez showed up with a book of wallpaper samples and was escorted into the office of the German in charge, an aging reserve colonel. While the officer was thumbing through the sample book, Duchez, pretending to be helpful, leaned over the colonel's shoulder and drooled saliva on his expensive tunic.

In the meantime, a subordinate entered the room, and, without paying any attention to Duchez, placed a stack of blueprints on the colonel's desk. René's sharp eye caught the wording on the top document: Atlantikwall.

Minutes later, the colonel was called out of the room leaving the "retarded" Frenchman alone with the top-secret map. Duchez's keen mind was spinning. Here was a once-in-a-lifetime chance. Should he steal the map? If so, how would he get it out of the building?

Duchez snatched the blueprint off the top of the stack and tucked it behind a wall mirror. Just then the colonel returned. The two men struck a deal. The German picked out his sample, and the Frenchman was to start working in the morning.

When the Centurie agent began papering the office, the colonel stayed away so as not to impede the work. Later in the afternoon the job was finished. Duchez retrieved the blueprint from behind the mirror and stuck it into an empty wallpaper container.

Whistling a tune, Duchez walked nonchalantly toward the front door of the building with the map under his arm. Outside, two German soldiers were standing guard. Grinning and drooling, the Frenchman could not resist talking with them. Edging up close, he let saliva drop on their uniforms before they could back off. Then bowing and saluting, the blueprint thief departed.

This highly unlikely spy had scored one of the great heists of any war. It would never be known how many Allied lives were saved when the Normandy invasion hit a year later. No doubt the total ran into the thousands.[13]

Eisenhower Disclosure
Stuns Reporters

AT HIS HEADQUARTERS in Algiers, North Africa, Supreme Commander Dwight Eisenhower stood before a large room full of reporters. Knowing that the Western Allies had been lying dormant since German and Italian forces in Tunisia had surrendered the previous month, the correspondents were expecting a routine announcement. It was June 10, 1943.

What the reporters received instead was a bombshell of a kind that had never exploded before and probably never would again.

"We will assault Sicily early in July, with the British Eighth Army under General [Bernard] Montgomery attacking the eastern beaches and the U.S. Seventh Army under General [George] Patton attacking the southern beaches," Eisenhower said.

Mouths fell open. An eerie hush pervaded the room. An official statement to scores of reporters one month in advance of a major military operation, including the target and time, stunned the listeners.

Eisenhower held back virtually nothing. Reporters ceased to scribble notes, because the supersecret information could not be sent to their newspapers, magazines, and radio outlets back home. Each correspondent realized that thousands of Allied lives and a crucial invasion could be the price paid for any inadvertent leaking of this awesome briefing.

Eisenhower left the room. Most of the correspondents remained in their chairs—dazed and silent. Then, individually and in twos and threes, they drifted away. Many resisted impulses to glance back over their shoulders to see if anyone was following them—German spies.

The supreme commander's thunderclap had not been loosed impulsively. It had been thoroughly debated with key staff officers. Curiously, the purpose of the unprecedented briefing was to maintain secrecy. With no major operation in progress, the reporters had to send regular dispatches back to the United States. Most of these stories were speculative in nature, as each reporter sought a new "angle," the traditional hallmark of a journalist.

Eisenhower's intelligence officers had noticed that some of these "guesses" were hitting quite close to the true plan, and it was feared that the crafty Germans might piece them together to pinpoint Sicily as the next invasion target.

Incredibly, perhaps, there would not be a single leak. When the Sicily assault erupted on July 10, the Germans and Italians on the triangular-shaped island were taken by total surprise.

Later, John H. "Beaver" Thompson, correspondent for the *Chicago Tribune*, told colleagues, only half in jest: "For a month I was afraid to go to bed at night. I thought I might talk in my sleep and spill the beans when a German spy was near."[14]

A Horrendous Bombing
Error Pays Off

LATE IN JUNE 1943, the sixty-ninth mission of the England-based U.S. Eighth Air Force was launched by its commander, General Ira C. Eaker. Fifty bombers were being sent to pound a German airfield on the outskirts of Brussels, the capital and second largest city of Belgium with a population of about one and a half million.

There was a haunting risk of killing Belgian civilians, because the approach to the German airfield would take the bombers directly over Brussels. That route was thought to be the safest, because the Germans seldom wasted antiaircraft guns protecting cities they occupied in Europe.

However, to be on the safe side, Eaker's crews had been warned at a briefing to be especially careful about dropping their bombs on anything but the designated airfield.

The flight lifted off from its base in England, and a short time later it was passing over Brussels. Bombardiers opened bomb-bay doors and checked their bombsights. Practicing for the real thing in a few minutes, the lead bombardier spotted a large park in the middle of a crowded residential area, and he used it as a simulated aiming point.

Suddenly, the young blond bombardier was stricken with fright: he felt the bomber shake as the bombs were released. As was the practice, the other bombardiers behind him in his combat group saw the explosives drop and they released their bombs. Looking downward, the horrified lead bombardier saw the park and the neighboring houses being devastated by the fiery explosions.

Back in England after the mission, the air base was wrapped in gloom. Never before had an entire group of bombers errantly dropped its collective payload that no doubt killed hundreds of civilians sympathetic to the Allies.

Two days later the pilots, navigators, and bombardiers in the Brussels mission were summoned to the headquarters of Brigadier General Robert Williams, leader of the 1st Bombardment Wing. The horrendous error would be reviewed, the fliers knew, and no doubt severe punishment would be meted out to the errant bombardier and possibly others.

"I don't know how it happened," the lead bombardier, barely out of his teens, testified in a low voice. "Whatever the cause, I alone am to blame." After pausing for several seconds, he added: "I can only say I regret the day I was born."

The room was silent as a tomb when the lieutenant had concluded his remarks. General Williams, who had lost an eye while serving as an observer during the Battle of Britain in 1940, scanned his fliers with his remaining orb.

Williams said that the Brussels mission had been "investigated" by Allied agents in Belgium and by "other intelligence sources." The latter category no doubt was referring to Ultra, the code name for the British interception and decoding of German radio messages.

Williams paused. His audience presumed that he was about to disclose the huge death toll among Brussels civilians. "We have learned that the results aren't nearly as bad as we had feared," he said. Another pause of several seconds.

"We have been informed that the German authorities in Brussels had felt the park and the upscale houses surrounding it were ideal for billeting troops," Williams continued. "So the entire circumference of the park was being used for that purpose. There were more than twelve hundred casualties among the German soldiers—and only a few Belgian civilians had been killed or injured.

"The mission has resulted in the German leaders in Belgium calling it a remarkable exhibition of American precision bombing," the general exclaimed. "Such are the fortunes of war. This incident is now closed."[15]

Freak Encounter in No-Man's-Land

PARATROOPERS OF THE ELITE but green U.S. 82nd Airborne Division received electrifying news at their bivouac area in Tunisia, North Africa. In forty-eight hours large numbers of them would spearhead Operation Husky, an Allied invasion of Sicily, a triangular-shaped island at the toe of Italy. It was July 8, 1943.

This was heady stuff. From the division commander, Major General Matthew B. Ridgway, on down the men were buoyed by the knowledge that they were on the brink of an historic mission. Not only would American paratroopers be cracking open Adolf Hitler's Festung Europa (Fortress Europe), but it would be the initial major combat jump by troops of any nation at night.

In the early morning darkness of D Day, Captain Edwin M. Sayre, a company commander in the 82nd Airborne, and fourteen of his men bailed out over Sicily and landed near a thick-walled, heavily fortified farmhouse on the heights known as Piano Lupo, inland from the coastal town of Gela, where the U.S. 1st Infantry Division was to storm ashore at dawn.

Holding a grenade in his teeth, another in one hand, and firing a pistol, the twenty-seven-year-old Sayre led a mad charge on the stronghold. Forty-three Italian and twelve German soldiers inside were captured, and fifteen others were killed. Four Americans were killed.

That night on Piano Lupo, Captain Sayre led a patrol into no-man's-land. It was pitch-black and the troopers edged along cautiously, weapons at the ready, eyes and ears alert. It was deathly still. Suddenly, the quiet was shattered. A machine gun to the front opened up withering bursts of fire at almost point-blank range. Sayre and his men flopped down.

While bullets hissed past their heads, the nine Americans began crawling and slithering toward the rear. After negotiating two hundred arduous yards, they reached a dry creek bed with five-foot-high banks and scrambled into its protective confines. Sprawled on the creek bottom to regain their breaths, the troopers heard shuffling sounds, and then ten dark figures leaped into the defile almost directly on top of them. Presumably, this was a 1st Infantry Division patrol seeking cover from the spurting machine gun.

The new men sat down and one called out in a hushed voice, *"Kompanie zu welcher Einheit gehosen Sie?"* (What company do you belong to?)

"They're Krauts!" an American shouted, whipping out his trench knife and plunging it into the nearest German. Now the creek bed was a whirling mass of thrashing, grunting, cursing bodies as men fought savagely with daggers, rifle butts, and swinging fists. Presently, surviving Germans wrenched loose and ran toward their own lines, leaving behind in the defile one dead and three wounded *Feldgrau* (field gray, the average German soldier).[16]

A Mule-Borne Commander

JUST AFTER MIDNIGHT, Captain Willard R. "Bill" Follmer, a company commander in the U.S. 82nd Airborne Division, was crawling along a dark hillside in Sicily. Parachuting to earth minutes earlier, he heard a loud snapping sound and felt a sharp pain race up his leg. His ankle had been broken in three places. It was July 10, 1943.

There in the blackness Follmer was worried. He had found himself alone and virtually immobile. Where were his men? Indeed, where were the thirty-five hundred other Americans in the 505th Parachute Infantry Regiment who were to have landed behind the invasion beaches? Had he been dropped by mistake on the wrong island?

Only later would the twenty-five-year-old Texan learn that heavy winds, inexperienced pilots and navigators, and darkness had resulted in the paratroopers being scattered along sixty miles of the Sicilian coast.

Now, after crawling for some one hundred arduous yards, the captain heard a faint rustling noise in the dark shadows. Whipping out his .45 Colt pistol, Follmer called out the password in a stage whisper: "George!" Came the reply: "Marshall!" Follmer felt a surge of relief when one of his sergeants emerged from the underbrush.

At the urging of the sergeant, Follmer climbed onto the other man, and in piggyback fashion the two troopers set out in search of the remainder of the company. As they trudged along, other men of Follmer's unit stepped out of the shadows. Within the hour, nearly all the company had assembled around their leader.

At the time the captain was unaware that his company was one of the few American parachute units to land on its designated drop zone.

Follmer's mission was to block roads to prevent enemy reinforcements inland from rushing to the beaches where amphibious forces would storm ashore after daylight. But how could the injured and immobile captain direct his company's actions?

His men had the answer. They "liberated" an ancient mule from a protesting farmer and hoisted the captain aboard.

No doubt Follmer was the only American officer in the war to lead his men into battle astride a mule.[17]

The Captain Refused to Be Killed

LATE ON THE NIGHT of July 11, 1943—D Day plus 1 for Operation Husky— an eerie silence blanketed the beachhead on Sicily's Gulf of Gela. Luftwaffe bombers had just flown away after pounding targets in the region for the fourth time in twelve hours. Ears were cocked for the sound of more German bombers. Jittery fingers were on triggers.

At 10:32 P.M. Captain Mack C. Shelley of the U.S. 504th Parachute Infantry Regiment was standing in the open door of his C-47 transport plane as it neared the dark and silent coast, where American amphibious forces had carved out a beachhead a day earlier. Shelley's flight was expected to be a "milk run," as a routine, uneventful mission was called. His regiment would jump *behind* American lines to reinforce the ground troops.

As Shelley's plane winged over the shore at seven hundred feet, American machine guns below began spitting streams of tracers skyward. Almost immediately, other guns followed suit. Then another and another. Soon, a wide sweep of the coast was aglow with a kaleidoscope of color. The C-47s flew directly into his hailstorm of fire.

Shelley had no way of knowing at the time that he was in the center of the most horrific friendly fire disaster of the war. He could see C-47s, with troopers and aircrews inside, burst into flame and plummet crazily to earth. Others received direct hits, exploding in midair and disintegrating.

Suddenly, Shelley felt an enormous jolt. His plane had been hit by a shell and had burst into flame. He was nearly blown out the open door but managed to grasp both sides of it and hold on. Fire engulfed the C-47. With the trooper still clinging to the open door, the plane glided to a crash landing.

Shelley was flung out the door and onto a heavy growth of brush that cushioned the impact. Yet he lost consciousness. An undetermined period of time later, he regained his senses, although his head was spinning and he was in great pain. He managed to shuck his parachute harness and crawl back to the burning wreckage to rescue comrades. Edging inside, he began tugging at

Captain Mack C. Shelley
"refused" to be killed on Sicily.
(Author's collection)

the first limp body. Moments later, there was an explosion, and again he was blown out of the aircraft.

Once more the captain blacked out. When he regained consciousness he became vaguely aware that two Italian soldiers were hovering over him. He understood their language sufficiently to know that they were arguing over whether or not to kill him. Again he passed out.

It was two days later, he learned, that he awakened in a German field hospital on the eastern coast of Sicily. His multiple injuries and burns were wrapped in yards of white gauze.

Despite his physical anguish, Shelley had been lucky. In the "milk run" flight, twenty-three C-47s had been shot down by friendly fire, killing ninety-seven paratroopers and sixty airmen. More than two hundred other Americans had been wounded.

Ten days after the paratroop captain had been carried into the field hospital, Canadian troops advancing up the east coast toward the major city of Messina freed the patients. Shelley was moved to a Canadian aid station, where he was told he would be evacuated to North Africa.

Despite agonizing pain from his burns and injuries, Shelley wanted to fight, so he ripped off his medical evacuation tag, put on his wrinkled, bloody, and dirty uniform that had been retrieved from a closet, and walked out of the aid station without authorization. After "liberating" the weapon of a wounded Canadian officer, the American hobbled off toward the front.

En route, he bumped into four Germans, and a shoot-out erupted. His right arm was badly burned, so he propped himself against a stone wall and blazed away with his good arm. When the four grenadiers charged firing Schmeisser machine pistols, the paratrooper killed three of them. The fourth hurled a potato-masher grenade, and the explosion sent a fragment tearing into Shelley's shoulder. However, he heaved a grenade that finished off the German.

Canadian medics found Shelley, barely conscious, and loaded him into an ambulance, which joined a road convoy heading for the British evacuation beach. Halfway on the trek, the Luftwaffe attacked the convoy, and a bomb exploded next to Shelley's ambulance, blowing him out through the back doors. He sustained yet another injury—a broken arm.

Picked up from the road, the American was placed in another ambulance, and this time he reached the shore. Captain Mack Shelley, who refused to be killed, finally arrived in North Africa on a hospital ship. He quipped to a comrade: "Hitler must have goofed. The Krauts didn't torpedo my ship!"[18]

Two GIs Beat Patton to Goal

THERE WAS NO KNOWN INSTANCE of anyone accusing U.S. General George S. Patton or British General Bernard L. Montgomery of being overburdened with humility. The two battle leaders despised each other.

In mid-August 1943, they were engaged in a "race" to be first to charge into Messina, the escape valve in the northeastern tip of Sicily through which the retreating German and Italian forces were being ferried across the two-mile-wide Strait of Messina to the Italian mainland.

A few days earlier Patton had captured the major city of Palermo in northwest Sicily, and then began attacking eastward along the coastal road toward Messina. At the same time, Montgomery was driving up the eastern shore toward the prized objective. Both of the Allied armies were slowed by German mines, demolitions, long-range artillery fire, and hostile terrain.

Meanwhile, south of Sicily across the Mediterranean Sea, thirty-one-year-old Captain Carlos C. Alden of the veteran U.S. 509th Parachute Infantry Battalion had grown restless and frustrated. He scribbled in his pocket diary: "This has been a tough time for morale in the 509th. While fighting is going on in Sicily, we sit here in a desolate, sun-scorched bivouac in Tunisia. Just sitting. Alerted for action. Rescinded. Alerted. Rescinded. Dry. Hot. Dusty. Boring."

Alden was the battalion surgeon, a free spirit who wore a red beret into battle instead of a helmet. A few months earlier he and his comrades had been fighting against General Erwin Rommel's vaunted Afrika Korps in Tunisia.

Captain Carlos C. Alden "welcomed" Patton's spearheads to Messina. (Author's collection)

Alden was always at the point of an attack or where the fighting was the heaviest. He had seen his unarmed medics, wearing Red Cross armbands and crosses painted on helmets, shot down. So he and his men ceased wearing medical identification on the battlefield and carried weapons, except for two men opposed to firearms on religious grounds.

Alden himself toted two pistols, a Tommy gun, and a trench knife. Moreover, he was an expert in their use.

Now Alden and the battalion's assistant surgeon, Captain A. A. Engleman, decided they would sneak into Sicily and, in Alden's words, "have a look around" where the fighting was raging. It was an unauthorized venture; they would be AWOL (absent without leave).

Early one morning Alden and Engleman hitched a ride on a U.S. cargo plane that landed on an improvised airstrip behind General Patton's Seventh Army. There they caught a ride in a truck that took them to near Patton's forward units. Then they began walking eastward for several miles, on past the front lines.

On their trek, the two paratroopers encountered German soldiers several times, but they paid no attention to the Americans, even though Alden was wearing his red beret and each man had a small American flag sewn to his jacket shoulder.

When the sun began sinking into the western horizon, the two officers knew they were far behind German lines when they reached a road sign with large letters: MESSINA.

They pushed on into the city. After nearly colliding with a German company marching along a street, Alden told his companion, "We'd better hold up here before our luck runs out!" Engleman agreed wholeheartedly.

The two doctors picked out an empty building and slipped inside. Now it was dark. While they were eating their field rations, artillery shells—Patton's shells—began crashing around their hideout and elsewhere in the city teeming with Germans.

Despite the explosions, both men were near exhaustion, and they dropped off into deep sleep. Shortly before dawn, they were awakened by more explosions. But there was a difference. "Those shells are coming from the [Italian] mainland across the strait!" Alden said. "They're German shells! All the Krauts in town must have pulled out during the night."

Within a few hours, tens of thousands of excited Sicilian men, women, and children packed the streets to cheer raucously and wave welcomes to General Patton's tank-tipped spearheads as they rolled into Messina. "Old Blood and Guts," as the flamboyant general was known, had beaten archrival Montgomery to Messina.

Like impish children, Alden and Engleman, grinning broadly, stood on a street corner and shouted at Patton's dust-caked tankers: "Where have you tourists been?"

Twenty-four hours later, the *New York Herald-Tribune* headline stated that Patton had beaten Montgomery to Messina. There was, of course, no mention about two venturesome American paratroopers being on hand to greet Patton's spearhead.[19]

"Prescriptions" for the Lady Spy

ONE OF THE U.S. Office of Strategic Services agents in Europe was a young American woman. She was strong, of strapping physique, highly athletic, and fluent in both French and German. Twice she had parachuted into occupied France on secret missions that were both highly important and hazardous beyond the norm.

Each time before departing for hostile territory, the young woman made only one demand: just before climbing into the airplane, she insisted on a heavy slug of brandy. She knew exactly how much to take to give her the added courage to leap into the dark unknown without dulling her perception to the danger point. When one high officer protested providing her with the "prescription" (as she called it), her reply was simple and to the point: "No brandy, no mission."[20]

Huge Bonus for a Jungle Spy

AUSTRALIAN COLONEL G. C. ROBERTS, controller of a widespread cloak-and-dagger apparatus, the Allied Intelligence Bureau (AIB), was seated at his desk in Brisbane perusing a radio message from Australian Navy Lieutenant Hugh MacKenzie. It was August 1943.

Turning to his deputy, Captain Allison Ind, Roberts said, "Kennedy's a blooming one-man army. Look at this!"

MacKenzie's message stated that New Zealander Donald Kennedy wanted the AIB to evacuate forty people who were living in his stockade and barracks on a copra plantation on New Georgia, in the southeastern Solomons. Kennedy's "boarders," as he called them, were twenty Japanese pilots who had been shot down, and the same number of American pilots who had been forced to bail out of crippled warplanes.

The energetic and resourceful Don Kennedy was a recruiter, a trainer, an observer, and a guerrilla leader with the Coastwatchers, a unique espionage network that had hundreds of agents on remote islands in a twenty-five-hundred-mile arc that covered the land, sea, and air approaches to Australia.

Before the war, the Australian government, with incredible foresight, had organized the Coastwatcher network. Military officers had fanned out into some of the world's most primitive islands to recruit jungle-wise gold miners, copra traders and planters, missionaries, telegraph operators, and administrators. Each Coastwatcher was intimately acquainted with his region and knew, if war broke out, which natives would be friendly to Caucasians and which would be hostile. After Pearl Harbor, the Coastwatcher network became a component of the AIB.

Don Kennedy was far more than just another Coastwatcher. Although his life was in danger almost constantly after the Japanese war machine engulfed the region north of Australia (Japanese patrols beat the bushes regularly in search of Coastwatchers), he had a much more comfortable life than did most of the jungle spies. He lived in a plantation house abandoned by the head of a copra firm.

Kennedy also had available the businessman's schooner, and, on occasion, the spy and a group of his native guerrillas sallied forth to shoot up Japanese shoreline positions and engage in pitched battles with enemy patrol boats.

Now in Brisbane, Captain Ind had finished reading the MacKenzie radio message, and Colonel Roberts grabbed a pencil and began calculating how much money AIB was going to owe the enterprising New Zealander. It had long been understood that a Coastwatcher was to receive a bonus for each rescued Allied pilot and captured Japanese airman.

Looking at Ind, Roberts said, "You Americans estimate that it costs $25,000 to train a pilot. That's $550,000 Kennedy has saved your taxpayers."

"How would you rate the Japanese pilots?" an officer asked.

"Same way," Roberts replied.

Two nights later a large Catalina flying boat, the type used extensively throughout the Pacific by the Allies, lifted off and set a course for New Georgia in one of the most curious missions of the war. On board was Kennedy's

The schooner used by Coastwatcher Donald Kennedy to raid Japanese positions lies at anchor in the Solomon Islands. (National Archives)

"bonus"—some $1 million (equivalent to about $10 million in 2002)—and two heavily armed soldiers to guard the Japanese "boarders" to be picked up.

Later that night, the Catalina touched down off the coast near the Kennedy plantation. The money bags were handed over to the New Zealander, and the Japanese captives—heavily trussed—and the twenty rescued U.S. pilots clambered aboard.[21]

"The Madame" Was a Secret Agent

SOON AFTER AMERICA was plunged into global war, a seventy-two-year-old widow who lived in Paris and on a country estate was recruited by undercover operatives of the U.S. Office of Strategic Services (OSS). Born in the United States, she had married a wealthy Frenchman after World War I, and had become so completely attuned to native life that friends forgot that she was an American.

After being contacted by the OSS agent at her chateau, the woman was asked if she would serve as a courier for the cloak-and-dagger agency. When she pointed to her age, the undercover operative assured her that the task would not be physically demanding. However, she would have to exercise courage, intelligence, and discretion. Her job would be to transmit secret messages between OSS agents in the Paris region.

After pondering the proposal for a few minutes, the woman accepted, even though it was pointed out that she would almost constantly be risking her life. The OSS never used her name, but referred to her respectfully as the Madame.

In the months ahead, the Madame took to her assignment as the proverbial duck takes to water. While carrying secret messages to various links in undercover cells in the Paris region, she invariably performed with a cool head and an enterprising mind.

On one occasion, while she was carrying an incriminating message in her pocketbook, two stern-looking German officers approached her on a Paris street. Her heart leaped into her mouth. It was too late to dispose of the damning piece of paper.

One of the officers tipped his hat in deference to the advanced age of the woman and asked politely for directions to a certain building. After breathing a sigh of relief, the Madame provided the information.

During a quiet period, the Madame decided to take a short trip to visit a personal friend. It was a scorching summer day. During her journey on a hot, sticky train packed with wall-to-wall humans, she had the need to go to the toilet. In wartime, lavatories on French trains were appalling. So the incisive woman spread a newspaper over the toilet seat before sitting down.

Soon after the Madame returned to her compartment, the train ground to a screeching halt at a small station. There were loud shouts as German soldiers scrambled into the coaches. Everyone was ordered off the train and into the station. Moments later, they were segregated; the women jammed into one large room, the men into another.

Two officious German females wearing Nazi uniforms loudly ordered all the women to strip totally naked. After the ritual had been completed, the German women began circulating through the room crowded with the assorted shapes of nude females, probing, inspecting body parts.

When the Nazis came to the Madame, she felt grateful that she had not been on an undercover mission. The inspectors ordered her to turn around. There were shouts of triumph from the Germans. One hurried from the room and returned minutes later with a small hand mirror.

Unceremoniously and to her embarrassment, the stylish, elegant but naked suspect was pushed facedown onto a table, while the Nazi women used the mirror to try to read the inverted "secret espionage message" on her ample bare behind. Presumably the Germans believed that they had detected a new technique that Allied spies were using to transmit secret messages. Actually, they were reading the morning news with the aid of the mirror.

The printing on her flesh had resulted from her use of the newspaper as a sanitary precaution on the Madame's visit to the train toilet. The moisture of her warm flesh in the stifling lavatory had picked up the newspaper ink. However, the Nazi women gleefully congratulated one another for discovering this new Allied technique.

The Madame had to lie in the exposed position for an hour, while the Nazis laboriously copied the morning news, word for word.

A half hour after the German women left the room, apparently to confer with their commanding officer, they returned, shouting for the passengers, including the Madame, to dress and get back on the train. The genteel, refined, aristocratic socialite-turned-spy chuckled to herself during the remainder of the trip. Clearly, the two German women's superior had not been impressed on reading the news from the Paris region.[22]

A Movie Fan on Bougainville

BOUGAINVILLE, the largest of the Solomon Islands in the southwest Pacific, had been fought over since the beginning of the war. Japanese forces had invaded the island and then the U.S. Marines stormed ashore in 1943 and carved out a large beachhead on which to build airstrips.

Living was still primitive for the Marines, but once the swamps were drained and huts were built, Bougainville was a relatively comfortable camp—by Pacific standards. It had the best climate in the Solomons, and the soil absorbed most of the furious cloudbursts instead of turning to knee-deep mud. A pleasant breeze blew steadily. Best of all, there was a minimum of malaria.

A Japanese soldier enjoyed American movies until he was caught.
(Rumsey Ewing)

The lone drawback to the easy living (by comparison) was the fact that Japanese occupied most of Bougainville, which has an area of about thirty-eight hundred square miles. Making themselves a nuisance, the Japanese snipers were active, and shellfire sporadically upset the peacefulness of the Marine camp.

So secure was the large beachhead, however, that outdoor movies were shown almost every night. On one occasion, a surprise inspection was made at the movies to make certain that every man was wearing his shoes and socks, as required by regulations. One man was found to be barefooted.

When he was taken into the light an amazing discovery was made: the barefoot man was a Japanese soldier. He explained that he had been hiding out in a foxhole in no-man's-land near the perimeter of the camp. After darkness fell, he would sneak through Marine lines and help himself to chow from the officers' galley. Then he attended the movies seated right in the middle of a couple of hundred Americans.

The enterprising Japanese soldier said he hadn't missed a show in a week.[23]

A GI Carries His Eyeball

MOUNT CROCE, soaring thirty-two hundred feet into the bleak, freezing sky of central Italy, had been part of German Field Marshal Albrecht Kesselring's so-called Winter Line. The towering elevation was to be held at all costs. But in November 1943, troopers of the veteran U.S. 509th Parachute Infantry Battalion drove a German force off the barren peak.

Three hours later the Germans launched a full-blooded counterattack to regain the elevation. Mortar and artillery shells exploded among the paratroopers. Bullets hissed into their positions. But the German force, which had been clawing its way upward on three sides, scurried back down Mount Croce under a hail of small arms fire.

For more than a week the paratroopers held on, almost constantly ducking shell bursts. Living conditions were miserable. Shallow slit trenches were lined with ice. Rations were frozen. Wounded men were likely to bleed to death before they could be tortuously carried down the mountain by medics or riflemen.

The walking wounded would live or die by their ability and strength to scramble back down the almost perpendicular mountainside to obtain medical aid in Venafro, a town at the bottom of Croce. One of those having an extremely difficult time in traversing the long descent—where mountain goats often stumbled—was Sergeant Robert Akers.

Shrapnel had peppered Akers in the face. Now, as he slipped and slid downward, he was holding his eyeball, still attached to its cords in his hand.

The fragment that had struck him had popped the eyeball out of its socket, and Akers had grabbed it.

Teenage Private Charles H. Doyle, who had been a lineman on his high school football team in Massachusetts only a year earlier, had been sent along to help the half-blind and bleeding Akers. While picking their way down-ward—the trek would require four hours for even an able-bodied soldier—Doyle had a disconcerting thought: "If Bob Akers collapses along the way, what'll I do with the eyeball he is carrying in his hand?"

But Sergeant Akers did make it to the bottom. From Venafro he was rushed to a field hospital where doctors popped the eyeball and its attached cords back into the socket.

Amazingly, Akers would regain full sight and be sent back into action before the war ended in Europe.[24]

Part Four

Beginning of the End

An Odd Place for Spying

ON JANUARY 16, 1944, General Dwight D. Eisenhower, the supreme commander for Operation Overlord, the looming invasion of Normandy, arrived in London. From that moment, Overlord began to dominate every respect of the war against Adolf Hitler. As Eisenhower would put it: "We are putting all our chips on the table!"

Much of the intensive and detailed planning took place behind the scenes: collecting crucial intelligence from along the English Channel coast in France. In one of the most daring and imaginative missions of the war, a team of two Allied agents produced a steady stream of information from the very midst of German forces.

All over northern France, especially in the small country towns, vendors of local wines used huge wooden casks mounted on a two-wheeled cart chassis. The vendors pushed the casks through town, selling direct to French civilians and German soldiers. The proper amount of wine was drawn from a bunghole at the bottom of the cask.

The pair of enterprising secret agents hatched a scheme in which an innocent-looking mobile cask would be the centerpiece. They built a dividing partition into the large container so that the bottom half could be filled with wine but the upper portion would remain dry.

In the top half, they installed a shortwave transmitter. Then, when all was ready, the radio operator climbed into the upper portion of the cask with his set. His teammate, with the bottom half of the cask filled with wine, began patrolling the streets of the region in search of the heaviest German activity.

Between customers, the cart pusher gave a running commentary of what he was seeing that might be of interest to Allied intelligence in London. The radio operator encoded the message, and then sent the message over his transmitter as the cask rolled along.

In an ongoing effort to thwart Allied espionage agents, the Germans employed D-F-ing trucks, whose direction-finding equipment pinpointed clandestine radio transmitters. The moving cask made it almost impossible for the trucks to locate the radio in the cask. When the agent pushing the cask spotted a D-F-er cruising the area, he would immediately halt. It was understood that the agent would transmit only when the cask was in motion.

A transmitter-receiver radio like this one was used by Allied agents in German-occupied Europe. (Phillips Publications)

Almost daily for months, this team sent London information on the movement of German units and armor. They told of the strength of the divisions, who the commanders were, and the morale of the troops. They pinpointed camouflaged supply dumps to be dealt with by Allied bombers. Command posts were located for the same purpose.

No doubt this two-man espionage team saved many lives when the invasion struck.[1]

Hitler's "Creatures" at Anzio

FIERCE FIGHTING WAS RAGING all along the U.S. 45th Infantry Division sector on the flaming Anzio beachhead, where Allied forces had landed on January 22, 1944, sixty miles behind German lines in central Italy. Peering through binoculars, the American artillery observers could not believe the sight that greeted their eyes a few hundred yards to the front.

What appeared to be miniature tanks, no more than five feet long and three feet high, were clanking toward the Americans. Unbeknownst to the perplexed observers, they were Adolf Hitler's latest "secret weapons," known as Goliaths. The mini-tanks were loaded with explosives and remotely controlled

Robot mini-tanks like these were sent against American lines on Anzio Beachhead. (U.S. Army)

by electrical impulses transmitted through a long cable connected to each unmanned armored vehicle.

Thirteen Goliaths were dispatched toward 45th Infantry Division lines that day, their function being to blow up strong points, explode minefields, rip up barbed wire, and in general clear a path for an infantry attack.

Five minutes after crawling out into no-man's-land and about halfway to the American positions, all thirteen Goliaths bogged down. Wide-eyed GIs along the front line had no way of knowing that German engineers considered the mini-tanks as "troublesome and dangerous toys." But they had to be employed at Anzio because they were creatures of the führer.[2]

American Spymaster Shocks London

WILLIAM J. "WILD BILL" DONOVAN was one of the world's most powerful men. When he had created the U.S. Office of Strategic Services (OSS) from scratch only four years earlier, it had consisted of himself and seven aides. His task had been mind-boggling: within months he was to create a global intelligence and sabotage organization that would try to catch up to those of Germany and other world powers whose clandestine groups had been in existence for centuries.

As a colonel in command of New York's "Fighting 69th" Infantry Regiment in World War I, he had earned the Congressional Medal of Honor, the Distinguished Service Cross, three Purple Hearts, and other combat decorations.

After the first global conflict, "Wild Bill," who had received his nickname while a football star at Columbia University, became a renowned Wall Street lawyer, and through shrewd investments he became a multimillionaire at a time there were not many of that breed in America. His close connections in the worlds of finance, commerce, and government in the United States and many foreign countries were legion. Among his foremost admirers was President Franklin D. Roosevelt.

Despite the enormous clout he wielded, Donovan remained modest and unassuming. His habit of ignoring danger was widely known. One longtime friend would claim that Wild Bill either didn't have a nerve in his body or he was crazy—"probably a little of each."

In early 1944, Donovan was flying into England for a round of discussions on the looming invasion of Normandy. He was perusing a stack of secret reports when the pilot came back to see him.

"What is it, Captain?" Donovan asked casually.

"Sir, a thick fog is blanketing the British Isles," was the alarming reply. "I've tried to get into every major airfield and they're all socked in!"

The general asked how much fuel was left, and was told about an hour's worth. "Well, keep looking for a field," Donovan said, turning back to reading his documents.

A half hour later the pilot returned. He explained that one remote field had a "small hole" over it, and he asked if he should try to land there. At best, it would be rough, he added.

The spymaster asked how far the field would be from London. When told seventy-five miles, he told the pilot to land there. "I don't mind a few bumps," he said casually. Presumably, it had not occurred to him that the landing would be fraught with danger.

The landing was agonizing for those aboard—except for Wild Bill. The plane had to be "talked" down from the ground to a runway the pilot knew was far too short, but the aircraft bumped along in a series of swerves.

Moments after the plane chugged to a halt, Donovan ordered an aide to scrape up transportation to London. At this remote, seldom used auxiliary airport, the vehicle pickings were strictly limited. Any kind would be fine, the spymaster said.

About three hours later, a dirt-spattered U.S. Army truck known as a four-by-four pulled up to the front door of Claridges, the lavish, prestigious London hotel that was patronized mainly by the highest-ranking military and government leaders.

Claridges' elegantly uniformed and impeccably mannered doorman frowned his disapproval over this filthy truck cluttering up his turf. He had long been accustomed to the arrival of clean limousines discharging the elite.

Doubtless the doorman's expression twisted into disbelief when he recognized General William Donovan, one of the world's most powerful and best-known figures, who deftly jumped over the truck's tailgate to the ground as though this style of arrival was quite routine.[3]

Exciting Races on a Beachhead

AS THE DAYS AND WEEKS PASSED on the stalemated Anzio Beachhead, where 100,000 British and American soldiers were penned in by the Germans on a narrow strip of Italian real estate thirty miles long, war weariness settled in on both sides. Like two gigantic prehistoric monsters bleeding, exhausted, and gasping for breath after a savage fight in which there was no winner, soldiers on each side were forced into static warfare. It was mid-March 1944.

An eerie lull had fallen over the killing grounds. It would last for several weeks. Recreation was created by the Allied soldiers as the Germans, perched on the heights a short distance inland, could look down on every move made on the beachhead. Seldom did the Germans try to disrupt the "recreation" activities.

Racing was the rage. The men of the elite American/Canadian First Special Service Force rounded up several sturdy steeds, usually in nighttime raids on Italian farm stables. A strip of ground was marked off as a track, the horses were lined up with mud-caked Forcemen as jockeys, and a rifle shot into the air sent the ponderous farm animals racing, more or less, along the track.

The Forcemen had heavy bets laid on these races, a factor that resulted in vocal cheering—and an occasional fistfight when a winner was disputed. In their balcony seats on the heights, the bored Germans may have also been laying bets on the same races.

Racing also was the rage in the British sector—beetle racing. It was a simple matter to locate contestants. All a Tommy (as a British soldier was called) had to do was to scoop out a shallow slit trench, and in seconds the bottom was lined with wiggling insects.

The beetle of each soldier was painted a different color, and all the race contestants were placed in a jar. The jar was put in the center of a ring some six feet in diameter, and as excitement rose among the onlookers, the starter lifted the jar. The Great Race was on.

Wild cheering and shouts of encouragement rang across the bleak landscape as the beetles scurried about. Pride was involved in the rabid rooting, but money played a role. Tommies placed bets on their favorites. The first beetle to cross the circular line was declared the winner.

A particular beetle won so often in the weeks ahead that he was pronounced the Grand Champion. Unfortunately his sudden fame was short-lived. Someone accidentally stepped on the Grand Champion.[4]

A Social Visit to the Enemy

AS AN EERIE LULL continued to hover over stalemated Anzio Beachhead in mid-1944, American and British soldiers began to think that they were destined to spend the remainder of the war—or perhaps their lifetimes—on that strip of Italian real estate. Perhaps the Germans, a few hundred yards away, had reached the same conclusion.

With endless time on their hands and throats becoming extremely parched, the Americans put their unexcelled scrounging talents to work. Soon makeshift distilleries popped up at many places. When a random German shell happened to score a direct hit on one distillery, the furious GIs branded the action a "war atrocity."

These distilleries consisted of five-gallon gasoline cans and tubing taken from wrecked airplanes, of which a good-sized number had been shot down over the beachhead. Out of these improvised apparatuses flowed a liquid concoction the men called Kickapoo Joy Juice, a term extracted from the popular stateside comic strip *Lil' Abner*.

Cut with grapefruit juice "liberated," usually at night, from supply dumps along the Anzio waterfront, thirsty GIs managed to get the drink down—and in most cases, keep it down.

One day a soldier in the U.S. 3rd Infantry Division fought an extended bout with a quantity of Kickapoo Joy Juice—and came out second best. Putting on a black civilian top hat and jauntily swinging a cane on one arm, he staggered across no-man's-land and into the arms of Germans manning an outpost. These particular Germans were among those caught up in the benign spirit that had infected both sides due to the greatly reduced casualty rate in the stalemate.

After talking casually with the GI for an hour, the Germans turned him around and, with his top hat still in place, sent him reeling back to American lines.[5]

The Spy Who Spent the War in Bed

ONE OF THE MOST important persons in France is the concierge, most likely a woman. Provided with a small apartment just inside the main door of nearly all office buildings, she or he guards the front portal, literally. Manually or with an electronic control, the concierge answers the doorbell and opens the huge doors, which keep the public out of most French buildings.

The concierge wields heavy clout, observing all comings and goings. Even with the German occupation, the concierges were left guarding the doors, even in the buildings that the Germans had taken over for their uses.

In Paris, the Luftwaffe had a large office building for a headquarters. The female concierge, who had been there for years prior to the occupation, still sat in the little glass box inside the door, keeping out any unauthorized persons.

In early 1944 a Frenchman working as an agent for the U.S. Office of Strategic Services (OSS) approached the concierge and her husband. Would they, as French patriots, give him a base from which to operate and a cover for his espionage mission? They would, although aware that they would be risking their lives.

One day the concierge "permitted" the spy to enter the building. With his forged documents in order, he called on the German officer who ruled on everything that had to do with the running of the Luftwaffe office. The Frenchman lied, saying that his house had been destroyed by British bombers and that he had come to Paris to live with his only "relatives," the concierge and her husband.

The German colonel examined the spy's fake documents, and then said that he had no objection. The agent moved into the concierge's three-room apartment.

For a few weeks, the OSS agent left for "work" each day, returning at about 6:00 P.M. The Germans in the building ignored his presence. Then, when he felt the time was right, the spy took to his bed. Her "cousin" had come down with a bad case of "la grippe," the concierge told everyone.

Prior to his "illness," the agent had installed a small induction microphone in the building running into the inner sanctums of the Luftwaffe headquarters. The hairlike wire from the delicate instrument could pick up conversations through a wall or through phone wires without direct tapping procedures. The wire tailed down to the agent's bed. Under the covers, he had a tiny radio shortwave transmitter.

All day long the seriously "ill" man lay in bed and eavesdropped on the top-secret matters of the Luftwaffe. (He spoke fluent German.) In the weeks prior to the Allied invasion of Normandy on June 6, 1944, he listened to the Luftwaffe's plans to thwart the looming amphibious and airborne operation.

Late at night, when most of the Germans had left the building, the Frenchman shortwaved the information to London from his "sickbed."

From the invasion through the Allied capture of Paris on August 22—a period of about three months—Supreme Commander Dwight Eisenhower's headquarters was provided with a running commentary of vital information from the heart of the German air effort against the Allies.[6]

Secret Agent Saved by a Blacksmith

BRITISH CAPTAIN George Donovan Jones had been transmitting secret messages by radio undisturbed to London since September 1942. A year and a half later, with Allied planners preparing for the invasion of northwestern France, Jones (code-named Isidore) was using his radio several times a day.

Jones was a key operative in the British underground network known as Stationer, which was of special importance to London. The espionage and sabotage circuit was located in south-central France, through which ran the crucial north-south roads and railway lines, over which the Germans could be expected to rush reinforcements northward to Normandy after the Allied landings.

One day in the spring of 1944, Jones took a bus to a nearby town to deliver a batch of important messages from London to the head of Stationer. The bus was halted by *miliciens*, the French police force serving the Germans. The coded notes were found on Jones. He was handcuffed and taken to Vichy, headquarters of the puppet French government.

The quick-witted Jones concocted a plausible story for his interrogators. He explained that he was an escaped British prisoner of war, and that he had fallen into a resistance group of which he knew only two or three members. He denied that he had played any role in espionage.

His French interrogators seemed to buy his story and said that he would be interned. But the Gestapo, meanwhile, had found his radio transmitter. For two months he was handcuffed and chained to the wall of a dark, wet dungeon cell, taken down only to be severely beaten each day.

One night, after Jones had absorbed his torture, the two Gestapo men, for whatever reason, decided to leave the interrogation room on the third floor after attaching their victim to a wood chair by his handcuffs.

Despite his enormous pain, Jones knew it was now or never. Amazingly, he had enough strength remaining to smash the chair and jump out a window to a roof and then to the dark street.

Expecting to hear German shouts at any moment, the Briton began walking and saw the silhouette of a man coming toward him. Hopefully, it was a Frenchman. With his manacled hands he grabbed the hat off the other's head, put it on, and said softly, "Please forgive me. The Gestapo is after me!" Jones then continued to walk down the street.

Soon he found a dark house that appeared to be unoccupied, and he hid in a small shed in the garden for two days, bruised and bleeding. Through cracks he could see Gestapo men darting about in search of the escapee.

Jones knew he had to move on. After a short sleep, he stole away and, through superhuman effort, walked for twelve miles, dodging patrols on occasion.

Nearing a small village, Jones decided to take a huge risk. He would confront the first Frenchman he saw, tell of his predicament, and ask for help.

If the fugitive were to avoid recapture and execution, he would have to find someone to cut off his handcuffs. But what were the odds that he could find that party? Or would he be contacting a traitor who would notify the Gestapo?

Just inside the village Jones saw a heavyset, middle-aged man and asked him for help. Luck was with Jones. The man was a member of the French resistance and also the village blacksmith. He quickly removed the manacles.

Then the benefactor contacted the underground circuit, and it sent men to take charge of Jones and help get him out of France and back to England.[7]

A Bomb Explodes Too Late

DURING THE SPRING OF 1944, tens of thousands of American soldiers and airmen were pouring into the British Isles. The entire world knew that the Western Allies were building up for a gargantuan attack across the English Channel against German-held territory. Code-named Overlord, the operation might decide the eventual outcome of the war in Europe.

Neptune, the assault phase of Overlord, would be unmatched in scope and complexity in the annals of warfare. The printed plan was five inches thick and even the typed list of American units—1,400 of them—required thirty-one pages.

There would be amphibious landings by five great naval forces in the Bay of the Seine, which was divided into the American assault area on the west (Utah and Omaha Beaches), and the British and Canadian assault area on the east (Gold, Sword, and Juno Beaches).

While feverish preparations were under way in London (D Day was tentatively set for the first week of June), the Merryweather firm, on Greenwich High Street, was engaged in a top-secret project on which the outcome of the invasion might rest. For more than a hundred years Merryweather had been specializing in building fire-fighting equipment.

Five hundred members of the firm, all sworn to secrecy, were engaged in developing one-hundred-foot telescopic steel ladders of the type fire departments around the world use to fight blazes in tall buildings. Only these particular ladders had to be improvised to be based in a DUKW (duck, as it was known), an American amphibious truck that was designed to carry a load of one and a half tons.

Early on Merryweather engineers had pointed out that the standard fire-fighting ladder and its mechanism weighed five tons, twice the weight that the ducks could carry. However, by discarding the normal raising mechanism and installing a different type, the weight was reduced by half.

Under clandestine conditions, tests were carried out using the one-hundred-foot turntable ladder of the Brighton Fire Department lashed to a

Fire-escape ladder mounted on a "duck" helped U.S. Rangers scale Pointe du Hoc at H Hour in Normandy. (National Archives)

duck. Merryweather was told to proceed at full speed, and five of the six ladders were ready in only five weeks—instead of the nine months a project like this would normally take.

Only after D Day did the employees of Merryweather learn the reason for the rush job of such a unique nature.

Soon after seven o'clock on the morning of D Day (June 6) American Rangers landed three miles west of Omaha Beach at the base of Pointe du Hoc, a sheer cliff a hundred feet high. Their mission was to silence a German artillery battery atop the heights that had the power and the range to wreak havoc on the landing beaches at Utah and Omaha, to either side of Pointe du Hoc.

During the planning stages for Neptune, it had appeared to Allied planners that Pointe du Hoc was unassailable. But now the Rangers hauled themselves to the top on rope ladders and scrambled up the Merryweather ladders.

Pointe du Hoc was cratered by bombs and shells, but the guns were gone. A mile inland the battery was discovered, but there was no sign of the crews.

The Merryweather team's timing had been amazing. Soon after it had completed construction of the crucial ladders, a German bomb scored a direct hit and destroyed the London factory.[8]

An Ingenious Escape Artist

PERHAPS THE MOST tenacious and innovative POW escape artists in World War II were the men of the Royal Air Force. However, only about 2 percent of the British airmen actually tried to escape, and of the 15,000 in permanent camps in Germany, only less than thirty actually got back to England or to neutral countries.

A few POWs tried to gain their freedom by outwitting German doctors, feigning illnesses to win repatriation. International laws for conducting warfare, the Geneva Convention, held that POWs were to be sent home if they were certified as severely ill by a panel consisting of doctors from the captor nation and the Red Cross.

One of those who had no intention of sitting out the war for months, maybe years, was an enterprising Royal Air Force sergeant, Richard Pape. He had broken out of his camp in Germany three times, but had been recaptured, once three hundred miles from his POW cage.

Pape decided that if he were to get back to England, he would have to change his technique and feign a serious kidney ailment. He somehow managed to eat yellow soap to cause his skin to look jaundiced, and he had a comrade flick his ankles repeatedly with a wet towel to make them swell.

When he decided he was "ill" enough to make his move, Pape created an artificial penis from a rubber hose and filled it with the urine of a friend who actually did suffer from a kidney ailment.

Pape reported on sick call. And when the German doctors asked for a urine sample, he secretly removed the cork from the rubber hose and provided the diseased specimen.

In May 1944, representatives of the International Red Cross recommended that Pape be repatriated in exchange for a German POW. Soon the "ailing" Briton climbed out of a boat at a port in neutral Sweden. Two weeks later he was back in England.[9]

A Prophetic German Cook

ALTHOUGH METEOROLOGISTS had assured the Wehrmacht high command that *der Grossinvasion* could not come on June 6, 1944, many German officers and soldiers defending the Atlantic Wall in Normandy seemed to sense that the great endeavor was about to be launched. No way, said the weather forecasters. The English Channel would be struck by shrieking storm devils, resulting in heavy winds and high waves.

Corporal Fritz Bayer, a cook in a German artillery battery a mile behind what the Allied planners had labeled Utah Beach, was among those who had an intuitive feeling that "something big" was about to strike. As had been his practice, just after 5:00 P.M. on June 5, the cook walked to the nearby farm owned by the Lavelle family to sip a jug of cider.

As he was leaving, the German surprised the French family. "This is certainly the last time I'll visit here," he said. "There is very bad news in store for us."

The cook was prophetic. He never returned. His corpse, mutilated by grenade fragments, would be found the next morning sprawled by his mobile kitchen. Thousands of Allied paratroopers had descended upon Normandy during the night.[10]

Gods Smile on Teddy Roosevelt Jr.

BRIGADIER GENERAL Theodore Roosevelt Jr., son of a former president of the United States, was short in physical stature and extremely long in heart. He had fought the Germans in North Africa as assistant commander of the 1st Infantry Division, where he gained wide fame as a fearless and inspirational combat leader.

Roosevelt was casual about his personal dress. On occasion he didn't bother to put on his general's stars when on field or combat duty. He often wore a wool knit cap and left a pant leg flopping over his leggings.

Such lack of discipline was greeted with a jaundiced eye by some high-ranking staff officers far removed from danger. The GIs loved the spunky, fifty-six-year-old Roosevelt. "He's got to go!" was the high-headquarters battle cry.

Consequently, Roosevelt was relieved from his post with the 1st Infantry Division in August 1943. After being shuttled around to a series of inconsequential jobs, the maverick finally was assigned to the 4th Infantry Division as a spare brigadier.

Commanded by Major General Raymond O. Barton, the "Ivy" division would make the assault landing on Utah Beach in Normandy.

Roosevelt had no troops to command and no assignment for the mightiest endeavor in military history. "Tubby, our boys are as green as the growing grass," he said to Barton. "The first men to hit Utah are going to be confused and scared to death. They need someone like me with them."

As Barton digested those words, Roosevelt resumed the attack: "Let me go in with the first wave. If the boys see an old son of a bitch like me standing up under it, they'll feel they can, too."

Rubbing his arthritic shoulder, Roosevelt had a twinkle in his eye as he added, "Besides, if the boys see a general on the beach, they'll think it's a safe place to be."

A major navigational error permitted the U.S. 4th Infantry Division assault troops to land on Utah Beach without heavy casualties. (U.S. Army)

Barton told him no several times. Utah Beach at H Hour was no place for an American general, he thought. But Roosevelt was persistent in the days ahead, and finally Barton reluctantly agreed.

At 4:45 A.M. on June 6, 1944, Teddy Roosevelt and his six hundred men, crammed thirty to an assault boat, roared off toward Utah Beach, eleven miles away and unseen in the darkness. At H Hour minus 40 minutes, a mighty roar erupted. Big guns on warships were pounding the shore and targets inland.

Three hundred yards from Utah, Teddy Roosevelt, clutching his walking cane, was peering intently ahead through the vision slot in the ramp. He was perplexed by what he saw—or didn't see. For countless hours he had studied photographs of Utah; now there was no landmark he recognized. Something definitely had gone wrong. He kept his apprehensions to himself for the moment.

At precisely H Hour—6:30 A.M.—Roosevelt's boat scraped bottom two hundred yards from his force's immediate goal, the seawall that ran for 10,000 yards along the edge of the sand dunes. Behind this barrier, the first wave could organize for the push inland.

Now Roosevelt and his six hundred men began wading ashore. They were at their most vulnerable point. No cover or concealment. The general recalled momentarily that some high officers in London had predicted ninety percent casualties in the first waves.

As the Americans scrambled across the wide beach to the seawall, a few random German shells exploded. Some GIs were hit. Behind the protection of the seawall, a soldier called out in disbelief, "What the hell's going on!" He and his comrades were amazed at the lightness of the fire they had met while wading ashore.

Hunkered down behind the concrete barricade, General Roosevelt was intently studying his map. "I don't know where in the hell we are; I'm convinced that we're about a mile and a quarter from where we're supposed to be," he told his two battalion commanders. "But if those German bastards want war, this is a hell of a good place to start it!"

In minutes shouted commands rang out along the seawall, and the men of the spearhead climbed to their feet and pushed inland with Roosevelt in the lead. Progress was impeded only by an occasional sniper and sporadic artillery fire.

Teddy Roosevelt Jr., trudging along with the aid of his cane, would learn later that the Gods of War had taken a hand in the Utah Beach assault—smiling on the Americans. A combination of tricky tides and the obliteration of terrain features by the heavy bombing and naval barrage caused the first wave to land where German defenses were light and thinly manned. Had the invaders come ashore on the true beach as planned, a mile and a half away, they would have bumped head-on against two concrete-encased batteries of .88-millimeter artillery pieces, thick minefields, and numerous machine-gun posts with interlocking fire. Roosevelt and his men no doubt would have been slaughtered and succeeding waves decimated.[11]

"Don't Worry . . . I'll Shoot You First!"

WILLIAM J. "WILD BILL" DONOVAN was deeply disappointed. D Day for the invasion of Normandy, the most monumental airborne and amphibious operation that history has known, was fast approaching—and he was being left outside looking in. The Office of Strategic Services (OSS) chief, who had been awarded the Congressional Medal of Honor in World War I, had been "grounded" for security reasons by Secretary of the Navy James V. Forrestal.

Donovan appealed to an old friend, the admiral in charge of naval forces in Europe, and he, too, rejected the appeal. If Donovan were captured, the Germans would reap a bonanza in top-secret intelligence matters.

Donovan hadn't gained wealth as a Wall Street lawyer nor as the founder and director of America's first cloak-and-dagger agency by taking "no" for an answer. So when the mighty invasion armada sailed for Normandy, Donovan was a stowaway on one ship. Along with him was Colonel David K. E. Bruce, the son of a U.S. senator and husband of steel baron Andrew Mellon's daughter, who was known as the "world's richest woman." The forty-four-year-old Bruce was the OSS chief in Europe.

Hard on the heels of assault troops, Donovan and Bruce had gone but a short distance inland when they had to flop to the ground when strafed by a Luftwaffe fighter plane. In the process, Bruce fell on his boss and gashed him badly on the throat with his steel helmet. Donovan was bleeding profusely, but he insisted on continuing inland. They came to a halt at an earthen hedgerow that was being raked by German machine-gun fire.

Sprawled facedown as bullets hissed just overhead, Donovan said, "David, we mustn't be captured, we know too much!" Bruce replied routinely, "Yes, sir."

"Have you your pill?" Donovan asked. Bruce had to admit that he did not have the cyanide pellet that would bring a quick death. "Well, I have two of them," Donovan said.

Still lying prone, the general searched his pockets, which were crammed with a wide array of papers. But no pills.

"Well, don't worry," Donovan said between machine-gun bursts. "I will shoot first!"

Bruce again replied, "Yes, sir, but can we do much with only our two pistols against that machine gun?"

"Oh, you don't understand," Donovan said. "I mean if we are about to be captured, I'll shoot you first. After all, I am your commanding officer."

No doubt General Donovan would have carried out the promise. But the two top OSS officers survived D Day.[12]

An Enemy Saves "Father Sam"

HEAVY GERMAN ACK-ACK FIRE was bursting about the C-47 transport plane as Captain Francis L. Sampson bailed out into the blackness. It was H Hour minus 6 for the invasion of Normandy, June 6, 1944. Floating earthward under his blossoming white parachute, he saw that he was going to land on the top of a tall tree, where he would be a prime target for German riflemen.

Captain Sampson, a Catholic chaplain in the U.S. 101st Airborne Division, tugged on the risers of his parachute and missed the tree. But he plunged into a stream with water over his head. The impact caused him to drop his Mass kit, an indispensable item for a Catholic padre.

The canopy of his parachute stayed open, and the strong wind caught it and blew him downstream. "Father Sam," as he was known to the troopers, thought he was a goner and said a quick Act of Contrition, a prayer for those in mortal danger. However, about a hundred yards downstream, his parachute was blown onto the riverbank, and he lay there for several minutes, exhausted. Heavy firing was raging on all sides.

Finally, he hacked himself free from his parachute harness with a knife and stumbled back to where he had hit the water to retrieve his Mass kit. After six dives, he found it.

Father Sam after his capture while looking for wounded comrades ahead of front lines in the Battle of the Bulge. (Author's collection)

During the night and throughout the day, hundreds of American para-troopers were lost and roaming the region after having been misdropped. In pairs and tiny bands, they stalked through the *boscage* (earthen hedgerow terrain). Death lurked everywhere. Often, Americans and Germans collided unexpectedly in this lethal game of hide-and-seek.

When dusk closed over Normandy on D Day, Father Sam was in a med-ical aid station in the village of Addeville. Wounded paratroopers, several of them dying, were sprawled on the filthy floor of the dilapidated house.

At dawn, the firing that had been raging around the medical station ceased. It was deathly still. Father Sam made a white flag from a sheet and hung it outside the door.

An hour later, Sampson heard voices and saw three Germans setting up a machine gun in the front yard. Grabbing the white flag, he went out to protest putting a weapon at a medical station in violation of the Geneva Con-vention rules.

Father Sam could tell by their distinctive bowl-like helmets and insignia that these were tough *Fallschirmjaeger* (paratroopers) and could sense that they were in a nasty mood. A German stuck a Schmeisser machine pistol in Sampson's stomach and snarled at him to start walking down the road. His pleas that he was a man of God taking care of seriously wounded men fell on deaf ears.

After marching for a quarter of a mile, Sampson was roughly forced against an earthen hedgerow. The three Germans pulled back the bolts of their weapons and took aim at the padre, who was reciting the Act of Contrition.

At that moment a shot rang out and a bullet zipped past just overhead. Sampson thought the Germans were amusing themselves by frightening him before riddling him with bullets. However, the shot had been fired by a German who wanted to attract the attention of the would-be executioners.

A husky, blond, handsome young sergeant strode up and spoke harshly to the other three Germans, and they sullenly walked away and disappeared from sight.

Like many Europeans, the sergeant spoke English and understood the language. Father Sam explained that he was a Catholic priest and showed him his military credentials. Much to the American's astonishment, the German paratrooper snapped to attention, saluted, and made a slight bow. Then he showed the padre a Catholic religious medal hidden out of sight inside his uniform.

"I am so glad that the Catholic Church is universal," Father Sam told comrades later in explaining his miraculous escape from certain death.[13]

Firefighters Center of Attention

SAVAGE FIGHTING had been raging since before dawn along one hundred miles of the English Channel in Normandy. On the eastern flank the Germans were trying desperately to hold the major city of Caen, capital of Normandy, fifteen miles inland from the invasion beach code-named Sword. It was June 6, 1944.

So hard did the Germans concentrate on defending the key road junction of Caen that the British and Canadians were able to fight their way into Bayeux, to the northwest. On D Day plus 2, a squadron of tanks, led by Lieutenant Colonel Stanley Christopherson, clanked into the center of town.

There was little shooting except for one diehard band of Germans firing a machine gun from a house. As a result of the tank shells being poured into the structure, it caught fire. But the German crew refused to emerge.

Minutes later there was the clanging of a bell and the Bayeux fire brigade charged onto the scene. It was manned by a full team of firefighters wearing bright red garb and shiny silver-colored helmets.

Perhaps pleased to be the center of attention, the firefighters bolted into the burning building, ignored the occasional bursts of machine-gun fire, and extinguished the blaze. Then the Frenchmen emerged—right in back of the German machine gunners they had "captured."[14]

The "Mess Sergeant" Was a Lady

FOR EIGHT CENTURIES, devout, hardworking citizens of Graignes, France, had endured life without the slightest hint of excitement. Suddenly, on the morning of June 6, 1944, all that changed. The community six miles south of the town of Carentan was electrified: hundreds of young Americans wearing waterlogged jump boots and baggy pants had appeared in their midst.

These newcomers had parachuted from the black sky into the swamps that ringed Graignes on three sides, in water ranging from one to five feet deep. Many drowned. Most of the others, aided by moonlight, spotted the belfry in the old Roman Catholic Church in Graignes and waded toward that landmark.

During the next forty-eight hours, paratroopers from the 82nd Airborne and 101st Airborne Divisions straggled into Graignes, until the mixed force had 14 officers and 168 men. All had landed eight to fifteen miles south of their true drop zones.

On the morning of D Day plus 1, Alphonse Voydie, the mayor, assembled nearly all of the town's citizens. Amid tears and applause, the Graigni agreed to give every possible help to their "guests" who had come from across the ocean to liberate France. Adults knew the penalty of aiding enemies of Nazi Germany—summary execution if caught.

Meanwhile, Major Charles D. Johnson, the ranking officer, took command of the isolated force and organized strong points all around Graignes, for a German assault could hit from any direction.

On D Day plus 2, Johnson and his troopers were confronted with a crisis: they had run out of food. Madame Germaine Boursier, the fifty-year-old greengrocer who ran a small café, leaped into the breach. Together with her two daughters and other women and older girls, Madame Boursier foraged for food and milk, prepared two meals daily and hand-carried them to the paratroopers in their observation and gun positions. Bread was nonexistent, but as the days passed, the café-and-grocery owner and some of her neighbors made periodic trips by horse cart to German-held Saint-Jean-de-Daye, five miles away, to bring back bread, which was hidden under hay or straw.

The trek to Saint-Jean-de-Daye was fraught with peril. Madame Boursier, her daughter, Odette Lelavechet, and other women traveled over poorly marked mined roads and through German roadblocks and past foot patrols. Once, a German group searched Madame Boursier's cart and found the bread. Her heart beat furiously, but outwardly, she was a portrait of serenity, explaining that the bread was merely for the citizens of Graignes. The Germans bid her good morning and waved her onward.

Madame Boursier no doubt was the only French woman to serve as a "mess sergeant" for an American outfit.[15]

Massacre in the Wrong Village

WITHIN HOURS OF the mighty Allied landings in Normandy on June 6, 1944, General Heinz Lammerding, commander of the elite 2nd SS Panzer Division, received urgent orders at his headquarters deep in southern France. His battle-hardened outfit, consisting of some 20,000 men, 75 self-propelled assault guns, and 163 tanks, began rolling northward that afternoon. Its mission was to reinforce the German army in Normandy.

Long before the invasion, Allied planners in London had anticipated that the 2nd SS Panzer would be rushed to Normandy. Along the routes the division would have to follow had been secreted numerous heavily armed French resistance bands whose task was to delay the movement of the German armored force.

Along the Germans' line of march, the Maquisards (French underground fighters) executed bloody ambushes, planted cyclonite land mines that looked like cow droppings, shot at tank commanders standing in their turrets, and held up the division by placing upturned soup plates, which looked like the humps of hurriedly buried land mines when viewed through a tank's periscope.

Soon the roads were littered with German corpses, the railway embankments dotted with locomotives and cars that had been derailed when filled with soldiers, and the roads were blocked with vehicles shot up by the Maquisards.

The harassment of the 2nd SS Panzer took many forms. Thirty Maquisards held up the leading elements of one German regiment for forty hours on the narrow road at the outskirts of the town of Souillac, while the rest of the division was bunched up on the roads to the rear and constantly pounded by Allied fighter-bombers.

Lammerding's force was to have been in Normandy and fighting the invaders forty-eight hours after leaving its assembly area in the south. Now it was D Day plus 7 and the division was still crawling along in fits and jerks. By this time, the temper of the SS men had become dangerously frayed.

While running the gauntlet of the French resistance fighters, a battalion commander, a highly popular man, was either sniped at and killed in his command vehicle or taken prisoner and shot in a small village. Early the next morning, a regiment under SS Major General Heinz von Brodowsky ringed the village of Oradour-sur-Glane to wreak vengeance for the German officer's death.

Almost all of the population of Oradour-sur-Glane was murdered. The men were machine-gunned to death; the women and children were locked in the church, which was set afire.

The massacre at Oradour-sur-Glane shocked the entire Allied world. Only later would it be known that the people were innocent of the "crime" of killing the German officer. He had met his death in nearby Oradour-sur-Vayres. The slaughter of innocents had taken place in the wrong village.[16]

A General Turned Fire Chief

A SHORT TIME before dusk in Normandy, a mud-splattered American armored car, trailing a towering plume of thick dust, clanked into the Saint-Jacques-de-Nehou square and ground to a halt. Out hopped forty-seven-year-old Major General J. Lawton "Lightning Joe" Collins, clad in his usual faded-salmon trench coat. Collins, the commander of the U.S. Seventh Corps, had already put in an eighteen-hour day, dashing about the zone of advance of the 8th Infantry Division, which was attacking westward from Utah Beach. It was June 9, 1944.

Colonel Frederick J. De Rohan's 60th Infantry Regiment had been involved in heavy fighting all day and bolted into Saint-Jacques-de-Nehou, where the exhausted men halted for the night. Now Lightning Joe Collins briskly strode up to the battalion commander, who was nearly out on his feet from almost constant movement and lack of sleep.

"The Krauts have pulled out of town and we've lost contact with them," the lieutenant colonel told Collins.

The Corps commander had his aide, Captain Jack Walsh, put in a call to Major General Manton S. Eddy, leader of the 9th Infantry Division. "Matt, I want you to meet me in Saint-Jacques as soon as possible," Collins said. He planned to tell Eddy to throw in fresh troops and continue the advance at dawn.

While waiting for Eddy, Collins turned his attention to the tower of the old stone church in the square. It was burning and spewing out thick clouds of black smoke. When the Germans pulled out of town a short time earlier, they had fired an 88-millimeter shell through the face of the clock on the tower, and the wooden clock supports had caught fire.

Residents were creeping out of their cellars and standing about in anguish and dismay, watching the old church go up in flames. General Collins, with time on his hands, could not stand idly by and watch the belfry being consumed by fire. So he rapidly organized a water-bucket fire brigade of townspeople, and they began to douse the burning debris in the belfry.

Only a few minutes before General Eddy sped into the square in a jeep, the brass bell in the tower crashed down in a shower of sparks, but no one was injured.

With the arrival of Eddy, Lightning Joe had to abdicate the role of Saint-Jacques fire chief. No doubt he was the only Corps commander in the war to serve as a volunteer fireman in a water-bucket brigade.[17]

The Great Soap Bubble Scheme

IT WAS A FEW MINUTES PAST 4:00 A.M. when an elderly volunteer in the Royal Observer Corps in southeastern England watched a strange object streaking through the dark sky toward London. Its dim contours resembled those of an airplane, but its exhaust was belching reddish orange flame, and it gave off a sputtering sound. It was June 13, 1944, one week after Allied armies had stormed ashore in Normandy.

Onward the object raced, and minutes later its preset timer cut off the motor; it crashed into the sleepy village of Swanscombe, some eighteen miles from its intended target, the Tower of London. The explosion rocked the region. England was under attack by lethal robots, Adolf Hitler's secret weapon code-named V-1 (V for vengeance).

Doodlebugs, the British would call the revolutionary contraptions. Buzz bombs, they were known to the Americans. By whatever name, these frightening pilotless aircraft had speeds of 440 miles per hour (faster than any Allied fighter plane could travel) and exploded with the impact of a 4,000-pound blockbuster.

Sprawling London lived in constant fear of chaos in the days and weeks ahead. Hundreds of the robots rained down on the capital, killing and wounding thousands of civilians. Huge numbers of people were homeless.

There seemed to be no defense against the diabolical robots. So any grain of an idea, no matter how illogical or lacking in scientific probability, that might counter the V-1 was given attention.

Not long after the robot barrage had been launched, Commander Charles Goodeve, a Canadian who headed the Directorate of Miscellaneous Weapons Development (DMWD), was presiding over an important conference in the Admiralty when he received word that a Mr. Real Big in the government hierarchy wanted to see him promptly. Annoyed to be taken away from his meeting, Goodeve walked down the hall of the Admiralty to the office of the high official.

Mr. Real Big introduced him to a stranger, a civilian, and said: "This gentleman has an idea I'd like for you to look at. It's a counter-measure to the doodlebugs. Take him along and let him show you the details."

Goodeve now was even more irritated. He would have to call off the crucial conference.

When the two men reached Goodeve's office, the stranger reached into his bulging briefcase, pulled out a large sheaf of papers, and spread them all over the floor. Goodeve strained to keep his composure.

Picking up a paper here and there, the stranger explained his revolutionary scheme: hundreds of barrage balloons would be sent aloft and across the routes of the flying robots. To the cable of each would be connected an apparatus of the type the stranger now displayed. It consisted of a cylinder of oxygen joined to a small benzene tank by an electromagnetic release valve. On the other side of the tank was a bath containing a soap solution.

"Do I make myself clear?" the inventor asked. Goodeve grunted something to the effect that he was grasping the explanation. The commander glanced at his watch, wondering if he would make his next conference on time.

"Now we come to the crux of the whole scheme," the stranger said with a ring of triumph in his voice. "The mixture finally emerges into the air in a series of huge bubbles."

Goodeve was startled. "I'm afraid I don't see how your bubbles can destroy flying bombs," he declared.

The inventor now gently scolded Goodeve: "Surely it must be obvious. When the robots fly over they suck my bubbles into their intake system. Then the bombs will explode in midair!"

Goodeve was speechless for long moments. Then, remembering that the stranger was a protégé of Mr. Real Big, the commander said it was an interesting theory and that he would like to consult some of his colleagues about the apparatus.

Goodeve was in a quandary. He knew that the scheme was ludicrous, but he had to treat the matter sympathetically. So later he sent a carefully worded letter to the inventor. In it, he stated that the apparatus might have merit, but suggested that it be resubmitted, not to the Admiralty but to the Air Ministry.

Goodeve heard no more about the Great Soap Bubble scheme.[18]

A Triumph for Two OSS Men

AFTER ALLIED FORCES stormed ashore in Normandy and carved out a beachhead in early June 1944, Americans of the Office of Strategic Services (OSS), who had parachuted deep behind German lines prior to D Day, were traveling with the Maquis (French underground) to "liberate" small towns.

The liberators, operating far from the landing beaches, came to expect wild receptions as conquering heroes. Champagne and wine flowed freely. Weeping women vied to see who could kiss the most liberators. Children thrust flowers and candy on the *parachutist Americans*.

At one celebration, the Maquis sang the French national anthem, the "Marseillaise," at the top of their voices. Then men of the Special Operations Executive (SOE), the British cloak-and-dagger agency, belted out "God Save the King."

Now all eyes focused on the two OSS officers, Lieutenant Reeve Schley, a Wall Street lawyer in peacetime, and Lieutenant John Alsop, the brother of the widely known journalist Joseph Alsop. Both men were Yale graduates and from wealthy families. Neither spoke French nor had a knack for music.

Alsop and Schley looked at one another sheepishly. Neither knew the words of "The Star-Spangled Banner." They would have to improvise. But only one song was known to both of them. Their British translators announced to the crowd that the Americans would render a specially composed anthem of international goodwill.

Singing with gusto, Schley and Alsop gave a rousing rendition of an obscene ballad they had learned in the bars of London: "Uncle George and Aunt Mable Fainted at the Breakfast Table . . . "

Never mind that the performers were far off-key, if indeed there was a tune. None of the French understood English. Members of the Maquis snapped to attention and saluted. Civilians were nearly overcome with emotion. Weeping women tossed flowers.

The OSS men had scored a magnificent triumph.[19]

Four Newsmen Bag
a German Platoon

SEVEN WEEKS AFTER Allied armies had invaded Normandy, a million and a half American, British, Canadian, and French soldiers were bottled up not far from the landing beaches. But on the morning of July 25, 1944, the stillness was shattered along a three-mile stretch on an east-west road running between St. Lô and Périers.

Germans dug in along the south side of the road were deluged by thousands of bombs and artillery shells. Although "friendly" bombs killed and wounded hundreds of American soldiers on the north side of the road, within two days Operation Cobra, the all-out effort to break out of the beachhead, had punched a wide hole in German lines. Tank-tipped American spearheads charged through the breach and headed southward.

On the fourth day of Cobra, John H. "Beaver" Thompson, a correspondent for the *Chicago Tribune*, and three other reporters were driving along in a jeep. They had not seen a single American soldier for the past ten miles. In pursuit of a story, they found themselves behind German lines.

Undecided on their next course of action, the newsmen in the jeep reached the village of Roncey, where the previous evening U.S. fighter-bombers had blasted a large German traffic jam and left it a pile of twisted metal. Hundreds of German corpses were sprawled about the wreckage. The pungent smell of death and burned flesh hovered over the area.

While Thompson and his three companions were prowling through the carnage, they glanced back up the road on which they had just entered Roncey. Hearts skipped a beat. Approaching were thirty-two German soldiers. Moments later the Americans breathed sighs of relief when they saw a large white sheet held aloft by the sergeant leading the group. But how would the Germans react when they got closer and realized they were confronted by four correspondents armed only with pencils?

Summoning his most authoritative manner, Thompson yelled, "*Halten!*" The Germans obediently stopped. Pointing up the road toward American

Chicago Tribune *war correspondent John H. "Beaver" Thompson "captured" a German platoon. (Author's collection)*

positions, he gave his best Prussian drill-instructor imitation and barked: "*Macht schnell!*" (Hurry, hurry!)

Apparently the German platoon was as lost as the Americans. When its members realized they were confronted by four correspondents, they must have thought they were far behind *American* lines. So in response to Beaver Thompson's stern order, the German platoon did an about-face and marched docilely back up the road.[20]

German Shoot-Out among Themselves

FRENCH MAJOR Marcel Rigaud and U.S. Navy Ensign Ralph Johnson were vigorously paddling a rubber dinghy toward a terrain feature known as the Bay of Rayol along the fabled French Riviera. It was pitch-black. Their crucial role was not to fight, but to flash green lights seaward to guide in the main body of French commandos. It was 1:00 A.M. on August 15, 1944.

Rigaud, who at forty-six was twice the age of his American companion, and Johnson would be the first Allied soldiers to land on the German-occupied Riviera. Hopefully, they would survive to savor that distinction. They were spearheading Operation Dragoon, the Allied invasion of southern France.

Second in scope only to Overlord, the invasion of Normandy, Dragoon would involve a force of three hundred thousand men, a thousand ships, and several thousand warplanes. The operation was designed to liberate the southern two-thirds of France and link up with Overlord armies in the north.

The French commandos were to land on the beach near Rayol, then scale nearby Cap Negre, towering three hundred and fifty feet into the black sky, and knock out a German gun battery that could pound Allied troops coming ashore after dawn.

Once that mission was accomplished the Frenchmen were to block the highway running along the coast to keep German reinforcements from rushing to the landing beaches from the major cities of Toulon and Marseilles. At the same time, a French detachment was to seize and hold a key height a mile inland.

Now Major Rigaud and Ensign Johnson in the rubber dinghy were close enough to glimpse the shoreline and the dim configurations of the terrain behind it. A deep surge of near-panic swept through Rigaud. In peacetime he had been to the bay at Rayol many times and knew the coastline intimately. He did not know where he and Johnson were touching shore, but this was *not* the bay at Rayol.

Time was crucial. The clock was ticking. After a half hour of feverish effort to orient himself, Rigaud whispered to Johnson, "We're one mile west of our target." Leaping into their dinghy, the two men frantically paddled along the shoreline. Reaching their destination, Rigaud again whispered, "This is it. No doubt about it."

The desperate pair began to blink the green glow of their flashlights out to sea. As the minutes raced by, Rigaud was flooded with waves of anxiety. There was only darkness. Now the flashlight batteries gave out. Tears of grief, rage, and frustration rolled down the French officer's ruddy cheeks.

Offshore in the blackness, Lieutenant Colonel Georges-Regis Bouvet, leader of the French commandos, was deeply concerned. In the bow of the first of twenty landing craft carrying his 620 elite fighting men, Bouvet could not detect the flashing green lights on shore. Had Rigaud and Johnson been killed? Drowned? Captured?

Bouvet could recognize no coastal landmark but decided to beach his flotilla. "Okay, take them on in here," he instructed the Canadian officer in charge of the group of landing craft.

"Can't do it," was the reply. "My orders are to wait for the flashing green lights on shore before landing."

Bouvet was furious. He whipped out his pistol, stuck it in the Canadian's stomach, and roared, "Well, here's *my* orders: Now take the damned boats onto the beaches."

The Canadian shrugged, and minutes later the twenty landing craft were on the sandy shore. Leaping stealthily onto the beach, the Frenchmen were nearly overcome with emotion on returning to their native land after years of exile. Many scooped up handfuls of wet sand and, with tears streaming down their blackened faces, pressed the soil of France to their lips.

Like Major Rigaud, Bouvet, too, knew the terrain and quickly oriented himself. While the main body of commandos silently marched off to scale Cap Negre, a company led by Captain Albert Thorel headed inland.

After reaching the east-west railroad line that ran along the coast, Thorel saw a dim light in the tiny railroad station in the village of Le Canadel. With his men remaining in the shadows, the captain banged on the door.

Inside, the stationmaster, Antoine Pergola, was on duty. The ominous knock in the night caused his heart to skip a beat. The Gestapo? This was the time that they customarily struck. He ambled to the locked door and called out, "Who is it?"

"The French army!" Captain Thorel replied.

Pergola was in a quandary. Was this a Gestapo trick to see if he would give aid to "terrorists"? Timidly, he opened the door.

Thorel explained his situation: the fleet would soon be shelling the coastline, and he and his men needed guidance to filter their way inland through German positions.

Seeing the shadowy figures of scores of French soldiers, Pergola agreed to guide the invaders to the coastal highway. Just as Thorel's column with the stationmaster in the lead started to march, an intensive crescendo of machine-gun fire and grenade and mortar explosions erupted far to the rear. A savage fight seemed to be in progress at the site where Colonel Bouvet's force had landed a short time before.

Only hours later would a puzzled Captain Thorel learn the cause of the full-fledged battle that had erupted along the beach far to his rear. A patrol of the German 918th Grenadiers had discovered a large amount of equipment discarded along the shore by Colonel Bouvet's commandos and rapidly spread the alarm that a large Allied force had landed.

Other German units rushed to the site. They grew panicky, and pandemonium erupted as German outfits began shooting at one another. Flares lighted the black sky. Shouted orders rang out over the sand dunes. Schmeisser machine pistols sent streams of bullets arching across the terrain.

By dawn, all was quiet. The German units that had been shooting at each other had left the scene, leaving a number of corpses of their comrades strewn over the landscape. There had not been a French soldier within a mile of the violent shoot-out.[21]

Ordeal for Missing Identical Twins

A sky train of C-47 transport planes, stretching for more than one hundred miles, was nearing the Riviera. On board were several thousand paratroopers of the 1st Airborne Task Force, which would spearhead Operation Dragoon. It was 3:00 A.M. on D Day.

Two members of the 460th Parachute Field Artillery Battalion, Roger and Richard Tallakson, were identical twins. They had asked to jump from separate airplanes so Mom and Pop wouldn't get a double jolt in a single telegram from the War Department in Washington, D.C.

When the green lights flashed in their respective C-47 cabins, they leaped into the dark unknown. Roger landed some twenty-five miles from his designated drop zone, and Richard crashed to earth thirty miles from his target field.

After daylight, each twin began asking other troopers for information on his missing brother. Richard heard that Roger had been killed, Roger was told that Richard had died.

Two days later, the twins were joyously reunited in an assembly area. Neither had been injured.[22]

Parachute Pack Saves Trooper

IN THE INKY PREDAWN of D Day for Dragoon, Technical Sergeant William W. Lumsden, a pathfinder of the U.S. 551st Parachute Infantry Battalion, was descending under his blossoming canopy. Pathfinders were a small, select group that jumped prior to the main body of their unit to mark the DZ (drop zone). It was not a task that promised longevity.

As the dark terrain rushed up to meet him, Lumsden plunged directly onto high-tension wires. He felt electric shocks nipping at his body, and moments later he fell some twenty feet onto railroad tracks. His binoculars had landed under him and were smashed almost flat, so great had been the impact. Lumsden was stunned by the electric shock and the force of his fall, but he was hazily aware that another American paratrooper had landed on the high-tension wires at about the same time he had.

Lumsden and the other trooper had come down directly on a railroad yard. Seconds later, pandemonium broke out. Men were dashing about, shouting and wildly firing machine pistols. The panicky German force guarding the rail yard apparently was convinced that a parachute assault had been launched against the facility, unaware that only two Americans had been misdropped there.

A German brandishing a Schmeisser machine pistol rushed up to where the dazed Sergeant Lumsden, still wearing his parachute harness and combat gear, was sprawled across the tracks. Firing from point-blank range, perhaps fifteen feet away, the German emptied the clip at the prone American. Lumsden felt a searing pain in his arm, as though a white-hot poker had been inserted into his elbow. A bullet had torn into his flesh and bone, and he felt warm blood flowing from the wound.

Having depleted his ammunition, the German spun around and began running. Still prone on the tracks, Lumsden pulled out his .45 Colt with his good arm and fired one round at the fleeing figure. A bullet tore through the back of his head, and the *Feldgrau* (field gray, the average German soldier) fell over dead.

As the wild shooting melee raged, Lumsden struggled to his feet. His knees felt jellylike and his head was groggy. A stream of tracer bullets hissed past him as he staggered to nearby woods, which swallowed him up.

Only after dawn would he discover four bullet holes in the reserve parachute pack worn on his chest. All the holes were in front. The tightly packed chute had absorbed the Schmeisser's four slugs and prevented them from ripping into Lumsden's body.[23]

Drone Boats Go Berserk

OFFSHORE FROM the French Riviera in the early morning hours of Operation Dragoon, a glittering galaxy of Allied brass was on the deck of the command ship *Catoctin* to observe the amphibious landings.

Dressed in khaki trousers and shirt open at the neck, a slight, gray-haired man went almost unnoticed amidst the crush of the immaculately clad generals and admirals with their silver stars and gold braid gleaming in the rays of the Mediterranean sun. This was the man largely responsible for the creation of the enormous U.S. fleet: Secretary of the Navy James Forrestal.

At two o'clock in the afternoon, elements of the U.S. 36th Infantry Division were to charge ashore and seize the small port of Frejus, which commanded not only the highway to the interior but also the east-west coastal road to the major ports of Toulon and Marseilles.

While the brass on the *Catoctin* watched, landing craft filled with assault troops circled several thousand yards offshore, while newly developed American drone boats headed toward the Frejus beach. These boats were remotely controlled and filled with high explosives to be detonated above underwater obstacles.

About halfway to the beach, the drone boats began to behave crazily. (Later the German radio operators would be credited with jamming the remote controls.) As one of the watching brass, General Lucian K. Truscott, commander of the U.S. ground assault forces, would explain it: "One [drone] went out of control, dashed wildly up and down the beach, turned back out to sea, much to our consternation."

Intimidated by the berserk drones, the landing craft with the assault troops continued to circle far from the shore.

Then the *Catoctin* brass viewed an astonishing sight. When a couple of the drones approached the landing craft, the entire flotilla turned about and headed far out to sea.

It developed that the assault boats had been ordered to "retreat" by Rear Admiral Spencer Lewis, a veteran of the decisive sea battle of Midway in the

Pacific. Unwilling to risk letting the landing craft run the gauntlet of wildly gyrating drones, Lewis had decided to alter the Frejus landing on his own responsibility. Instead of the designated beach, the assault troops were put ashore on a nearby beach, and they quickly captured Frejus with minimal losses.

Doubtless it had been the first time in history that a major military operation had suddenly been altered because of berserk robot boats.[24]

"Am I Having Hallucinations?"

AT DAWN ON D Day plus 1 for Dragoon, Staff Sergeant Paul Roberson of Cedartown, Georgia, was emerging from the effects of morphine administered to help relieve the excruciating pain from two broken ankles received when he jumped the previous day with the 596th Parachute Combat Engineer Company. Wandering in extreme pain for two hours after the parachute jump, Roberson came upon a medic who gave him first aid and ordered his evacuation. Now, in his fuzzy-minded condition, the blond, fair-complexioned sergeant recalled that he had been brought to a hospital ship lying offshore, but as he looked around the ward at some thirty wounded men stretched out on litters, all seemed to be wearing the gray-green uniform of the Wehrmacht. And when they spoke to each other, it was definitely in the German language.

Roberson was confused. Am I having hallucinations? he reflected. Or had the American hospital vessel been sunk and he had been taken prisoner while unconscious?

Only later would Sergeant Roberson learn what had happened. With his almost yellow hair, fair complexion, his uniform soiled and torn, black camouflage paint streaking his face, and his coveted jump boots missing to relieve the stress on his broken ankles, Roberson had been mistaken for an enemy soldier by Navy medics and placed in the German ward.

When a Navy doctor stopped to treat the American, Roberson asked, "What in the hell am I doing here?"

Ignoring the question, the physician asked one of his own: "Where did you learn to speak such good English?"

Roberson snapped: "Cedartown, Georgia, by God!"[25]

A Doctor Captures a German Hospital

THIRTY HOURS AFTER the U.S. 551st Parachute Infantry Battalion had jumped behind German lines along the French Riviera, the paratroopers fought their way into Draguignan, a town ten miles inland from the invasion beaches. It was night. Lieutenant Colonel Wood G. Joerg, the outfit's leader, set up his command post in the Hotel Madeline.

Fighting was raging throughout the town as Joerg radioed Captain Jud Chalkley, one of the battalion's two surgeons, to hurry into Draguignan. Casualties were mounting.

Chalkley and the other combat doctor, Captain John Y. Battenfield, were about two miles from Draguignan at the time. The two men had worked out a system whereby they would leapfrog each other during an attack, with one working the rear area and the other the point of the assault.

Fire fights erupted all around them as Chalkley and his medics trudged into Draguignan. At the Hotel Madeline, the doctor was told by Colonel Joerg that the paratroopers had captured a French hospital in town, and the American casualties were being taken there.

Chalkley went immediately to the French hospital, which was crowded with both American and German wounded soldiers. Needing more medical assistance, Chalkley radioed the other battalion doctor, Captain Battenfield, to move forward with his medics and "join me at the hospital in Draguignan."

Battenfield and his men promptly started forward. What neither doctor knew was that there were *two* civilian hospitals in Draguignan—one that the Americans had taken over, and the other still held by the Germans.

Reaching the outskirts of Draguignan, Battenfield told his French guide, "Take us to the hospital." Clearly unaware that there were two hospitals, the Frenchman led Battenfield and his medics through the dark, ominous streets and pointed to the shadowy silhouette of a large structure—the German-held hospital.

Battenfield walked up to the front door and found that it was locked. Near exhaustion and without sleep for many hours, the doctor irritably pounded on the door and shouted: "Let me in, goddamn it!"

Moments later the door slowly opened and Battenfield and a medic named Perkins found themselves face-to-face with a German officer. The adversaries stared at one another for several seconds. Recognizing that a serious mistake had been made, the quick-witted Battenfield demanded that the Germans in the hospital surrender to him immediately.

"We have your hospital surrounded by an entire company," the American bluffed. "There is no way you can escape alive." Actually, the only Americans nearby were Battenfield and Perkins, both unarmed.

Hearing loud voices at the door, a German lieutenant colonel appeared and was told of the surrender demand. Behind the German in the dim light, Battenfield could see the forms of numerous armed Germans.

"We will surrender only to your senior commander!" the German colonel declared haughtily.

Continuing his charade, Battenfield shouted back angrily: "Like hell you will. Either you surrender to me immediately or my paratroopers will storm this building and wipe all of you out!" The American remained stone-faced. He could feel his heart thumping wildly.

Captain John Y. Battenfield captured a German hospital and 200 armed troops. (Author's collection)

Several seconds passed. Then the German colonel, speaking flawless English, declared resignedly, "All right, to save lives I hereby surrender the hospital to your force."

Outwardly calm and confident, Battenfield strode inside the hospital and whispered to Perkins to go out and round up some armed American paratroopers. Much to the relief of Battenfield, Perkins showed up fifteen minutes later with a squad of troopers, who proceeded to disarm some two hundred German soldiers who had taken refuge in the hospital.[26]

A Colonel's Unique "Uniform"

PLATOON SERGEANT Robert Van Horssen and his men of the U.S. 551st Parachute Infantry Battalion were cautiously looking for Germans along the streets in Draguignan. It was the second night of the invasion of southern France.

At one house, Van Horssen and another trooper stole inside and kicked open a door. They charged into the room, weapons at the ready. A figure asleep in a bed in his underwear abruptly popped up on hearing the Americans crash into the room. He was a German lieutenant colonel who apparently had lost a bout against cheap French whiskey and had slept through the fierce fire fight that had been raging in Draguignan.

"Let's go, Adolf!" Sergeant Van Horssen barked, pointing to the door. The startled German, in his underwear, grabbed his tunic and quickly slipped it on. The Americans noticed that the blouse was covered with ribbon decorations— "fruit salad" to the GIs.

The two paratroopers chuckled on seeing that the German was wearing bright red undershorts. Again Van Horssen snapped, "Let's go!" The German protested, insisting that he wanted to put on his uniform pants.

"Hell, where you're going, Adolf, you won't need any pants," the sergeant declared.

The two paratroopers marched their high-ranking prisoner down a hill and into the Draguignan jail, which was serving as a POW enclosure. With as much dignity as the captive could muster, he joined some forty German soldiers behind bars, painfully aware that the other POWs were snickering inwardly over the bizarre sight of a once dignified German officer clad in an expensive, ribbon-festooned tunic and flaming red undershorts.[27]

Part Five

Allied Road to Victory

Banzai Charge in a POW Camp

MOONLIGHT BATHED the camp near Cowra, Australia, where a large number of Japanese prisoners of war were confined. Suddenly, just at 2:00 A.M., the quiet was shattered by the raucous sound of a bugle. It was August 18, 1944.

Even before the final note rang out, some one thousand Japanese inmates, shouting "*Banzai!*," their traditional battle cry, charged toward the barbed-wire fence. Wielding baseball bats, clubs, kitchen knives, and other improvised weapons, the POWs were met by a hail of bullets from Australian guards. But the heavy fire failed to even slow down the charge.

Wave after wave of frenzied Japanese reached the fence, climbing over the bodies of dead and dying comrades, and were mowed down. Before the escape effort dwindled away, 231 Japanese had been killed and another 107 wounded.

More than 330 POWs managed to break out of the camp. But Australian patrols fanned out after daylight and all of the escapees were killed or recaptured, most betrayed by their Oriental features.

The Australians later learned the purpose of the mass uprising: the Japanese planned to take over the camp, seize weapons, and wipe out a nearby Australian infantry training center.

Surviving POWs were gripped by shame. They had failed to carry out the dictates of *Bushido*, an ancient Japanese code of conduct that equated failure to die for the emperor as a dishonor. Many sought to redeem their dignity: They committed *hara-kiri*, the historic suicide, to end their disgrace.[1]

A Nazi Zealot Obeys His Führer

TWO WEEKS AFTER Allied forces invaded southern France on August 15, 1944, French troops were assaulting the major Mediterranean port of Toulon from the north and the west. French warships were pounding German strong points and the heavy bunkers that surrounded the city on three sides.

The German commander of Toulon, Rear Admiral Heinrich Ruhfus, had at his disposal some 25,000 men, about one hundred light guns and sixty heavy ones, and scores of minefields. He also had a stern order from Adolf Hitler: hold Toulon to the last man and the last bullet.

141

Despite the führer's demand, Toulon was isolated and doomed. But savage fighting would rage for another week.

Meanwhile, a German-speaking French colonel tapped the telephone line leading to a large fort and told the Nazi commander that new orders had been received from the führer. The German officer was being directed to shout "Heil, Hitler!" three times, blow up his guns, and surrender the fort.

The zealous Nazi officer obeyed to the letter.[2]

Miracle Saves Woman Spy's Life

GERTRUDE SANFORD LEGENDRE was an American sportswoman of international renown. Several big-game hunting expeditions into Africa before the war had marked her as a woman of courage, resourcefulness, and daring. So it was only natural that she had joined the Office of Strategic Services (OSS) soon after the United States got involved in the global shooting conflict.

Despite her athletic background, Legendre would not seem to be a typical volunteer for the OSS. A member of a wealthy family, she had graduated from fashionable Foxcroft in Virginia. Later she married Sidney Legendre, and the couple lived on their historic plantation, Medway, in South Carolina.

After Pearl Harbor, Sidney joined the Navy at the same time his wife enlisted in the OSS and became a file clerk in Washington. Medway was closed for the duration, and the two Legendre children began living with an aunt and a nanny in New Orleans.

Through dint of diligent effort and brains, Gertrude worked her way up the promotion ladder from file clerk to head of the Cable Desk at OSS headquarters in Paris, which had just been liberated, in September 1944.

On orders from the Allied high command, all civilian OSS personnel were to wear uniforms. So Gertrude donned the garb of a Women's Army Corps (WAC) second lieutenant.

In her role as head of the Paris Cable Desk, Legendre saw almost every top-secret message that was received or sent. She was a walking encyclopedia of Allied intelligence matters.

In late September, Gertrude was issued a five-day pass. Typical of high-spirited people, she sought even more adventure. So with two OSS male companions she decided to drive a jeep toward the front lines because she wanted to "smell the battle." She was making the hazardous trek without official permission.

A few days later, the entire OSS apparatus, from Washington to Paris, was rocked by blockbuster news over Radio Hamburg: an American woman, Gertrude Legendre, had been captured in Luxembourg. Paris and Washington gave brief sighs of relief when the radio broadcast identified their captive as "an interpreter for an American naval officer."

Gertrude's husband was now a lieutenant commander serving in the Pacific. When notified of his wife's precarious predicament, he paid the ultimate tribute to her courage and daring with the comment: "God help the Germans!"

Gertrude was driven to a thirteenth-century castle in Germany and confined to Cell 38. Each night she was questioned for hours by an army lieutenant who said his name was William Gosewisch. He said he lived in the United States for eighteen years, had taken a bachelor of arts degree in psychology at Columbia University in New York City, and had married an American woman.

In 1939, Gosewisch had brought his wife and their two American children to Germany to visit relatives. When Adolf Hitler launched what would be known as World War II by invading Poland on September 1, 1939, Gosewisch was dragooned into the army.

After a number of mild questioning sessions, Gosewisch told Gertrude that the Gestapo was trying to get custody of her because it believed she was a spy.

Within six weeks, Gosewisch and Legendre were on a first-name basis. He told her one night that while he loved his native land, he was opposed to the Nazi regime and hoped the democracies would win the war.

One day Gosewisch informed her that he was being sent to the front, but that he believed he had convinced the Gestapo and his superiors that she was just what she claimed to be: a file clerk.

Within hours of Gosewisch's departure, Gertrude was hustled out of the castle, driven deeper into Germany, where she spent four more months locked up in prison. Lucky for her, the Battle of the Bulge had smashed Adolf Hitler's hopes for victory, so she largely escaped more intense grilling.

Now Dame Fate smiled on Legendre. With Allied forces preparing to storm cross the Rhine River, she was moved to Kronberg, where she was given a room at the home of Dr. and Mrs. Hans Grieme. He was head of a large factory and had connections high up in the Nazi Foreign Office. Miraculously, through Grieme's efforts, Gertrude was able to contact her old friend, Lieutenant Gosewisch, who had been reassigned from the front and was in a nearby castle.

Gosewisch immediately came to see her at Kronberg. With the help of Dr. Grieme, a hair-raising escape from captivity was planned.

Gertrude was picked up by a stranger in civilian clothes and driven in a small automobile through the war-ravaged country to a spot near the Swiss border. There, as told, she boarded a train for Switzerland. She noticed that a tall man in a light raincoat was tailing her.

After a short trip through the night over battered tracks, the train halted. Gertrude moved to the door and could see the white gates of the Swiss frontier in the bright moonlight, although the train was still in Germany.

Legendre slipped out the door and began sneaking along the tracks. She halted to consider her next move, and looked around to see the tall mystery man in the light raincoat. "Run!" he called out in a stage whisper. Then her unknown benefactor vanished.

Gertrude started running. Moments later a German border guard began chasing her, shouting *"Halten!"* repeatedly. Why he didn't shoot, Gertrude would never know.

As she shouted "American! American!" the Swiss guard raised the gate and she ran under it to freedom.

Gertrude was sent back to the United States, where she and her husband were reunited. When the war ended, he was mustered out of the Navy.

It was not until five years after the war before Gertrude was able to return to Germany and try to locate the man who no doubt had saved her life, William Gosewisch. She found the former army lieutenant and his family broke and living in squalor in the basement of a bombed-out building.

Gertrude arranged to bring the Gosewisch family to South Carolina, where they were put up in a nice home on the Medway plantation. William was given a job working for Sidney Legendre in his business.[3]

The War's Unexplained Mystery

THESE WERE HEADY DAYS in the ivory towers of the Supreme Headquarters, Allied Expeditionary Force in suburban Paris. Hotly pursued eastward across France by five armies, the Wehrmacht was retreating rapidly to the borders of the Third Reich. General Dwight D. Eisenhower's peppery chief of staff, Lieutenant Walter B. "Beetle" Smith, airily told reporters: "Militarily, the war in Europe is won." It was September 10, 1944.

That same day, Field Marshal Bernard L. Montgomery (he had just been promoted and now outranked his boss, Eisenhower) called on the supreme commander to present a bold plan of action to bring the European war to a quick end. Eisenhower was astonished by the audacity of the plan, code-named Operation Market-Garden.

Customarily cautious and methodical in battle, Montgomery now proposed dropping huge numbers of paratroopers and landing gliders behind German units, like pieces on a checkerboard hopping over their opposition, to seize a number of key bridges over the multitude of waterways that crisscrossed Holland.

But in war, unlike checkers, the enemy pieces that have been hopped over are not thereby swept from the board. They have to be removed by force. So it would be the job of Brian Horrocks's British XXX Corps, paced by the crack Guards Armored Division, to dash through the sixty-mile-long dotted line traced by the airborne troops and bolt over the Rhine (known in this region as the Neder Rijn) on the big bridge at Arnhem. Then spearheads would wheel eastward and head toward Berlin.

Eisenhower bought Monty's pitch and approved the massive and complicated operation. D Day for Market-Garden was set for September 17.

Although few in the Allied high command recognized the chilling fact at the time, Montgomery and his planners ignored the alarming intelligence collected by Colonel J. M. Somer, chief of Dutch intelligence, and his one thousand secret agents in the Netherlands.

For the past month Somer's undercover operatives had been drawing maps and sketches, taking photos, writing reports, and manning a score of radio transmitters. By the time Eisenhower approved Market-Garden, the Dutch had laid out the disposition of German forces in the country down to the last company and gun emplacement.

During the crucial week before the attack, Somer's men accelerated their snooping. Monty and his generals apparently turned a blind eye to the fact that the barracks near Arnhem could house ten thousand soldiers safe from air reconnaissance photos, and that thousands of others could be lodged in the good-sized city.

Heavily wooded areas could conceal large numbers of panzers, but the Allied photo interpreters concluded that there were only a few tanks and several thousand German soldiers to confront the invaders. Dutch spies on the ground reported large numbers of German panzers and SS groups in the Arnhem vicinity.

A young British officer, Major Brian Urquhart, became a lone voice crying in the wilderness. From a wide array of intelligence items, he concluded that the crack 2nd SS Panzer Corps, which had pulled out of Normandy when the Allies broke out of the bridgehead and was then "lost," was concentrated around Arnhem.

Urquhart, examining hundreds of air photos, even spotted several panzers squatting on the drop zone itself. Deeply worried, he took his concerns to Major General Frederick A. "Boy" Browning, commander of Montgomery's airborne outfits. Urquhart's concerns were brushed aside, and he was told that he "needed a rest." Translation: Browning was accusing the major of, in essence, hallucinations.

On the heels of Urquhart's being shot down, the ominous warnings multiplied. Dutch undercover operatives definitely identified the 9th Panzer Division near Arnhem. North of London in top-secret Bletchley Park, which intercepted and decoded German wireless messages, an unbuttoned signal disclosed that Field Marshal Walther Model, commander of Army Group B in Holland and Belgium, had set up headquarters at Oosterbeeck—three miles west of Arnhem.

Meanwhile, British officers under Montgomery studied the same pictures that Major Urquhart had scrutinized and concluded that they revealed no panzers on the drop zone.

Montgomery would not be denied. He listened to no one and to nothing that cast doubt on his plan for "ending the war in Europe" in one fell swoop. Hitting the retreating Germans hard before they could regroup, he felt confident, was far more crucial than painstakingly studying intelligence reports.

Allied intelligence on roads, terrain, and antiaircraft defenses was uniformly poor or nonexistent. Yet Montgomery and his planners did not ask the Dutch what they knew.

Had the Dutch been consulted, some of Monty's blunders might have been avoided—such as dropping British paratroopers eight miles west of the key bridge at Arnhem and virtually on top of two SS Panzer divisions—just as Major Urquhart had predicted.

After the Allied airborne divisions landed in Holland, General Brian Horrocks's tanks and infantrymen, who were supposed to be "rushing" to link up with the British Red Devils at Arnhem, were mired in a twenty-thousand-vehicle traffic jam on the single road north.

The Western Allies' euphoric hopes of ending the war in 1944 ground to a halt before the flaming guns of Tiger tanks. Why the huge amount of solid evidence had been disregarded would forever remain one of the war's most bizarre mysteries.[4]

Dutch Boys Capture Nine Germans

IN EARLY SEPTEMBER 1944, two Dutch boys, each seventeen years of age, decided that they would launch their own private war against the hated German occupiers. The lads were members of the underground in Veghel, a picturesque little city in which the natives scrubbed their sidewalks daily.

At night, on the pretext that they knew where there was a large cache of liquor, the teenagers enticed German soldiers, one at a time, to the place of this hidden treasure. Once they got a soldier into the basement of the house, they hit him over the head with a club, just hard enough to knock him unconscious.

Then the boys bound and gagged the German and dragged him into a basement room that was securely locked and escape-proof, even should the soldier regain consciousness, shuck his bonds, and try to get out.

Now that the Dutch boys had nine Germans locked up, they weren't quite sure how to dispose of them. Killing them was out of the question; such an act would be cold-blooded murder.

Then providence took a hand when a mighty Allied airborne army landed in Holland, and elements of the U.S. 101st Airborne Division assembled outside Veghel. The Dutch teenagers handed over the nine trussed-up and embarrassed Germans to the Americans.[5]

Luck Runs Out for the Blue Goose

THE AMERICAN light cruiser *Honolulu* had been bombarding the invasion beaches in Leyte Gulf as a prelude to General Douglas MacArthur's vaunted return to the Philippines. Now those on board the Blue Goose (as the crew called her) were relaxing as the ship stood by offshore for the next firing mission. It was A Day—October 20, 1944. (MacArthur never used the term D Day.)

The Blue Goose had long led a charmed life, having been involved in countless engagements and escaping unscathed time and again as sister ships around her were severely damaged or sunk. Amazingly, she had never lost a man—to accidents or to enemy action.

Now there were shouts from the lookout on the Blue Goose: "Torpedo plane! Torpedo plane! Port quarter!"

Captain H. Ray Thurber, the ship's skipper, was getting a haircut in his cabin. He dashed out and onto the bridge and saw the low-flying airplane racing directly toward him.

Moments later, he saw the torpedo drop, the splash as it hit the water, and a wake coming toward the Blue Goose. Thurber shouted orders to take evasive action—but it was too late. There was a gigantic explosion and the cruiser shook violently. The torpedo had ripped into the ship on the port side, gouging out a hole some twenty feet by twenty feet in size.

Lady luck had finally turned her back on the charmed life of the seemingly indestructible Blue Goose. Sixty officers and sailors had been killed; scores of others were badly injured.

Yet the intrepid ship failed to go down. She limped away under her own power to the relative protection of the shoal water near the beach.

While American soldiers were digging foxholes in which to spend their first night on liberated Philippines soil, out on Leyte Gulf admirals and sea men alike were growing nervous. They knew that the Japanese air force would be back, that it liked to strike under the cover of night.

An order was flashed to the hundreds of immobile ships: "Begin smoke operations!" Generators on many vessels began grinding away to lay a blanket over the standing fleet, an action that continued until midnight. If the thick smoke shielded the fleet, it also made antiaircraft gunners even more jittery.

Their anxiety grew more tense as a result of periodic calls over loud-speakers: "Flash red! Flash red!" (unidentified aircraft approaching). None was ever actually sighted. Yet a few gunners with itchy trigger fingers opened fire—at American ships in Leyte Gulf.

Guns aboard an unknown ship raked the wounded Blue Goose with 20-millimeter projectiles. Five men were killed and eleven wounded by the "friendly fire."[6]

"Baby Patrol" in No-Man's-Land

AFTER THE WESTERN ALLIES broke out of the Normandy bridgehead where they had been bottled up for six weeks after D Day, Lieutenant General George S. Patton's U.S. Third Army wheeled eastward, skirted Paris to the south, and headed hell-bent for Nancy, France, a city of some 200,000 people.

As Patton's spearheads neared the city in mid-October 1944, many worried parents sent their young children to a school outside of Nancy as a safety precaution. Unbeknownst to Patton's leading elements, they had trapped more than eighty Nancy children, between the ages of two and six, in no-man's-land between American and German forces.

A Third Army company commander, Captain George Schneider, became aware of the potential disastrous situation, and he called for volunteers for the dangerous task of rescuing the helpless and no doubt frightened kids.

Schneider and ten volunteers slipped into the blackness of no-man's-land and headed for the school, a half mile ahead. The GIs expected to be raked by machine-gun fire at any moment, but they arrived at their destination safely.

The patrol stole into the dark building, where they were greeted by four French nurses who had been taking care of the youngsters. By the light of two candles, the children gawked at the apparitions that had suddenly appeared out of the ominous night. There were only a few whimpers, even when artillery muzzle blasts shook the building.

Almost as though the scenario had been rehearsed many times, each soldier cradled two of the tiny kids in his arms. Other small tikes rode piggyback on the GIs. The older children grabbed tightly to the soldiers' jackets and belts, as told.

In single file the group moved out of the building. Moments later a flare from one combatant or the other turned the landscape into daylight. The GIs flopped to the ground, careful not to hurt their charges. Shells began crashing around them—but not one child cried or let out a scream. Perhaps they were too bewildered and frightened to even utter a sound.

When the flare's iridescence vanished, Captain Schneider called out in a stage whisper, "Let's go." After trudging in the darkness for a few hundred yards, the Americans heard a voice call out: "Halt, who is there!"

Schneider softly gave the password, and the procession continued into American positions. Soon the group arrived at a field hospital, and the begrimed, bearded, nearly exhausted soldiers tenderly put their sleepy companions to bed. After daylight, the children were back with their parents in Nancy.

The "Baby Patrol" had been unique. Perhaps it had been the only instance in which American soldiers risked their lives to save so many children they had never known and would never see again.[7]

Providence Saves a Polish Spy

ALL ALONG THE FRONT, from Holland in the north to the Swiss border in the south, the Western Allies were stalled by bad weather, extended supply lines, and tenacious German resistance. Now Supreme Commander Dwight D. Eisenhower, at his headquarters in the ornate Versailles Palace outside Paris, needed high-grade intelligence on what was taking place inside Adolf Hitler's Third Reich. It was the fall of 1944.

A decision was made to mount an almost-overnight operation to penetrate the tightest police state the world had known. Masterminding this perilous and complex intelligence operation was thirty-two-year-old William J. Casey, chief of Secret Intelligence in Europe, whose office was on Grosvenor Street in London. His organization was a branch of the Office of Strategic Services (OSS), America's cloak-and-dagger agency.

Penetrating the heart of Nazi Germany would require enormous courage and ingenuity on the part of the secret agents. They would have to parachute right into the crowded midst of not only the German armed forces, but also a hostile civilian population numbering in the tens of millions. Casey's spies would bail out "blind," that is, not having a reception committee on the ground to provide them safe houses and information on the local situation.

In March 1945, a Pole code-named Adrian leaped out of a transport plane near Augsburg, deep in the Third Reich. On him was a phony document prepared by OSS craftsmen in London. In civilian life, the forty-one-year-old spy had been a railroad technician, so his fake papers stated that the German government had ordered him to take a job on the railroad at Augsburg.

After landing safely—and alone—Adrian buried his parachute and set out on a two-mile walk into Augsburg. On the way he passed a major airfield and made a sketch of it.

Reaching the city, he had his papers checked routinely by police. His cover story was shattered. Although he supposedly had been ordered to Augsburg, there were no documents authorizing travel to that city.

Adrian was arrested by the Gestapo and taken by train to the town of Halle for further interrogation. On the way, he swallowed, piece by piece, the drawing he had made of the airfield.

At Gestapo headquarters in Halle, Adrian's clothes and shoes were cut up into tiny pieces. But nothing incriminating was discovered. Convinced that their prisoner was a spy, the Gestapo ordered him to drink a liquid laxative. When he refused, Adrian was smashed in the mouth by a rifle butt, knocking out several teeth.

Adrian then drank the concoction, but the Gestapo found nothing in the body residue. Then the interrogators placed the Pole between large rubber rollers and moved his body between them until he vomited. Using a large magnifying glass, the Gestapo agents inspected the stomach contents and found parts of the telltale map. That disclosure seemed to doom the prisoner.

Hoping to obtain more information, the Germans beat Adrian with clubs for the next five days, but he denied any knowledge of spying or that he had any confederates in the Reich.

A day later Providence took a hand in Adrian's predicament. A flight of American B-17 Flying Fortresses flew over Halle and dropped its lethal cargoes. One bomb, miraculously, blew out the doors of the section of the prison where the Pole was awaiting execution. Adrian and a few other prisoners simply walked away.

Gaunt, half-starved, nearly exhausted, Adrian fell asleep in a thick forest outside Halle. There he was found by Polish laborers who had been conscripted by the Germans. They hid him in a house until spearheads of the U.S. Army overran the region in mid-April.

The Counterintelligence Corps (CIC) gave Adrian the task of identifying hard-core Nazis from large numbers of Germans being hauled in for questioning. In one group, the Pole recognized two men—they were the ones who had beaten and tortured him.

Without a word, Adrian slipped a pistol from the holster of one of the CIC agents and fired two bullets, point-blank, into each of the Gestapo men.

Curiously, the CIC agents had suddenly gone blind and deaf. As the two corpses were being hauled away, the Americans continued with their work.[8]

The Choirboys Plot to Doom Hitler

ALTHOUGH MOST OF Major General William Donovan's U.S. Office of Strategic Services (OSS) operatives spied, conducted sabotage, and collected intelligence behind enemy lines—they were known as Cowboys—a large number of others were assigned to Dr. Stanley Lovell's Research and Development Division. These were largely inventors, scientists, geographers, psychologists, linguists, historians, and anthropologists. They came to be known as the Choirboys.

The job of the Choirboys was to conduct studies and to dream up unorthodox and devious plots to undermine and befuddle the enemy.

After Adolf Hitler's army in the West had been chased eastward across France by the Allies in the summer of 1944, the Choirboys in Washington, D.C., came up with an amazing plot based on the premise that Germany would promptly collapse if only the führer could be demoralized—"driven crazy," is the way one Choirboy described it.

The way to get Hitler out of the picture was to expose him to a flood of pornography. Leaping into action, the OSS men collected the largest amount of German smut ever assembled in the United States. This mountain of materials was to be dropped by airplanes around Hitler's headquarters. Presumably, the German leader would stroll outside, pick up some of the smut, and immediately be stricken by total madness.

The Choirboys were enthusiastic about the plot, and an Army Air Corps colonel was called in by the pornography collectors and briefed on the number and type of aircraft needed. The colonel was astonished and thrown into near-madness himself.

Rising from his chair, the Air Corps officer shouted that Bill Donovan's men were a bunch of maniacs, and that the Air Corps would not risk the life of a single man for such an insane machination.

The colonel stomped out of the room. With his departure, the pornography plot died a natural death.[9]

"Kidnapping" a Thirty-Ton Tank

IN THE FALL OF 1944, in Europe, General Omar N. Bradley, commander of the million-man U.S. 12th Army Group, took what he called a "calculated risk." He assembled the bulk of his forces in the Aachen-Julich sector along the northern part of his long line and was preparing a massive offensive across the Cologne Plain to the Rhine River, Germany's historic barrier to invasion from the West.

South of the region from which Bradley would launch his Sunday punch was the Ardennes of Belgium and Luxembourg. This seventy-five-mile-long sector was so hilly and heavily forested that the Allies considered it to be "impassible." So Bradley thinly manned what came to be known as the Ghost Front with green divisions "just off the boat" and veteran outfits exhausted from heavy fighting.

The Germans used the Ghost Front for the same purposes: to rest decimated combat units and to "blood," that is, test lightly in combat, newly formed divisions.

Although within rifle distance of each other, American and German soldiers along the sector evolved something of an unwritten "gentlemen's agreement": you don't shoot at us and we won't shoot at you. Consequently, it was normal for soldiers on both sides to emerge from their houses each morning and wave in friendly fashion to their opponents.

One American squad, to while away the long and boring days, hooked up a loudspeaker to a record player and sent the melodic strains of famed American band leader Glenn Miller's "In the Mood" drifting across no-man's-land to the ears of the Germans. This gesture would be returned by the *Feldgrau* (field gray, the average German soldier), and the GIs would recognize the beautiful German ballad "Lili Marlene."

Along the Ghost Front, there were gaps of two or three miles between American units. It was rumored that some Belgians conscripted against their will into the German army were slipping through these wide openings in the front and visiting wives, girlfriends, or relatives behind American lines.

In this curious, even eerie, frontline atmosphere, each side appeared to take precautions that nothing was done that would upset the tranquil co-existence. However, both the Americans and the Germans sent patrols through the frontline gaps as a sort of on-the-job training for green soldiers.

On one occasion, a German patrol behind American lines came upon a thirty-ton Sherman tank, which presumably had been parked while its crew went into a nearby house for a respite from the cold and perhaps a few belts of cognac or vino.

Somehow, the Germans managed to start the iron monster. Then they proceeded to "kidnap" the tank and bring it back through American positions to their own lines without once being challenged.[10]

A Hero "Resigns" from the Navy

IN OCTOBER 1944, Lieutenant Commander John D. Bulkeley, skipper of the destroyer USS *Endicott*, received orders to sail to the United States after his ship had been involved in Operation Dragoon, the massive invasion of south-ern France. During that action the thirty-three-year-old Bulkeley had received widespread media recognition when the *Endicott* sank two German warships in one battle.

Although he had never sought it, fame and public recognition was noth-ing new to Bulkeley. Since his days in the Philippines early in the war, he had received the Congressional Medal of Honor and every other decoration for valor—some of them two or three times.

Most of Bulkeley's renown had come from being skipper of PT-boat squadrons in the Philippines and the southwest Pacific, and later to spearhead the invasion of Normandy in June 1944. It had never been known why this warrior had been shifted to destroyer duty, but he had accepted the challenge and excelled at it.

Now, en route to the United States, the *Endicott* made a stopover in Tangier, Morocco, a city lying opposite Gibraltar at the western opening of the Mediterranean Sea. Most of Tangier's residents were Moslem Berbers and Arabs, many of whom hated the United States.

There would be a forty-eight-hour layover in Tangier to refuel and resup-ply the *Endicott*. So while ashore on liberty, two *Endicott* sailors were badly beaten up in a sleazy bar by a pair of Moroccan thugs.

Bulkeley was furious. Yet he knew that an official protest through diplo-matic channels would be futile. So the skipper shed his uniform, put on civil-ian clothes, and went alone into Tangier in this disguise. In essence, he had "resigned" from the U.S. Navy.

Lieutenant Commander John D. Bulkeley "resigned" from the Navy to take care of a task in Tangier. (Author's collection)

Bulkeley made a beeline for the saloon where his two men had been set on by surprise and mauled. He identified the pair of native hoodlums and, in the words of an officer on the *Endicott*, he "beat the hell out of them."

Returning to his ship, Bulkeley took off his civilian clothes, put on his uniform, and "rejoined" the Navy.[11]

A Jeep Bonanza for "Scarface Otto"

HULKING OBERSTURMBANNFÜHRER (SS Lieutenant Colonel) Otto Skorzeny was one of the war's boldest and most widely known warriors. In Germany, he was a folk hero after he had pulled off an electrifying rescue of deposed Italian dictator Benito Mussolini and later had kidnapped Admiral Nicholaus Horthy, the regent of Hungary, who was planning to defect from the German side.

In the Allied world, the 6-foot-5, 250-pound Skorzeny was a villain, although held in a degree of awe. He was known by the sinister nickname "Scarface Otto." As a teenage engineering student in Vienna, he received a slashed cheek during one of the fifteen saber duels he had fought. The deep wound was sewn up on the spot without anesthetic, and Skorzeny resumed the encounter.

*The fate of one of SS Lieutenant Colonel Otto Skorzeny's American
jeeps; the dead soldier is a German in a genuine U.S. uniform.
(U.S. Army)*

In mid-October 1944, Adolf Hitler, the warrior's greatest admirer, summoned the thirty-six-year-old Skorzeny. "Colonel, I have a mission for you that
may well decide whether Germany lives or dies!" the führer declared.

During the next hour Hitler described plans for a mighty surprise offensive that would strike the unsuspecting Americans in mid-December. Skorzeny
was to collect and train a force of English-speaking German soldiers, who would
be equipped with authentic American weapons, jeeps, armored cars, and even
two Sherman tanks.

When the mighty blow was struck, Hitler explained, Skorzeny's imposters,
two or three in a jeep, were to fan out behind American lines in the Ardennes
Forest of Belgium and Luxembourg, create fear and confusion, engage in sabotage, and perpetrate mayhem.

Now General Alfred Jodl, Hitler's astute chief of operations, put out an
order that all captured American vehicles should be turned in to specified cen-
ters so that they could be sent to Skorzeny's secret outfit.

The vehicles were steadily rounded up—except for jeeps, the small,
speedy, tough, all-purpose conveyances. Skorzeny knew that many German
combat officers had been using captured jeeps, and the vehicles were highly
prized by them. So when Jodl's order circulated, jeeps mysteriously vanished
from the German army in the West.

Skorzeny knew that his unorthodox mission would fail unless a good-
sized number of American jeeps could be found. Success would depend upon
speed and maneuverability, and only the jeeps could provide those dimensions.

So the colonel sent out teams of his men on scavenger hunts to try to locate jeeps—a seemingly hopeless task—because he knew the German officers had hidden their prized possessions. However, the gods of battle smiled on Skorzeny. His foragers discovered eighteen jeeps, all in good condition, hidden in a barn.[12]

A Peculiar Reception Committee

EARLY ON THE MORNING of December 12, 1944, in the Pacific, an American invasion force of old battleships, cruisers, destroyers, and a few "jeeps" (baby aircraft carriers) edged out of Leyte Gulf in the Philippines for the 550-mile trek to southern Mindoro Island. General Douglas MacArthur's eye had focused on the main Philippine island of Luzon for nearly three years, but first he would have to capture Mindoro to provide airstrips for the leap northward to Manila, Bataan, and Corregidor on Luzon.

At dawn on N Day (December 15), Rear Admiral Arthur D. Struble's armada was lying off Mindoro and preparing to blast the invasion beach. Suddenly, an urgent warning echoed through the warships: "Hold your fire! Hold your fire!"

Large numbers of Filipino men, women, and children, many waving American flags, were prancing along the targeted beach to greet the invaders. Eight or ten caribou were also lumbering up and down the sandy shore, perhaps eagerly anticipating a renewal of their favorite sport, chasing and butting American soldiers.

Joyous Filipino civilians on the beach held up the American invasion. (U.S. Army)

Admiral Struble was puzzled and frustrated. Courses at the U.S. Naval Academy had never taught how to handle a situation in which a specific time and place for an invasion had been planned, yet friendly civilians and hopefully friendly animals were gyrating on the shoreline.

Struble and his staff hurriedly discussed what action could be taken. Finally, it was decided to fire airbursts high in the sky over the beach to frighten off the reception committee. Struble cautioned the gunners, "Make sure you don't hit natives or animals."

Several destroyers fired warning shots. Much to the relief of all hands, Filipinos and caribou rapidly scurried inland. The war could resume.[13]

Hitler Humbles His Generals

ON DECEMBER 12, 1944, German field marshals and top generals along the Western Front received mystifying—and unprecedented—orders. Each was to report to Ziegenberg Castle, near Frankfurt, that day. There was not a hint about the purpose of this curious order. Each was told not to bring a single aide with him, also an unprecedented directive.

One by one the field marshals and generals, driven by chauffeurs, arrived at medieval, towering Ziegenberg Castle. Thus began one of the most peculiar scenarios of the war.

Hushed and guarded conversations among the commanders failed to unravel this highly unusual event. Each was aware that a spiteful Adolf Hitler had in the past ordered the execution of German generals who he felt had betrayed him.

Late in the afternoon, the commanders assembled in a cavernous room. There a stern-faced SS captain addressed the gathering, "Gentlemen, I have received orders from higher authority," he said. "Each of you is to deposit your sidearm and briefcase with me."

A detail of armed SS men then circulated through the room and collected the items, storing them in a locked cloakroom. And the humiliation of the proud field marshals and generals was only beginning.

Next a junior SS officer "ordered" the high brass to don topcoats and hats. Then the commanders were herded out the front door by the black-uniformed SS men, much like a group of hardened convicts being transferred from one prison compound to another. A cold, heavy rain was beating down on the commanders as they headed toward a large, old, war-weary bus that was parked in front of the castle. As the group marched along, their every move was scrutinized by the heavily armed SS men who lined their path.

Interspersed with the SS troopers were raincoat-clad agents of the Geheime Staatzpolizei (Gestapo), who were feared by even the highest-ranking Nazis.

Adolf Hitler, führer of Greater Germany, supreme commander of the armed forces, and chairman of the Nazi Party. (Author's collection)

Planners of this mystery-shrouded operation were taking no chances that the German commanders might try to kill the führer.

Now the bus began to move, and each field marshal and general sat silently, immersed in his own thought. For a half hour, the vehicle chugged around the countryside as the Gestapo and SS officers kept watch on the passengers. Some of the brass noticed that the vehicle was traveling on a circuitous course and they passed the same point several times during the meandering.

Finally, the bus ground to a halt in front of a thick-walled bunker, which the passengers recognized as the Eagle's Nest. It was from that command post that Hitler had directed the invasion of France and the Low Countries four years earlier.

The pride of the German military tradition were ordered to leave the bus, and the commanders walked the short distance to the bunker between two rows of SS men and Gestapo agents. Inside, the field marshals and generals were led to a large conference room and told to take their seats. Chairs had been arranged in rows, like those in a children's school, with each chair spaced three feet apart. In the front of the room was a rectangular table some ten feet long, behind which were three chairs.

After the field marshals and generals (numbering about sixty) were seated, a door at the front of the room opened and through it strode Adolf Hitler and two of his trusted confidants, Field Marshal Wilhelm Keitel and General Alfred Jodl.

Hitler had always trusted only a few of his generals. That distrust turned to paranoia the previous July when a conspiracy of German military, government, and civic leaders known as the Schwarze Kapelle (Black Orchestra) exploded a bomb that nearly killed the führer at his headquarters behind the Eastern Front.

Now an eerie hush hovered over the room as Hitler began to speak. For an hour he rambled on about a confused series of inconsequential matters. Although most of the commanders had heard all of this before, each appeared to listen intently. None dared to fidget in his hard wooden chair or even reach for a handkerchief for fear that such a gesture might be interpreted by the hawk-eyed SS men lining the room as going for a hidden pistol.

Suddenly, the führer paused dramatically. Finally, he said, "I have made a momentous decision. I will take the offensive in the West!" Pausing again, he pointed a finger at a wall map of the Western Front. "I will strike here—in the Ardennes!"

As Hitler continued to relate details of the mighty assault code named Wacht am Rein (Watch on the Rhine), skepticism invaded the thoughts of most of the audience, except for the most rabid Nazis. Although the Ardennes was known as the Ghost Front and held lightly by a few exhausted American divisions, the veteran strategists in the audience felt that the enemy would have enough resources, firepower, and troops to eventually smash Wacht am Rein.

Despite the reservations of most, none of the Wehrmacht leaders stood up and voiced an objection. To do so, they no doubt realized, would be signing their own death warrants.

Hitler exhorted his commanders to give their all: "This battle will decide whether Germany lives or dies!"

The die was cast. With a final roll of the dice Hitler was bent on reversing the fortunes of a nearly beaten Third Reich. O Tag (D Day) was eighty hours away.

As an elated führer, face flushed with the scent of victory, withdrew from the room, the field marshals and generals leaped to their feet as one, clicked their heels in unison, and shouted "Heil Hitler!" as they raised their arms in the Nazi salute.[14]

History Repeats
for German Colonel

Two hours after midnight on December 16, 1944, twelve hundred German paratroopers, burdened with heavy combat gear, waddled into big Junkers

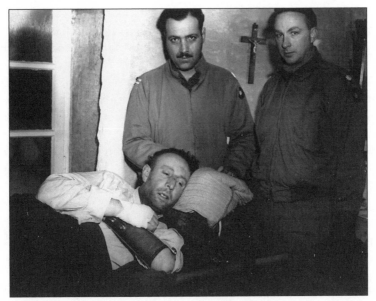

Exhausted, frost-bitten, and starving, German Lieutenant Colonel Friedrich von der Heydte (in U.S. aid station) surrendered. (U.S. Army)

transport planes at Lippsprings and Padderborn, two hundred miles behind the Western Front. It was O Tag for Operation Wacht am Rein.

Leading the parachute *Kampfgruppe* (battle group) was thirty-five-year-old Lieutenant Colonel Friedrich August Baron von der Heydte, who had recently organized the unit and hardly knew the names of the officers.

At dawn, tens of thousands of German assault infantrymen and pioneers (engineers), supported by one thousand panzers, were to plunge through the thin American lines along the Ghost Front of the Ardennes in Belgium and Luxembourg. Colonel von der Heydte's men were to bail out over a crossroads in a desolate area near Malmedy, Belgium, and block American reinforcements that would be rushing southward to meet the oncoming German ground units.

Now, as the German sky trains carrying the paratroopers lifted off and set a course for Belgium, von der Heydte reflected that his luck was bound to change for the better in this, his second, combat jump. Back in May 1941, he had parachuted onto the Mediterranean island of Crete as the leader of a Kampfgruppe of some two thousand paratroopers. After hitting the ground, he scrambled to his feet, looked around, and saw that he was alone.

Now, three and a half years later, the Junkers carrying von der Heydte and his troopers crossed the Belgian border. Minutes later, the plodding transports were raked by bursts of machine-gun tracer bullets. A few planes plummeted like flaming torches. Others scattered.

At 3:30 A.M. the baron was standing in the door of his plane. Rapidly he tightened the sling on his heavily taped left arm. A fleeting thought reminded him that he would probably be the first parachute commander to jump into battle with a broken arm.

A green light flashed in the cabin, and von der Heydte bailed out into the dark unknown. He hit the ground hard and was dazed. But he pressed the two buttons on his chest and unstrapped the belts at his thighs, freeing him from the parachute.

Bruised and aching, the colonel struggled to his feet and looked around for his paratroopers. It was Crete all over again: von der Heydte was alone.[15]

A Jinxed Town in Belgium

WITHIN HOURS AFTER the German juggernaut charged through American lines in Belgium to launch the Battle of the Bulge, Malmedy, a picture-book town right out of Hansel and Gretel, was under attack. But stubborn soldiers of the U.S. 30th Infantry Division stayed put and beat back the German force bent on capturing Malmedy.

On the afternoon of December 23, 1944, a flight of six U.S. B-26 bombers was winging above the snow-covered forest. Even though the weather had cleared after a week of thick clouds, the flight leader was unable to pinpoint his primary target, Zulpich, Germany, a railhead for supplies pouring into the Ardennes. He and his navigator concluded that they were over Lammersum, Germany, six miles northeast of the target.

As the flight flew over the town scores of bombs fell to earth, causing a rash of explosions that seemed from the air to have virtually wiped out the community.

Soon soldiers of the 30th Infantry Division and hundreds of dazed and battered civilians were crawling from the carnage inflicted on Malmedy, Belgium—forty miles from Lammersum. Scores were dead among the ruins.

A short time later, Major General Leland Hobbs, commander of the 30th Division, was on the telephone berating the leader of the Ninth Air Force, General Elwood "Pete" Quesada. "What's going on?" Hobbs shouted. The bombs had killed some forty of his men.

Quesada was horrified. "It can't happen again," he assured Hobbs. Forty-eight hours later an effort was being made to celebrate Christmas Eve in Malmedy. An American truck loaded with presents drove up to the civilian hospital in the town. The GIs of the 30th Infantry Division had given up their own Red Cross Christmas presents to express their sorrow for the scores of civilians who had been killed earlier that day in the accidental bombing of Malmedy by the U.S. Ninth Air Force—the second one in two days.

Under a dull moon on Christmas night, men of the 30th Division and civilians were digging for survivors of another "friendly" bombing of Malmedy—the third one in three days.[16]

A Belgian Woman Halts the Panzers

DURING THE HOURS BEFORE DAWN on December 24, 1944, the spearhead of the crack German 2nd Panzer Division was charging along a fog-blanketed road leading to the Meuse River. There had been no resistance. Looking at his map by flashlight, the task force commander saw that it was only a few miles to the Meuse.

That river had been a key initial objective of Adolf Hitler's surprise offensive. Once across the Meuse, German spearheads were to race on northward and capture the port of Antwerp, thereby cutting American forces away from the British armies. Perhaps the panzer leader already could envision the führer pinning a high decoration on him for reaching Antwerp first.

At this locale stood the Pavilion Ardennais, owned by Madame Marthe Monrique, who, in peacetime, enjoyed a brisk business. A day earlier she had looked on as a few American engineers planted a couple of mines in front of the inn, then scurried off toward the Meuse.

A courageous Belgian woman halted a German tank-tipped spearhead like this one. (National Archives)

Madame Monrique had been urged by frightened neighbors to flee from the oncoming German tide. But she refused, determined to protect her property.

At 6:00 A.M. the proprietress was still sleeping when there was a ham-fisted knock on the front door. She turned on the light and answered the summons. Two German officers walked in. "How many kilometers to Celles?" they demanded to know in a harsh tone. From Celles it was only a stone's throw to the Meuse.

Madame Monrique, who spoke fluent German, replied truthfully, "Ten kilometers," seemingly wanting to be helpful.

"How's the road?"

The madame was a skilled actress. "The Americans have been working night and day planting mines in the road, for miles ahead," she lied. After a brief pause, she added, "And there are thousands of American soldiers hiding just up the road." As she had suspected, there wasn't an American between her inn and the Meuse.

The two Germans appeared to be startled by the disclosures: hundreds of buried mines, thousands of American troops.

After the pair left, Madame Monrique heard orders being shouted. Peeking out a window, she was elated to see that the entire column of panzers had turned off the road and into a woods. There the tanks hid for hours until patrols had reconnoitered the region ahead in search of an alternate route to the Meuse.[17]

Hex by a Lieutenant's Pal

KNEE-DEEP IN SNOW and laced by icy arctic blasts, men of the veteran U.S. 509th Parachute Infantry Battalion were near exhaustion after having spent two bitter hours battling elements of the 2nd SS Panzer Division for the Belgian village of Sadzot. Lieutenant Hoyt R. Livingston, commander of A Company, turned to his radio operator: "Tell battalion that Sadzot is secure."

It was December 28, 1944, the thirteenth day that the Battle of the Bulge had been raging.

Soon A Company's executive officer, Lieutenant Kenneth R. Shaker, approached, and the two men began discussing the situation. Shaker had been a teenaged soldier of fortune who had served as an infantry private during the Spanish Civil War.

Now in freezing Belgium, Lieutenant Livingston felt slightly uneasy standing next to his good friend, Ken Shaker, in a combat situation. Twice in previous campaigns Livingston had been wounded, and each time he was talking to Shaker.

The next day, savage fighting erupted when the Germans tried to recapture Sadzot. For the third time during the war Livingston was wounded—his pal Ken Shaker was again nearby.[18]

A Fluke Halts Eisenhower Trip

ON THE FRIGID MORNING of December 26, 1944, Allied Supreme Commander Dwight D. Eisenhower was preparing to leave his quarters in suburban Paris for the railway station. There he would board a special train that would take him to Belgium for a conference with British Field Marshal Bernard L. Montgomery, commander of Allied forces in the north in what came to be known as the Battle of the Bulge.

Just before Eisenhower would head for the Paris railway station, an urgent message arrived. In a million-to-one shot, a random Luftwaffe bomb had struck the parked train he was to take. The supreme commander's trek had to be postponed for twenty-four hours until another train was brought in.[19]

A GI "Division" of Thieves

WHILE HALF-FROZEN American soldiers were knee-deep in snow and engaged in a savage, no-holds-barred struggle with German forces in December and in January, 1945, thousands of "saboteurs" in the Paris region were giving a mighty boost to the Werhmacht. Some twenty thousand American deserters— more men than in a combat division—were stealing supplies badly needed by the embattled GIs in the Ardennes.

These American scoundrels were pilfering everything from food to trucks and selling their ill-gotten gains on the Paris black market. "The bastards would have stolen tanks," said a captain in the provost marshal's office in Paris, "but there were no buyers for those items."

However, the thieves wearing GI clothing were making a gigantic haul in a commodity that was particularly needed at the front. They were stealing about a thousand gallons of gasoline each day, which accounted for the large number of civilian automobiles that suddenly had begun to appear on Paris streets.

Not all of the American culprits were roaming loose to ply their newfound profession. Nearly fourteen hundred of them had been arrested and confined to guarded barracks. In a second POW enclosure in Paris, nearly two hundred officers and a handful of enlisted men were charged with an amazing crime: stealing an entire trainload of soap, candy, food, cigarettes, and other supplies. When arrested each of these miscreants had about $5,000 (equivalent to some $60,000 in the year 2002) in his possession. Before being collared, one major had sent home $36,000 in only three weeks.[20]

The Miracle of Wiltz

SO RAPID HAD BEEN the German advance in the Battle of the Bulge that four thousand civilians were trapped in their basements in Wiltz, Luxembourg, as fighting raged in and around the town. After Wiltz was captured by the Germans, the civilians lived like animals in icy cellars. Above them in the arctic cold, death continued to hover.

As shells whistled into Wiltz, the spirits of the civilians plummeted. They were aware that a strong German force was occupying their town, and it seemed evident that the Americans could never recapture it and rescue the citizens.

Despite the ongoing danger, the local pastor, sixty-three-year-old Canon Prosper Colling, traipsed from cellar to cellar to try to uplift spirits. One day he climbed down into a dark, cold, wet basement and saw the occupants crying and staring at him with terror. "We're all doomed!" one called out.

The small, wiry Colling made no reply. But he put a piece of paper onto an overturned barrel and began to write. The refugees looked at him as though he had lost his mind.

Minutes later the canon handed the sheet to an assistant and told him to go to the parish office and type the wording. Soon the typewritten copy was returned to the cellar. Waving the sheet of paper, Colling said, "I am making a promise to Our Lady of Fatima to build a shrine to the Sacred Heart and Our Lady of Fatima in Wiltz, if we are all saved."

He signed the paper. The gloom in the cellar had vanished. The canon had given his word, and it could always be believed.

Then Colling told the young men in the cellar to tell the people that he had created a special prayer. Every day they were to pray to St. Sebastian, the patron saint of Wiltz, then recite a prayer for repentance. The information spread through town like a wildfire on a dry prairie. People became convinced that if they kept the pledge to build the shrine, the Germans would pull out of town on January 20, the birthday of St. Sebastian—just as Canon Colling had promised.

On the morning of January 20, 1945—the day the "Miracle of Wiltz" was scheduled to occur—Canon Colling was singing High Mass. He became irritated. There was much whispering going on among the congregation in the badly damaged church. The canon turned to reprimand the worshipers when everyone grew silent. Outside could be heard the sound of many hobnail boots on the cobblestone streets and then the roar of tank motors.

Moments later a man dashed into the church and shouted: "The Germans are leaving! The Germans are leaving!"

Closing his eyes, Canon Colling thanked God for delivering the Miracle of Wiltz in such timely fashion.[21]

Unique Distinction for a Survivor

ADMIRAL WILLIAM F. "BULL" HALSEY was at his post on the battleship *New Jersey* off the Philippines. His carrier planes provided cover for General Douglas MacArthur's invasion forces. It was late December 1944.

Stouthearted Bull Halsey tried to mask the deep concerns that gripped him. He had just finished his eighth cup of coffee and thirtieth cigarette. There was good reason for his worry: meteorologists had advised him that a typhoon was charging toward the Third Fleet.

A few hours later, the storm struck in all its fury. Men were washed overboard. Planes on carriers broke loose from tiedowns and plunged overboard. Fires erupted on flight decks. Winds reached ninety miles per hour. Seventy-foot waves jolted the fleet.

At the height of the typhoon's savagery, several ships capsized. Among them was the destroyer *Hull*, grizzled veteran of Guadalcanal, Wake Island, the Marshalls, and the Marianas. Of two hundred and fifty men, fifty-four would survive.

Nicholas Nagurney, a fireman on the *Hull*, was among the handful of men on one raft. They spent a terrifying night. Each time an angry wave would jolt the raft, some of the men were swept overboard, never to be heard from again.

Dawn brought a calming of the water, and renewed horrors. Several men died of wounds they had sustained earlier; others were afflicted by curious hallucinations. One man spotted land that was not there; a scantily clad Japanese woman suddenly appeared with fresh drinking water; a Russian submarine arrived to rescue the survivors.

In real life, sharks moved relentlessly around the raft, intensifying the delusions that gripped the men. Glenn Wilkerson called out to Nagurney, "See how deep the water is, Nick." Without hesitation, Nagurney thrust his arm into the water. It was nipped by a shark. Nagurney let out a howl and quickly pulled back his arm.

Nagurney and the others examined his bleeding arm. The shark had bitten a thin slab off the top of the forearm; on the underside were teeth marks half an inch deep.

Soon a Navy lieutenant on the raft became delirious and took several long gulps of seawater, which would make him deathly ill. Nagurney pounced on him and rammed his finger down the officer's throat to make him vomit. The deranged lieutenant bit Nagurney's finger.

Later, after being rescued, Nagurney said to his bedraggled raft mates, "I am probably the only guy that's ever been bit by a shark and a lieutenant on the same day!"[22]

Digging Up a Revered German Hero

EARLY IN 1945, powerful Soviet armies were charging westward and approaching Königsberg, a port on the Baltic Sea, an arm of the Atlantic Ocean enclosed by Denmark and the Scandinavian peninsula. For four years the Baltic had been a German lake, but now it was about to be controlled by the surging Red Army.

On January 15, the skipper of the German cruiser *Emden* was ordered to proceed at once to Königsberg. On arrival at the port, he received a second order: Stand by to sail on an hour's notice. There was no hint of the secret mission.

In the meantime, a strange activity was taking place at the town of Tannenberg, seventy miles inland in East Prussia, where an ornate mausoleum held the remains of a revered German hero, Field Marshal Paul Ludwig von Beneckendorff Hindenburg, and his wife, Gertrud.

It was at Tannenberg, in World War I, that Hindenburg and his army had scored a brilliant victory over a far superior Soviet force.

Hindenburg had been a great military commander, but in 1925 the seventy-nine-year-old Prussian native suddenly became a political leader. Elected president of the Weimar Republic, the government imposed by the victorious Allies on vanquished Germany after World War I, the field marshal had to confront problems he could not understand, including massive unemployment.

Largely because of his hero image, the field marshal, now eighty-five years of age, was reelected president in 1932. At this election, the National Socialist German Workers' Party (Nazis), led by a firebrand named Adolf Hitler, polled 14 million votes and gained 230 seats to make it the largest party in the Reichstag (legislature).

On January 30, 1933, the senile Hindenburg appointed Hitler to be chancellor, and it was the World War I corporal who actually ran Germany behind the scenes. The field marshal died on August 2, 1934. On that same afternoon, Hitler proclaimed himself führer (a new title) and ordered the armed forces to swear an oath of allegiance to him alone—not to the nation nor the constitution.

Now, ten and a half years later, the secret work party at the Tannenberg mausoleum, protected by a circle of armed guards, broke into the enclosure and removed the caskets holding the remains of Hindenburg and his wife. In two trucks, the containers were driven to Königsberg, where the cruiser *Emden* was standing by.

At three o'clock in the morning on January 24, 1945, the puzzled *Emden* skipper stood on deck and watched the approach along the quay of two trucks heavily guarded by armed SS soldiers. The arrival of the mystery vehicles was veiled by a heavy snowstorm. Off in the distance could be heard the dull rumble of Soviet artillery.

The two large caskets containing the remains of Field Marshal von Hindenburg and his wife were taken from the truck beds and covered with large Nazi flags bearing the swastika. The caskets were taken aboard by the SS men.

Then the *Emden* sailed under secret orders to be opened by the warship's captain when two hours out of port. The Hindenburgs were to be reburied at an undisclosed location.

This remarkable scenario to keep the German national hero out of the clutches of the oncoming Red Army was unique in history. The entire operation was cloaked in mystery. It would never be known who had ordered the mission at a time that Germany was teetering on the brink of collapse.[23]

An Unlikely Battlefield Hero

ON JANUARY 12, 1945, the Soviet army launched an all-out drive on a front some two thousand miles long. Much of the bloodiest fighting raged in Hungary.

During the drive across Hungary, Booty, a large, brown dog of questionable pedigree, rode on the Soviet tank driven by Eugen Dormidontov. Booty had been found shaking from the bitter cold and near starvation a month earlier, and the tank outfit promptly adopted him.

Dormidontov's tank was in reserve when he received a radioed order to go northward for three miles to duel with German panzers that were holding up a Soviet column. Eugen never took the pooch into battle, so he told him to get off the tank and await his return.

Dormidontov's tank was gone for nearly four hours, and when it failed to return, a squad was sent out to hunt for the missing crew and vehicle. Three hours later the search party came back: it had seen no trace of the driver nor the tank.

One of the returning soldiers had an idea. "Send Booty out," he said. "Booty always recognizes Eugen's tank, even from a distance."

Wagging his tail furiously, Booty dashed away and was soon out of sight. About an hour later, he was back. He sank his teeth into a soldier's trouser legs and tried to drag him.

"Booty's found Eugen!" the soldier called out to comrades. The dog barked loudly in agreement, then led two of the Soviets about a mile to the edge of a woods.

While the two soldiers waited, Booty scampered into the forest. "He's following Eugen's tank tracks," one man exclaimed.

A short time later the dog came thrashing back through the woods. In his mouth was Eugen's wallet, to which a handwritten message was pinned.

"Send up some bullets with Booty," the note stated. "We're alive but under attack and almost out of ammunition."

A container of bullets was strapped to the dog, and he bounced away. Twice he returned for more ammunition.

When Booty came back a third time, he was badly burned and flopped to the ground in pain. A note was fastened to his collar. "These are our last moments," it stated. "They are setting our tank on fire. Greetings to our families. Booty will break through. Farewell." The message was signed by Eugen Dormidontov and his three gunners.

Minutes later Booty, a faithful and courageous soldier, died from his wounds.[24]

Part Six

A Shaky World Peace

Amazing Scenario in Manila

In a sugarcane field sixty miles north of Manila, lanky Lieutenant Colonel Haskett "Hack" Conner, a squadron leader in the U.S. 1st Cavalry Division, gathered his unit officers around him. A murmur of excitement erupted when Conner disclosed the mission.

In a modern-day charge in tanks, halftracks, and armored cars instead of horses, the squadron was to plunge through Japanese-infested territory, bolt into Manila, and rescue some thirty-seven hundred American men, women, and children who had been imprisoned at Santo Tomas University for more than three years. It was now midnight, January 31, 1945.

Minutes later Hack Conner's flying column, some seven hundred men strong, roared southward in what quickly became a crazy kind of operation. At some points the column attained high speeds on highways, at other times it was slowed to a crawl when forced to use caribou paths where there were no roads.

Often the cavalrymen had to halt and engage in skirmishes with ambushing Japanese, battles that took a stiff toll on both sides. As each pocket of resistance was wiped out, the cavalrymen leaped back into the vehicles like pony express riders and charged onward.

Seventy-two hours after Hack Conner's flying column had left the sugarcane field, its leading tanks reached the walls surrounding Santo Tomas University. Inside, the American civilians wept and shouted with joy. Soon the elation vanished. Colonel Toshio Hayashi, the POW camp commandant, and sixty of his soldiers had herded 267 inmates, mostly women and children, into the steel-and-concrete Education Building, where they were holding them hostage on the third floor.

Meanwhile, Conner's men had entered the compound and tried to break into the building. But finally the effort had to be called off out of fear for the hostages' safety. The only hope for saving the hostages was through negotiations with the Japanese. But in the savage war in the Pacific, such parlays were unheard of.

Other American outfits reached Santo Tomas, and Lieutenant Colonel Charles E. Brady, executive officer of the 1st Cavalry Brigade, was named to try to negotiate with Colonel Hayashi.

One of the Pacific war's strangest episodes: armed Americans (in files to either side) provide an escort from Santo Tomas prison camp for armed Japanese (in center). (U.S. Army)

That night, holding a white flag, Brady, unarmed and with only an interpreter, entered the Education Building. Hayashi kept him waiting for twenty minutes. When the Japanese colonel entered the room, he had an escort of six armed soldiers.

Both Brady and Hayashi were ill at ease under these unprecedented circumstances in the Pacific. Aware that he was holding the aces, Hayashi set down his demands for the release of the hostages: he and his sixty men, carrying their weapons and grenades, would be allowed to march unmolested out of the university grounds.

After much haggling, Brady agreed to an unusual arrangement. The hostages would be left unharmed, the Japanese would be permitted to depart carrying only personal firearms, and then be escorted through American "lines" and released.

At dawn on February 5, Colonel Hayashi, wearing his samurai saber, walked out of the Education Building followed by his armed contingent. As they appeared, Americans outside tensed and fingers played across triggers. If a single shot was fired by either, a bloody catastrophe could result.

The Americans, veterans of heavy fighting, were amazed at the scenario. None had ever remembered seeing an armed Japanese soldier without shooting at him.

The Japanese quickly formed up three abreast, and Hayashi took his place at the head of the column. In rapid order, as though they had rehearsed such a scenario many times, Americans, also with loaded rifles, moved into single files, one on each side of the Japanese. Colonel Brady then walked to the head of the combined Japanese American formation, alongside Hayashi, and the bitter enemies marched out through the front gate.

As the group headed down the street, Hayashi appeared to grow nervous. He kept insisting that Brady and his men conduct them farther and farther. Finally, Brady called a halt.

"This is as far as we're going," Brady told Hayashi, who spoke fluent English. "This is the front line. This is where we leave you." Actually, the "front" at this time was anyone's guess.

Hayashi called out a command, then turned to Brady and saluted smartly. The action took the American by surprise. He paused briefly, then returned the salute.

The Japanese column marched off, and as each man passed he either bowed or saluted Lieutenant Colonel Brady.[1]

Death Stalks a Navy Pilot

ON FEBRUARY 10, 1945, history was being made in the Pacific. A group of carriers designated Task Force 58, under Vice Admiral Marc A. "Pete" Mitscher, sailed for a series of air strikes against Tokyo and its environs. It would be the first bombing of the Japanese capital since U.S. Lieutenant Colonel James H. "Jimmy" Doolittle and his handful of two-engine bombers hit Tokyo in April 1942, a raid that electrified the Allied world.

Now, after dawn on February 16, fighter planes began taking off from the carriers in Task Force 58, which had "sneaked" undetected to within sixty miles of Japan's shoreline and only one hundred twenty miles from Tokyo. As expected, the intruders were soon discovered, and Japanese fighter planes filled the sky to combat this challenge to the home islands.

For two days, swarms of Mitscher's planes strafed, bombed, and rocketed aircraft plants, dock facilities, ships at anchor, and army barracks.

During the savage duels in the sky, Ensign Louis A. Menard Jr. found himself in serious trouble when his Hellcat fighter plane was struck by an antiaircraft shell burst at six thousand feet above Tokyo Bay. The Hellcat began to tumble crazily, but Menard somehow managed to straighten it out at two thousand feet.

His right aileron had been smashed, he discovered, but, amazingly, he was able to fly the plane if he kept the speed below one hundred eighty miles per hour. He headed out to sea, knowing that he could not jeopardize lives and other planes by trying to land on a carrier deck with his badly damaged Hellcat.

Menard hoped to parachute near some ship, and he finally located the destroyer *Taussig*. When he prepared to bail out, he tried to open the plane's canopy, but it was stuck on a jagged piece of metal that had been twisted by the shell burst.

Frantically, the pilot started tugging at the pins that secured the canopy, a difficult maneuver because of his cold fingers. The pins were rusty, but he managed to break the canopy loose. As it flew into space, the canopy pulled a safety cable across his chest, pinning him in the cockpit.

Somehow Menard extracted a jackknife from his bulky flight garb, and he freed himself by hacking through the sturdy cable. Moments later he climbed onto the wing, leaped, and pulled the rip cord of his parachute.

When he splashed into the water, the parachute failed to collapse. He reached for his jackknife to cut himself loose from the harness, but remembered it had been left in the cockpit. Then he labored to inflate his life jacket. But before he could achieve that task, enormous gusts of wind began dragging the blossomed parachute and Menard along the water.

Weak and dazed, the pilot began a roller-coaster type of ordeal. The waves were large. He would plunge through one, then skip along the trough before plowing into another huge wave. Finally, Menard lost consciousness.

Lady Luck now smiled on the presumably doomed pilot. The skipper of the *Taussig*, Commander Josephus A. Robbins, had been watching the episode. He rapidly maneuvered the destroyer to a halt with its stern downwind from Menard's billowing parachute. The action was something of a gamble, because the *Taussig*, dead in the water, would have been a juicy target for any lurking Japanese submarine.

Menard's parachute collapsed on the ship's fantail, and sailors hauled the unconscious pilot aboard. Pharmacist's mates (medical personnel) worked on Menard for more than an hour and revived him. Forty-eight hours later he was aboard his own ship, the carrier *Randolph*, ready for another mission.[2]

Shoot-Out at a Boxcar

EARLY ON THE CLEAR BLUE morning of February 16, 1945, a sky armada approached Corregidor, a fortress three and a half miles long perched in the mouth of Manila Bay, in the Philippines. Soon men of the U.S. 503rd Parachute Infantry Regiment began bailing out over a terrain feature known as Topside, rising five hundred feet above the water.

Two hours later landing craft crammed with grim soldiers of Lieutenant Colonel Edward M. Postlethwait's battalion of the U.S. 24th Infantry Division headed for Black Beach, a strip on Bottomside, the lowest part of the Rock, as the island was called.

General Douglas MacArthur, Allied commander in the Southwest Pacific, had long called the tiny island "the Holy Grail." It had been captured from the Americans in the spring of 1942, and MacArthur had pledged to one day return.

Fighting became savage. U.S. intelligence had estimated that there were six to eight hundred Japanese on Corregidor. Actually, there were some six thousand warriors, all pledged to die for their emperor if need be.

On D Day plus 2, thirty-four-year-old Colonel George M. Jones, leader of the 503rd Parachute Infantry and also designated Rock Force commander, left on foot from his CP (command post) on Topside and headed for the road that led down to Bottomside. He was bent on determining the progress, or lack of it, of the 24th Infantry Division battalion that had been confronted by tenacious Japanese dug into spider holes (foxholes).

An overpowering stench hung over Corregidor. Dead Japanese—some eight hundred of them—were strewn about the bleak, rocky landscape. The smell of decaying corpses caused many GIs to vomit. Crewmen on destroyers a mile offshore were nauseated by the putrid smell. Flies, tens of millions of them, were a constant source of torment to Americans and Japanese alike.

Striding along briskly, Jones finally reached Bottomside. He learned that a continuous front line was almost nonexistent, and that tiny bands of 24th Infantry Division men were engaged in skirmishes with clusters of two or three Japanese.

A shoot-out was in progress. Ten or twelve GIs were attacking an old ice plant in which Japanese had holed up. On a hill about two hundred feet above the ice plant, a band of Japanese had gathered around a boxcar on a railroad spur and were pouring small arms fire at the Americans around the plant.

Seeing that his men were pinned down around the ice plant, the Rock Force commander decided that he would personally lead an assault against the Japanese at the boxcar.

Quickly rounding up a squad of 24th Division men, he briefed them tersely on his assault plan. "We'll creep up on them, pitch smoke grenades, then when the smoke has cleared, we'll charge the Nips at the boxcar," Jones explained.

Jones sensed that the infantrymen, most quite young and new to combat, were far from enthusiastic. The colonel was not wearing his insignia rank, and the GIs had never laid eyes on him before.

"Okay, follow me!" Jones called out, as he started trudging up the steep slope. Smoke grenades were hurled—but there was no charge. The Japanese at the boxcar opened fire, and the squad had vanished.

Undaunted, the colonel acquired another squad and started up the hill again. When the smoke cleared, Jones moved forward and reached the boxcar. Looking back, he found that he again was alone.

After his one-on-one shoot-out with a Japanese Marine, Colonel George M. Jones (left, wearing helmet) tours Corregidor with General Douglas MacArthur. (Author's collection)

Jones edged around the end of the boxcar and suddenly found himself face-to-face with an Imperial Marine in a spider hole. One antagonist was as startled as the other. Before the Japanese could react, Jones scrambled for cover. Moments later the American colonel in command on Corregidor and a Japanese private were blasting away at each other with their weapons.

Unbeknownst to the colonel, up on the edge of Topside Lieutenant Dick Williams, leader of a Signal Corps trio that had parachuted onto Corregidor after only twenty minutes of instruction, was photographing the two-man shoot-out far below with a telescopic lens.

After some fifteen minutes, the colonel decided that a dead Rock Force commander would be of little use in the battle to capture Corregidor. So he slithered away and headed for his CP on Topside. During the trek, he quipped to an aide, "It's a good thing I'm the Rock Force commander. I guess one could say that as a squad leader, I'm a flop!"

Flop or not, perhaps it was the only time during the war in the Pacific that an American commander of such a large force was out in front of his troops alone and engaging in a shoot-out with a Japanese private—one on one.[3]

MacArthur Recaptures His Home

FIVE-STAR GENERAL Douglas MacArthur had just entered Japanese-held Manila with his spearheads of the U.S. 1st Cavalry Division when he learned that an assault was being planned against the red-roofed Manila Hotel, once the finest in the Philippines. It was February 17, 1945.

MacArthur, his wife Jean, and the couple's young son Arthur had lived in the six-room, air-conditioned penthouse before being forced to flee Manila when the invading Japanese army arrived on Christmas Eve 1941.

The penthouse, with its multitude of red drapes and French mirrors, held fond memories for MacArthur. It had been filled with countless memorabilia and personal belongings collected over a lifetime. As far as the general knew, these priceless artifacts were still there, even though the premises had been occupied by a series of Japanese military and government brass.

The Manila Hotel would be a tough nut for the Americans to crack. It featured a number of strong points, especially in the tunnels that ran beneath the sturdy, five-story structure.

At daybreak, a company of the 1st Cavalry was preparing to assault the hotel. The young soldiers were astonished to see that an outsider had joined them for the assault—General MacArthur, who would assume the role of rifleman. Perhaps this was the only time in the war where a five-star officer became, in essence, a private taking part in an assault.

Minutes later the lieutenant leading the attack gave a signal and the cavalrymen charged the front door and barged inside the lobby. On their heels was MacArthur, who was armed only with a small-caliber pistol he carried in his trousers pocket. A firefight erupted, and four or five Japanese were gunned down.

Then the GIs headed up the stairs. MacArthur was with them. At each level there was a shoot-out. The route to the upper floors was strewn with Japanese bodies, causing concern among the officers that one might be shamming and could suddenly gun down one of America's most brilliant generals.

When MacArthur reached his old penthouse home he found that the Japanese had set fire to it, and many of his precious belongings had been destroyed. A dead Japanese colonel was stretched out across the threshold of the open doorway. A cavalry lieutenant, clutching a Tommy gun in one hand, looked down at the bloody corpse of the Japanese colonel and called out to MacArthur: "Nice going, sir!"[4]

Offering Up a Bonfire of Money

BOTH AMERICANS AND JAPANESE agreed that Iwo Jima was one of nature's lesser triumphs. U.S. B-14 Liberator bomber pilots, who had flown nearly two thousand missions to "soften" the eight-square-mile island in December 1944 and January 1945, were convinced it was the ugliest piece of real estate on planet Earth.

Lieutenant General Tadamichi Kuribayashi, who commanded the Japanese garrison on Iwo, entertained a new staff officer, Major Yoshitaka Horie, for dinner one night. Booze flowed freely. So did the conversation. The general asked the junior officer for his opinion of the island that was pockmarked with deep gulches and had soil of gray volcanic ash.

As in most armies, a junior officer would have been reluctant to offer advice to his superior, but in the relaxed mood of the night Major Horie did so.

"The best thing to do with Iwo," he said, pausing only to take a long snifter of sake, "would be to sink it to the bottom of the sea!"

General Kuribayashi may have agreed with the major's suggestion for the barren, waterless pile of ash, but he knew that the Americans would come soon to try to capture a base for fighter planes to escort huge B-29 Superfortress bombers that had been raining explosives and incendiary devices on Japan.

Kuribayashi knew more about Americans and their ways than most other Japanese officers. As a captain in the late 1920s he had taken cavalry training at Fort Bliss, Texas. Later, as military attaché at the Japanese Embassy in Canada, he often visited the United States and became friends with many American army officers.

These travels left him with an enormous respect for the U.S. industrial potential and the great energy of its leaders and people. Only to his wife did Kuribayashi confess his true feelings: "The United States is the last country in the world Japan would want to fight."

Despite his high opinion of the enemy, Kuribayashi was determined to kill as many Americans as possible. Iwo Jima, he often stated, would be a dagger aimed at the heart of Japan, only a few hundred miles to the north. He was determined to convert Iwo into a rock fortress anchored in the sea.

When the invasion neared, Kuribayashi said, "Every man will resist until the end, making his position his tomb!"

At 8:59 A.M. on February 19, 1945, the first assault waves of U.S. Marines stormed ashore. Bitter fighting soon erupted and continued all day. By 5:00 P.M. thirty thousand Marines were ashore.

American commanders predicted a typical mass *banzai* assault during the night, but only a steady pounding of the Marines by huge mortars occurred. Curiously, the Iwo commander was busy with a strange task.

Collecting all the Japanese currency on the island—120,000 yen (equivalent to about $3 million in the year 2002)—the general initiated a short ceremony, then lit a match to the pile of currency.

Presumably Kuribayashi didn't want the money to fall into the hands of the enemy, although the currency would be of no use to the Americans on godforsaken Iwo Jima.

By radio, the Japanese commander informed the armed forces headquarters outside Tokyo that the bonfire was a gift to the National Treasury from Iwo's doomed warriors.

It was not clear how a pile of currency ashes could improve the Japanese financial situation.[5]

A Tommy-Gunning Pilot

BY SUNDOWN on February 26, 1945—D Day plus 10—organized resistance on Corregidor had ceased. Almost six thousand Japanese had died defending the tiny rock island.

Early the next morning Americans on Topside, the highest elevation on the island, could see a few hundred diehard Japanese warriors, knowing that the end was near on Corregidor, trying to swim to the Bataan peninsula on the mainland, a distance of two to three miles.

PT-boat crews patrolling around the Rock were leery about fishing Japanese out of the water. Long ago Americans had learned that a Japanese soldier or sailor often carried a hand grenade and would blow himself up along with those trying to rescue him. So most of the Corregidor escapees were fair game while swimming.

One of those involved in the "Jap hunt" in Manila Bay was Lieutenant James R. Thomas, a pilot of the 462nd Parachute Artillery Battalion's spotter plane. In a paratroop outfit rife with colorful, even oddball, characters, Thomas was one of the most flamboyant. He packed a pair of pearl-handled revolvers and wore white silk laces in his jump boots.

Thomas had gone to flight school to become a fighter pilot, but one day he couldn't resist the temptation of flying—upside down—under a railroad bridge. So he was booted out of the flight school, but his carefree spirit and venturesome qualities earned him a home in a paratroop outfit, where feats of derring-do were the norm.

Now Jim Thomas was in his element over Manila Bay. With no artillery targets to spot, he flew his Cub with one hand and clutched a Tommy gun with the other while zipping along just above the water. Back and forth he flew over the swimming Japanese, leaning out the window and squeezing off bursts from his automatic weapon.

When an American destroyer tried to usurp a Japanese swimmer Lieutenant Thomas had earmarked for himself, he angrily buzzed the ship at mast level, wig-wagging the Cub's wings vigorously until the Navy gunners ceased firing.

With the cowboy-pilot swooping repeatedly across Manila Bay and GIs on Topside blasting away with machine guns, few, if any, of the Japanese swimmers reached Bataan.[6]

Gods Smile on German General

WALTHER MODEL, who at fifty-four was Germany's youngest field marshal, had gained his exalted rank partly through achievements on the battlefield but also through his fanatic devotion to Adolf Hitler. When the führer had miraculously escaped being killed in the July 20, 1944, bomb plot by a conspiracy of

German military and government leaders, Model had been the first officer to send a message to the shaken leader, pledging his undying loyalty. Come what may, Walther Model could be counted on to fight to the end.

Now, in late February 1945, General Erich Brandenberger, a bespectacled, portly leader of the Seventh Army, contacted his superior, Field Marshal Model. Brandenberger's exhausted men had been battling to hold back repeated assaults by General George S. Patton's U.S. Third Army against the key German towns of Prum and Bitburg, only seventy-five miles west of the Rhine River. Could the Seventh Army pull back to more defensible positions? Brandenberger asked.

Hitler's standing order was: "Don't give up a foot of ground!" So Model, face flushed with anger, adjusted his monocle and angrily snapped: "*Nein!*"

A few days later Model was presiding at a solemn conference of his division and corps leaders. Mincing no words, Model accused Brandenberger, whom the Allies regarded as one of Germany's most capable commanders, of incompetence and cowardice. He concluded his tirade by sacking Brandenberger on the spot and replacing him with Lieutenant General Hans Felber, a corps commander, as Felber looked on in embarrassed silence.

Brandenberger promptly left the building after his public humiliation by the acid-tongued Model. Moments later an American fighter-bomber dived and dropped a five-hundred-pound explosive directly onto the structure. The blast rocked the building, showering those inside with broken timbers and masonry. Model escaped serious injury but was badly shaken, and several officers were killed and wounded.

Whatever he thought about the disgrace of being fired in front of fellow generals for "incompetence and cowardice" (charges other German leaders branded as false), General Brandenberger no doubt realized that his life had been saved by the Gods of War. Had he not been sacked, he would have been inside the building when the bomb hit and probably killed.[7]

A Tail Gunner's Miraculous Survival

AFTER MORE THAN FOUR YEARS of pounding by bombers of Britain's Royal Air Force and later the U.S. Eighth Air Force, Adolf Hitler's Third Reich, which he once had boasted would "last for a thousand years," was teetering on the brink of total destruction. Yet, spurred by the führer's belief that his revolutionary new Me-262 jet fighter planes could still gain him at least a negotiated peace with the Western Allies, the Germans continued to fight.

In an amazing survival, the tail gunner of a U.S. Flying Fortress like this one was trapped in the rear section (left of dotted line) when it was shot away from the fuselage and tumbled thousands of feet to the ground in Belgium. (U.S. Air Force)

Early on the morning of March 1, 1945, an Eighth Air Force B-17 Flying Fortress lifted off from its base at Great Ashfield, England. Piloted by Lieutenant Charles Armbruster Jr., the four-engine craft formed up with its group and set a course for Ulm, in southeastern Germany.

The flight had not yet seen the jet fighters that had been intercepting bomber streams of late, but over Belgium Armbruster's plane was involved in a freak collision with another B-17 at 13,500 feet. The tail unit of Armbruster's bomber, with rear gunner Sergeant Joe F. Jones inside it, was hacked off as though a huge supernatural meat-ax had been wielded.

Trapped, Jones floated down inside the turret. Its plunge through space was slowed because it spun around in a circular motion. Finally, the tail section hit the ground. The sergeant, not long out of his teens, was stunned and bruised—but alive.

A Belgian couple, Henri and Sophie Ryjkeboer, and their five young children had watched the tail unit spin to the ground. They rushed to the site and pulled Sergeant Jones from his trap.

Jones's escape from seeming certain death was one of the most remarkable incidents of its kind during the air war in Europe. In six weeks, he was back with his comrades at Great Ashfield. No doubt he reflected often on the highly appropriate name that had been painted on the nose of his bomber before the mission—Lucky Lady.[8]

Curious Incident
in a Command Post

MAJOR HAYNES W. DUGAN, assistant G-2 (intelligence officer) of the U.S. 3rd Armored Division, and his driver jeeped into Niederaussen hard on the heels of a task force that had just captured the German town in the great Allied push to the Rhine River. They drove directly to the forward CP (command post) of the division leader, Major General Maurice Rose. It was March 2, 1945.

The CP was located in a small hotel on the northeast corner of the town's main intersection. A church with a tall steeple—ideal for artillery observers, as the Germans well knew—and a graveyard were across the intersection.

Climbing out of the jeep, Major Dugan glanced around. His experienced eye didn't like what it saw. "If Kraut artillery ever had an ideal target to zero in on, this CP is it!" he told his driver. Main intersection. Church steeple. Both excellent aiming points.

Small arms fire erupted up ahead as Dugan strolled into the hotel and saw Lieutenant Colonel Wesley A. Sweat pinning a large map to the wall. With a black crayon he circled the next objective.

Sweat, the 3rd Armored operations officers, Dugan, and several other officers were studying the map when the old hotel was rocked by German shells exploding outside. Those in the room instinctively flopped to the floor as a rain of shrapnel clattered against the building.

A short time later, when the barrage ceased, the Americans scrambled to their feet. They stared at the wall map in disbelief: a large shell splinter had flown through an open window and embedded itself in the map—directly in the crayoned circle marking the 3rd Armored's next objective.[9]

Hoax to Seize a Rhine Bridge

LIEUTENANT GENERAL William H. "Big Bill" Simpson was at his headquarters in the German town of Neuss, ten miles west of the Rhine River, mulling over a tactical problem unique in American history. Across the Rhine lay the great Ruhr basin, where most of Adolf Hitler's accoutrements of war had been and were still being manufactured. It was March 1, 1945.

Supreme Commander Dwight D. Eisenhower's grand design for crossing the broad Rhine had excluded a frontal assault on the Ruhr. In that densely built-up industrial complex, the Americans could get bogged down fighting for every factory and mill. Rather, the master plan called for surrounding the Ruhr by assaulting the Rhine north and south of that region.

Tall, gangling Bill Simpson, commander of the Ninth Army, would follow the grand design—except he saw no harm, in the meantime, of nibbling away at the Ruhr. So he hoped to sneak a force across the river barrier rapidly before the Germans could blow up a bridge at Oberkassel.

No doubt Simpson made sure he could plead ignorance of a masterful hoax, but underlings disguised a task force of the 83rd Infantry Division as a German column. The imposters were to sneak through enemy lines and grab the Oberkassel Bridge before it could be destroyed.

In the predawn blackness of March 2, the masqueraders set out for the Rhine. GI foot soldiers were wearing ankle-length overcoats and helmets "borrowed" from German prisoners. Soldiers fluent in German were put at the head of the column to do any talking that might be necessary.

Clanking along with the foot soldiers was a squadron of American Sherman tanks, which had been altered to resemble German panzers. The U.S. white-star insignia on the tanks had been painted over and replaced by German crosses.

As Simpson's task force moved ahead, strict discipline prevailed. There was no smoking. The only talking was a muttered *"Heil Hitler"* when the column passed a German outpost in the darkness. On one stretch of road, a German infantry company trudged along in the opposite direction.

About two hours after leaving American lines, the imposters reached Oberkassel without a shot being fired. Now they were far behind German lines.

Soon after dawn, a *Feldgrau* (field gray, the average German soldier) halted his bicycle and stared at the disguised Americans. He became deeply suspicious, and peddled off to sound the alarm. A GI brought the soldier down with a rifle shot, but the ruse had been unmasked. In Oberkassel the air-raid sirens screeched as the intruders were hurrying through the town.

Just as the first American tanks reached the Rhine, there was an enormous explosion. German engineers had blown the key bridge.

After seeing their target crash into the Rhine, the American imposters turned around quickly and headed back for their own lines. In the confusion, the column reached safety without even being shot at.[10]

Churchill "Consecrates" the Siegfried Line

ADOLF HITLER'S VAUNTED Siegfried Line was a formidable barrier bristling with thick-walled bunkers, gun emplacements, and two sets of "dragon's teeth," tank obstacles of reinforced concrete. Built in the late 1930s as the führer prepared for war, the barricade ran continuously for more than four hundred miles, along the western frontier of the Third Reich, from the Swiss border in the south to Holland.

Hitler considered the chain of fortifications to be impossible for an enemy to crack. So he named the daunting obstacle after the mythical German hero, Siegfried, who had forged a mighty sword from the broken one of his father and killed a dragon with this powerful weapon.

Even in the Allied world the Siegfried Line had taken on a mystical aura of seeming German invincibility.

By early March 1945, after a month of savage fighting, divisions of British Field Marshal Bernard L. Montgomery's 21st Army Group in the north had fought their way almost to the Rhine River. A brutal price had been paid. Montgomery's First Canadian Army, U.S. Ninth Army, and British forces had suffered nearly 25,000 casualties battling against the Siegfried Line.

On March 3, British Prime Minister Winston Churchill arrived at Field Marshal Montgomery's headquarters to inspect the battlefield and to congratulate the 21st Army Group for its notable achievement of breaking through the Siegfried Line.

Then Churchill, Montgomery, and Field Marshal Alan Brooke, the chief of the Imperial General Staff, climbed into a Rolls Royce and set out for the headquarters of Lieutenant General William Simpson, commander of the Ninth Army, in Maastrict, Holland.

After about an hour at Simpson's command post, the Allied brass prepared to head for the front. Churchill demanded to see for himself the battle that continued to rage west of the historic Rhine. Simpson asked the prime minister if he wanted to visit the men's room before leaving.

Captured Germans walk through the Siegfried Line's concrete "dragon's teeth." (U.S. Army)

Churchill asked: "How far is it to the Siegfried Line?" About a half-hour drive, Simpson replied. "In that case, I'll wait," the portly, spry, seventy-year-old Briton declared.

In the convoy of twenty vehicles, Churchill sat next to General Simpson in the back seat of the Rolls Royce. After a routine drive, the American said, "Mr. Prime Minister, the Siegfried Line is just ahead, past that small bridge."

"Halt the car!" Churchill exclaimed. He alighted and, with the aid of a cane, strolled forward to a long row of concrete dragon's teeth. The other brass trailed him.

"Gentlemen," the prime minister proclaimed with an impish grin, "I'd like to invite you to join me." With that he fumbled with the fly on his trousers. "Let us all urinate on Adolf Hitler's Siegfried Line!"

That remark triggered one of the war's most unique episodes: the highest of Allied leaders standing mutely and "consecrating" the dragon's teeth. "An historic operation," Churchill quipped.[11]

An Airman Dodges Certain Death

AT THE MAZE OF AIRFIELDS in eastern England, swarms of B-24 Liberators and B-17 Flying Fortresses of the U.S. Eighth Air Force were taxiing from their hardstands to take up assigned positions on the runways. Crew members were gripped by mixed emotions. They were elated to be part of the seven hundred and thirty heavy bombers, escorted by eight hundred fighter planes, that were to hit the Big-B—Berlin. Yet the airmen were apprehensive, knowing that the German capital was ringed by scores of antiaircraft guns and that the bomber streams would be pounced on by the new Me-262 jet aircraft. It was March 6, 1945.

Leading the bomber stream was a Fortress piloted by Major Fred A. Rabbo. His crew included Lieutenant John C. Morgan, a husky, red-haired Texan who had flown with the Royal Canadian Air Force for seven months before transferring to the U.S. Eighth.

Morgan was a celebrity of sorts in his unit. Several months earlier, on December 18, 1943, he had received the Congressional Medal of Honor, America's highest award for valor, in a special ceremony at Eighth Air Force headquarters.

During a mission against targets at Hanover, Germany, on the previous July 26, Morgan had been copilot of *Ruthie II*, piloted by Lieutenant Robert L. Campbell. Over the English Channel, *Ruthie II* was attacked by a group of Luftwaffe fighter planes. A shell tore through the fuselage, zipped past Morgan, and struck Campbell, ripping off the back of his head.

Morgan had to take over the controls with one hand, while holding off the slumping, half-dead Campbell with the other. Instead of turning back, the

Texan kept the bomber in formation while flying with one hand, reached the target, and made it back to England—a time frame of two hours.

Making Morgan's feat all the more phenomenal was the fact that German shells and bullets had smashed the radio and the intercom system with which a pilot kept in touch with other bombers and his crew.

Now, seven months after that astonishing episode that had earned Lieutenant Morgan the Medal of Honor, the B-17 being piloted by Major Fred Rabbo, with Morgan aboard, was approaching Berlin when the formation was raked by antiaircraft fire from the ground. The Fortress was hit and seriously damaged, but continued on the bomb run with one engine ablaze.

After the bomber began to lose altitude, Rabbo gave the order to bail out. But before anyone could jump, a shell scored a direct hit, killing eight of the twelve-man crew. Incredibly, John Morgan was blown out of the bomber with his parachute under his arm. Somehow, while plunging through space, he managed to put on the parachute and landed safely.

Morgan spent the remaining two months of the war in Europe as a "guest" of the German government. He made no mention of his miraculous escape from death to fellow POWs, knowing that they would not believe him.[12]

Pilot's Prayer Gets Results

NAZI GERMANY WAS hemmed in by Allied armies on three sides. Now its hard-pressed *Heer* (army) deployed along the eastern bank of the historic Rhine River was about to be struck by an enormous thunderclap from the blue, the mightiest simultaneous airborne assault that history had known. It was code-named Operation Varsity.

Within a time span of about two and a half hours, 17,122 American and British paratroopers and glider soldiers would land on an airhead measuring five miles deep and six miles wide. It would be the most congested concentration of airborne warriors ever attempted.

Early on the morning of March 24, 1945, the U.S. 17th "Thunder from Heaven" Airborne Division began lifting off from airfields in central France. At the same time, the British 6th "Red Devils" Airborne Division took to the skies from airfields in southeastern England. The two flights rendezvoused over Belgium and the 1,545 aircraft carrying the paratroopers and towing about 1,300 gliders formed a stream stretching back for a hundred miles.

At about 10 o'clock in the morning, scores of gliders were cut loose from their tug planes, east of the Rhine, and they began crash landings at speeds up to ninety miles per hour.

Flight Officer Harold W. Morgan, whose glider was packed with mortar shells, brought his craft to a hard but otherwise routine landing. That in itself was a feat. Most glider pilots felt that a successful landing was one in which they suffered only two broken legs.

Morgan, his copilot, and four glider soldiers had no time to offer up thanks for their good fortune. They recognized that they had come to a halt less than a hundred yards from a house filled with German soldiers, who began raking the Americans with small-arms fire.

The four passengers scrambled out of the glider without being hit, but the copilot was struck by bullets in the chest and throat as he was going out the door. Morgan jumped out right behind the seriously wounded man and was not hit.

As streams of bullets poured into the glider, the six Americans were sprawled facedown only yards away. Aware that the craft was loaded with mortar shells, Morgan called out, "We're going to have to get the hell out of here before she blows up!"

"Hey, you guys," the injured copilot pleaded, "don't leave me, I'm dying!"

Now the German fire was growing more intense. Morgan glanced upward and said, "Please, God, get us out of here alive—and help me find a medic for my copilot."

Morgan said to the injured man, "You're going to have to get to your feet and run with us to that pond over there, or we'll all get blown to hell when this thing explodes!"

Gritting his teeth in agony, the copilot pulled himself up, and the six beleaguered Americans made it safely to the pond fifty yards away.

Moments after reaching the pond, Morgan's prayer was answered favorably. A glider crammed with medics crunched to a halt alongside the prone men. Two of the passengers leaped out and began ministering aid to the copilot, saving his life.[13]

Glider Used as a Weapon

IN THE SKIES OVER THE REGION east of the Rhine, scores of American gliders were cut loose from their C-47 transport plane tugs and their pilots were searching for suitable strips of ground on which to crash-land. It was D Day for Operation Varsity, March 24, 1945.

One of the glider pilots was Lieutenant Robert H. Price, a veteran of three previous combat missions in Europe. Although glider pilots assume the role of infantryman once they have brought their craft to a halt and discharged soldiers and cargo, Price had never as much as fired his Tommy gun at a German soldier.

Price's glider was drifting toward a landing when a German soldier leaped from a foxhole in the glider path and began dashing toward a house a short distance away. Seeing the glider bearing down on him, the German glanced over his shoulder, squeezed off two wild shots from his rifle, and began zigzagging.

Price was determined to personally bag at least one enemy soldier during his combat in Europe, so he altered the rudder to pursue the panicky soldier. Again, the German fired a couple of rounds, and then changed his course again. Price realigned his craft on the quarry.

Moments later, the duel was over. Price slammed the glider into the German. This may have been the only time in the war that an American pilot dispatched an armed enemy soldier with a glider.[14]

His Masseur Coerces Himmler

Felix kersten, a mild-mannered, short man, had a unique place in the Nazi scheme of things. He had no medical degree, but he called himself Doctor, as did his wealthy and influential clients in the Third Reich who flocked to him for his "manual therapy" services. Kersten, no doubt, was the only masseur in Germany who held such a lofty title.

Kersten's most famous client was Reichsführer Heinrich Himmler, a one-time chicken farmer who rose in influence and prestige after hooking up with a promising politician named Adolf Hitler in the mid-1920s. Himmler clawed his way to near the top of the Nazi totem pole, and as commander of the Schutzstaffel (SS) elite military force and chief of the Geheime Staatzpolizei (Gestapo) he became the Third Reich's second most powerful leader.

Just before Adolf Hitler had ignited war in Europe by invading Poland on September 1, 1939, Himmler was stricken with severe stomach pains. Physicians had failed to relieve his suffering, so Felix Kersten was called in. He treated the patient with such success that Himmler would be dependent on him during the years ahead.

In March 1945, Reichsführer Himmler was devoting most of his time and energy to saving his own skin. It was clear that Nazi Germany was on the brink of total collapse, but Hitler had ordered the Gestapo head to murder the hundreds of thousands of prisoners in concentration camps before they could be liberated by the Allies.

Himmler, again bothered by stomach pains, was being treated by Dr. Kersten, who had become quite influential with his celebrated patient. In fact, the masseur was one of the few men in Germany who could speak his mind, even criticize, the reichsführer without fear of being executed.

Now Kersten apparently brought up the topic of the concentration camp prisoners. Himmler told him of Hitler's extermination order, and the masseur pleaded with him to ignore the directive. "Those are the führer's direct orders," Himmler said testily, "and I must see to it that they are carried out."

Reichsführer Heinrich Himmler was influenced by his masseur to spare Jews. (National Archives)

Undaunted, Kersten kept hammering away at his patient through manual therapy sessions during the next two weeks. The two men had heated arguments. But finally, the persistent masseur won out. He coerced Himmler into writing on paper a personal pledge to Kersten that he would not have prisoners killed, and that they would remain in the camps to be handed over to the Allies in orderly fashion.

After completing the amazing document, Himmler stared at it for perhaps a minute. Presumably, he didn't believe that he, himself, had made such a pledge, much less put it on paper. But finally he signed the paper, and Kersten politely took it from his patient's hand.

Kersten had scored an extraordinary coup, but he was not finished. During the next few days, as the Third Reich continue to disintegrate, he obtained ever more humanitarian concessions from this patient. He persuaded Himmler to countermand Hitler's order to destroy The Hague and the Zuyder Zee Dam in the Netherlands, and to draft a strict order forbidding cruelty to Jews.

Now Kersten asked the man under whose orders hundreds of thousands of Jews had been murdered in concentration camps to meet face-to-face with Hilel Storch, a leader in the World Jewish Congress, a global organization whose mission was trying to save as many Jews as possible from the Nazi vengeance.

Himmler was shocked. He even seemed to turn whiter. "I can never receive a Jew!" he blurted. "If the führer heard of it, he would have me shot dead on the spot!"

Now Kersten turned to subtle blackmail, reminding the Nazi official that he had already compromised himself by writing and signing several documents in which he pledged to disobey Hitler.

In a weak voice, Himmler gave his consent to set up the meeting with the Jew.

Never in history, perhaps, had a person with such a modest status wrangled such far-reaching concessions from a man with such enormous power.[15]

A Surrender-by-Telephone Tactic

NAZI GERMANY WAS hemmed in on all sides by hostile forces and teetering on the brink of collapse. Powerful Soviet armies were knocking on the gates of Berlin in the east. American, British, Canadian, and French armies were across the broad Rhine River, Germany's traditional barrier to invasion, along a 450-mile front and were plunging deep into the Third Reich. It was late March 1945.

What the Western Allies came to call the Great Rat Race was on. Never in history had so many men—about a million of them—moved so rapidly. All along the front the offensive had taken on the aura of a gigantic contest. Each division was determined to be the first to reach the major objective: the Elbe River about ninety miles from Berlin.

The German opposition was totally unpredictable. Many areas surrendered without a shot being fired. Other cities, mainly those defended by SS troops, fought savagely until wiped out.

In this fluid and crazy tactical situation, creative techniques were employed to secure bloodless surrenders. Captain Francis Schommer of the U.S. 83rd Infantry Division came up with an especially ingenious scheme. Schommer, who spoke fluent German, launched a "surrender-by-telephone" strategy.

Schommer would enter a building where a captured *burgomaster* (mayor) was being held. He would point his pistol at the frightened official and tell him: "It might be a good idea if you telephoned the burgomaster in the next town. Tell him if he wants anything left standing, he better surrender the place—right now. Tell him to get the people to hang white bed sheets from their windows—or there's going to be hell to pay!"

The nervous burgomaster would usually greatly exaggerate the situation to please his captors—and presumably to save his own life. He would tell his neighbor on the telephone that the Americans in his town had hundreds of tanks and artillery pieces, and thousands of soldiers. Actually, there might be a platoon or two of GIs and a couple of tanks.

Captain Schommer's hoax worked time and again. No doubt many American—and German—lives were saved.[16]

Kidnapping Polish Underground Leaders

IN LATE MARCH 1945, Soviet Field Marshal Georgy Konstantinovich Zhukov, perhaps the most successful of Russian generals, was given the honor by Premier Josef Stalin to capture Berlin, now a crumbling mass of ruins after countless Allied bombing attacks. Zhukov's spearheads were only forty miles from the Reich Chancellery, where Adolf Hitler and his entourage were holed up in a bunker.

In the wake of Zhukov's advances, Soviet commissars (political leaders) had fanned out over Poland to solidify the Communists' hold on that peaceful nation. Earlier Stalin had given his word to U.S. President Franklin D. Roosevelt and British Prime Minister Winston S. Churchill that the Red Army would eventually withdraw and Poland would revert to a free nation.

Zhukov's officers had gotten word to leaders of the Polish underground, who had fought the occupying Germans for five years, that the field marshal would like to confer with the Poles to discuss the nation's security and postwar role.

Most of the Pole leaders were hesitant about coming out of hiding, fearing a devious Soviet plot. But other Poles pointed out that the Russians had shown their goodwill by promising to release captured Pole underground leaders, including Alexander Zwierzynski, chairman of a group known as the National Democrats.

The Soviet proposal appeared too good to be true. After the conference with Field Marshal Zhukov the top underground leaders would be flown to London to confer on postwar plans with the Polish government-in-exile.

After much solemn discussion, twelve underground leaders agreed to be taken to see Zhukov. They boarded a Soviet transport plane at the Warsaw airport and received their first indication that all was not going to be as promised. Lying on the floor of the aircraft was Alexander Zwierzynski, who seemed to be in a hazy frame of mind. He told his comrades that the Soviets had kept him in a cell and beaten him regularly. But suddenly he had been hauled out of the enclosure and, without explanation, driven to the airport and hurled aboard the plane.

After the transport was airborne and heading east, a Soviet captain came back into the cabin from the cockpit and announced that there had been a change of plans. Field Marshal Zhukov was too busy to see them, and they were going to Moscow. Now the alarmed Poles were convinced that they were not guests of the Soviets, that they were being kidnapped.

Exhausted and hungry, the Poles reached the Moscow airport. Zbigniew Stypulkowski and two other underground leaders were put into the first automobile. As the small caravan drove through the bleak and cold streets they passed the Foreign Office, which, the Poles had been told, was their destination.

A half hour later the string of cars reached a large, stone building, guarded by Red soldiers. The gate was opened and the caravan entered a yard surrounded by walls with windows covered by steel bars.

Now any hope the bewildered Poles had that they had been flown to Moscow for friendly discussion vanished like wisps of smoke in a hurricane. They realized there they were in the dreaded Lubianka Prison, which held Russia's most hardened criminals along with "enemies of the people," such as the twelve Pole leaders.[17]

El Darbo's Charmed Life

AMERICAN COLONEL William O. Darby was a classic warrior who had led a charmed life on many battlefields in Europe and the Mediterranean. Barrel-chested and energetic, he had formed the commando-like Rangers in mid-1942 and later led them in combat. His men held their leader in great affection and called him El Darbo.

His narrow brushes with death became a legend among the Rangers. In the savage struggle on the Anzio beachhead, a mortar barrage struck his command post near the front lines. His close friend through many battles, Major Bill Martin, was standing next to Darby. One shell killed Martin instantly, but Darby did not receive a scratch.

A short time later, more mortar rounds exploded on Darby's CP (command post) while the colonel was talking to his loyal runner, Corporal Presley Stroud, who was mortally wounded. Three medics were also killed. Darby was unscathed.

On another occasion, the charismatic Ranger leader was in the front lines atop an Italian mountain when a German artillery barrage shook the ground around him. Two Rangers were killed. Shell fragments literally ripped Darby's pants to ribbons, but he did not receive as much as a scratch.

In mid-1944, the American high brass presumably realized that Darby had far exceeded his good fortune, and he was ordered to return to Washington, D.C., to man a desk in the Pentagon. His constant badgering to be sent back to "my boys" fell on deaf ears.

When he did return to Italy in April 1945 it was in the ignominious (to him) role of escorting a group of Pentagon officers on an inspection trip. "A nursemaid," he told a friend.

However, he got a chance to get back into action, but not with the Rangers. The assistant commander of the 10th Mountain Division had been wounded, and Darby was assigned to take his place.

*Colonel William O.
Darby's charmed life
came to an abrupt halt.
(U.S. Army)*

Soon after Darby reached the front lines, a single, random shell hissed in. El Darbo's charmed life was over, and he was killed instantly. Two days later the German army in Italy surrendered.[18]

Air Dogfight with Pistols

HIGH ABOVE AND OUT IN FRONT of the numerous Allied spearheads charging eastward into the Third Reich were Piper Cubs: light, slow, unarmed planes. In one of these craft, U.S. Lieutenant Duane Francies, the pilot, and his observer, Lieutenant William S. Martin, were scouting for the 5th Armored Division. It was April 12, 1945.

The job of the two men was to scour the region for German strong points, tank concentrations, or other targets. They would radio this information to officers riding at the tip of the advancing armored column.

Near the end of one mission, Francies was about ready to head back to a landing in some pasture near the 5th Armored when he looked down and saw a Fieseler Storch, a German spotter plane. It was winging along only a few hundred feet above the ground, no doubt seeking to avoid detection.

Francies knew all about the Storch. It was larger than his Cub and could fly thirty miles per hour faster. Yet, almost in unison Francies and Martin called out to one another, "Let's get the bastard!"

While Francies threw the Cub into a dive, Martin got the side doors open. Steering in a tight circle above the Storch, both Americans leaned out and emptied clips from their .45 Colts. They knew that the pistols were inaccurate and would carry only a short distance, but they hoped to confuse the German pilot into flying even lower where machine gunners in the 5th Armored could blast the Storch out of the sky.

No doubt surprised by the unexpected attack from above, the Storch pilot, instead of flying onward and away from the armored column, began circling wildly. Even as Francies and Martin reloaded their automatics time and again and fired away, the German kept circling.

Dropping to only some twenty-five feet above the Storch, the two Americans pumped bullets into the German's windshield. Martin yelled into his radio, "We got the bastard! We got the bastard!"

The Storch cartwheeled down and crash-landed in a pasture. Francies set his Cub down in an adjoining field, and the two Americans ran to the downed plane. The German pilot and his observer had already climbed out and were holding up their hands in surrender.

Francies and Martin had fought what may have been the final dogfight of the war in Europe. More importantly to the two men, they no doubt were the only airmen in the conflict to shoot down a German plane with a pistol.[19]

Comic Opera in the Bavarian Alps

ON THE NIGHT OF MAY 3, 1945, men of Colonel Robert F. "Bounding Bob" Sink's U.S. 506th Parachute Infantry Regiment were electrified. Only days earlier the outfit had been rushed from northern Germany on a three-hundred-mile trek southeast to the Bavarian Alps. Its mission was to help mop up the remaining German troops in that mountainous region.

Now Colonel Sink received orders directing his regiment to capture Berchtesgaden, the charming Alpine village indelibly linked with Adolf Hitler and Nazism. On a towering peak overlooking the town was the Adlerhorst (Eagle's Nest), the führer's secluded retreat.

Early the next morning, Sink and his men were in a truck convoy hightailing it toward Berchtesgaden, sixty-five miles away. Some seventeen miles from the village, the convoy ground to a new halt. The narrow roads were clogged with General Jacques LeClerc's French 2nd Armored Division and Major General John W. "Iron Mike" O'Daniel's U.S. 3rd Infantry Division.

At General Alexander Patch's U.S. Seventh Army headquarters, a harried staff officer moaned: "Everybody and his brother is trying to get into Berchtesgaden!"

All the while, Germans in the region were surrendering in droves. Then a dramatic message was received by Seventh Army units: "Effective immediately all troops will stand fast. German Army Group B in this sector has surrendered. No firing on Germans unless fired on."

Now rumors were rampant that numerous Nazi bigshots were holed up in the Berchtesgaden region. Colonel Bob Sink received a tip that one of the biggest fish, Field Marshal Albrecht Kesselring, was comfortably ensconced in the *Brunswick*, his private nine-car train parked nearby.

Kesselring, known to the Western Allies as "Smiling Al," had been regarded as one of Germany's most capable commanders. At this time he held the post of Oberfehlshaber Westen (supreme commander in the West).

At the same time Sink was informed about Kesselring's presence, other outfits in the area received similar information, and a mad dash for the *Brunswick* erupted.

A comic-opera scenario unfolded. Within minutes Kesselring's train was ringed by the field marshal's own armed German guards, by soldiers from a U.S. cavalry unit, by GIs from an infantry division, and by Colonel Sink's paratroopers. Except for the grim German bodyguards, everyone was trying to coax Smiling Al out of his private car without creating a ruckus.

While the mixed bag of armed combatants from both sides milled about, reports surfaced that diehard SS troops in the region were planning to launch a raid to "kidnap" Kesselring and keep him out of the clutches of the Americans. Then, the rumor had it, the field marshal would be spirited off high into the Bavarian Alps where he could easily be hidden from the Americans.

For two days, negotiations for the field marshal's surrender continued in his ornate coach. In between sessions, American war correspondents slipped inside to interview one of Germany's most famous and successful commanders. The civilian reporters were wearing American military uniforms, and the German guards apparently presumed them to be high-ranking officers of some kind. So the Germans at the door to Kesselring's coach snapped to attention and saluted each time the newsmen entered or departed.

Finally, the standoff was resolved. Kesselring agreed to surrender, but only to Major General Maxwell D. Taylor, leader of the U.S. 101st "Screaming Eagles" Airborne Division.

The curtain came down on the comic opera.[20]

Collaring a Nazi Bigwig

AT THE COMMAND POST of the U.S. 502nd Parachute Infantry Regiment in Bavaria, Major Henry G. Plitt received an anonymous telephone tip. Julius Streicher, perhaps the most notorious figure in the Third Reich, was holed up in a farmhouse near Waldring. It was May 6, 1945.

*Top Nazi Julius Streicher,
self-styled "Jew-baiter
Number One." (National
Archives)*

Streicher had founded an anti-Semitic party after World War I, and he gave up that organization to join the Nazi Party two years later. At Nuremberg he founded and edited a weekly newspaper, *Der Stürmer,* which was labeled the "world's best-known anti-Jewish publication." It featured crude cartoons, grotesque pictures of Jews, and stories blaming Jews for murders and the spread of pornography.

Streicher was highly regarded by Adolf Hitler, and the coarse, foul-mouthed, self-styled Jew-baiter was among the few the führer addressed with the familiar *Du.*

Now, at his command post, Major Plitt was not too elated about the tip he had received. Tips of Nazi bigshots hiding out in the region flooded American units. However, the report would have to be investigated, so Plitt and a few paratroopers headed for the farmhouse.

There they found a middle-aged bearded man leisurely creating a painting on canvas. He said his name was Erich Sailor.

Major Plitt had seen many photos of Streicher, all without a beard. But after studying the German's face for a few moments, he suddenly exploded: "You're Julius Streicher, you bastard!"

"No, no!" the man protested. "I am a painter. I have never had any interest in politics."

Plitt kept hammering away, and finally the German admitted that he was the Jew-baiter.

No doubt his capture was of special satisfaction to Major Plitt, a highly decorated Jewish officer.[21]

Peculiar "Capture"
of an SS Colonel

THE WAR IN EUROPE had been over for a week when Standartenführer (SS Colonel) Otto Skorzeny and three aides, all in uniform and armed, came down from their hideout in the Bavarian Alps of southern Germany with the intention of surrendering to the Americans. It was May 13, 1945.

Soon the four Germans realized it wouldn't be all that simple. Skorzeny identified himself to an American sergeant, who was one of the few human beings who had never heard of the "Most Dangerous Man in Europe," as Skorzeny was known to the Western Allies. The GI said he had things to do other than hassle with prisoners, but he did obtain a jeep ride for the Germans to Salzburg, where a major U.S. headquarters was located.

Skorzeny and his men tried to enter the building, but were told they would have to wait outside until the American officers in the headquarters had finished their lunch.

Finally a bored American major sauntered outside and he, too, presumably didn't know Skorzeny by reputation. He sent the SS colonel and his companions to another town to pick up orders accepting him as a captive.

One of war's boldest warriors, German SS Colonel Otto Skorzeny, relaxes after his surrender. (U.S. Army)

By the time the Most Dangerous Man in Europe returned to Salzburg, the Americans had awakened from their stupor. The Germans were ordered to wait in a large room off the lobby of the headquarters, and their sidearms were removed before they entered.

Moments later there were loud crashes. In a finely tuned military operation, seven or eight GIs, all armed to the teeth, burst through doors and windows. They surrounded the puzzled and unarmed Skorzeny and aimed their weapons directly at him from a few feet away. They had "captured" the German they now knew was the Most Dangerous Man in Europe.[22]

Stalin's Son in Strange Mission

LATE IN MAY 1945, after Victory in Europe Day, Soviet Army technical intelligence teams were sifting through tons of scientific documents in the Russian-occupied zone of the Third Reich. In the library of one Nazi scientist, who apparently had fled in a hurry on the approach of the Red Army, these experts discovered a design for a revolutionary rocket-powered bomber.

This material was sent to Moscow, where a Soviet expert translated it into Russian and compiled a condensed descriptive report. It was passed up the chain of command and finally reached Iosif Vissarionovich Dzhugashvili, known to the world as Josef Stalin.

The short, shrewd, and ruthless Soviet dictator was intrigued by the report and called a secret conference to discuss it. Among those present were Vasily Stalin, son of the *voshd* (boss); Vyacheslav Molotov, Stalin's secretary and a power in the Communist Party; Lavrenty Beria, chief of the Soviet secret police; and several scientists and technical experts.

In the discussions, Stalin learned that the rocket-bomber concept had been developed over a period of many years by the brilliant German team of Eugen Sänger and Irene Bredt. It envisioned a ninety-two-foot bomber weighing 220,000 pounds, to be launched from a sled driven by power rockets developing 1.3 million pounds of thrust.

The sled would hurl the bomber into the air at 1,000 miles per hour, then its own 200,000-pound-thrust liquid oxygen rocket engine would boost it to a speed of 13,700 miles per hour and an altitude of more than 160 miles.

If built, the manned rocket-bomber would skip along the top of the atmosphere (where no human had ever been) like a stone skipping along a pond. It could reach New York City or Washington, D.C., with a bomb load of six tons, sufficient to cause horrendous damage and casualties.

Sänger and Bredt had calculated that the entire flight, from takeoff to a return landing in Germany, would require only eighty minutes.

Later, Stalin would learn that the fantastic scheme had been finalized too late to help Adolf Hitler. One hundred copies of the Sänger-Bredt report had

Vasily Stalin, the Soviet dictator's son, failed on a secret mission. (National Archives)

been made, marked Top Secret, and circulated to eighty VIPs, a list that read like a Who's Who in German rocket and aircraft design. But in the beleaguered Reich, with enemy armies closing in on three sides, few, if any, of the recipients had the time or inclination to wade through 409 pages of technical detail.

Now, in the Kremlin in Moscow, scientists had finished their briefings on the Sänger-Bredt report. Josef Stalin was fascinated by the potential of a craft that could bomb targets a few thousand miles away and was so speedy it could not even be seen, much less shot down or otherwise impeded.

Stalin wanted to know the whereabouts of Eugen Sänger. Secret Police Chief Beria had to confess that he did not know.

"Then have somebody find Sänger and bring him to Moscow," the dictator ordered, adding, "in a voluntary-compulsory manner."

Twenty-four-year-old Vasily Stalin, the dictator's son, either volunteered or was designated to spearhead the hunt for Sänger. A pilot in the Soviet air force, young Stalin flew to Berlin in strict incognito, and called at the headquarters of General I. A. Serov, the commander of the Russian-occupied zone of the city.

Serov sent for Serge Tokaev, his technical advisor, and instructed him to join with Vasily Stalin in tracking down Sänger, who, presumably, was somewhere in Western Europe. If Sänger refused to come along, the general stressed, he was to be kidnapped. "Remember," he added, "Comrade [Josef] Stalin relies on you to produce results."

Lieutenant Colonel Tokaev and young Stalin proved to be birds of a feather. They spent several weeks in the search, first in Berlin, then in Paris. Alarming reports began to float back to General Serov in Berlin: The two investigators were spending more time in German and French nightclubs and assorted shady dives with shady women than they were devoting to the task of locating Eugen Sänger.

Finally, Vasily Stalin and Tokaev reported back to Serov that their mission was a failure. The seemingly elusive target was probably dead, they concluded.

Their failure was a curious one. Sänger and Irene Bredt, a mathematical whiz, had been married in recent months and were living quite openly, with no secrecy, under their real names.

When Americans combing the Third Reich for scientists began looking for Sänger, they had no trouble locating him. Interrogated at length, the scientist was highly cooperative. He even gave a copy of his rocket-bomber report to the U.S. officers.

In the next few years, the Sänger report played a major role when scientists in the United States were developing a huge rocket with sufficient thrust to lift it to the moon.[23]

A Scheme to Blow Up Japan

AFTER THE SURRENDER of Germany in May 1945, the focus of the Americans shifted to smashing Japan and destroying her still powerful armed forces. Toward that goal twenty-eight-year-old Navy Commander John Sheehan, an operative of the U.S. Office of Strategic Services (OSS), hatched an incredible scheme.

Sheehan planned to destroy two concrete tubes that provided transportation between the Japanese home islands of Honshu and Kyushu. Such an operation would create turmoil just before General Douglas MacArthur's forces would invade Japan that fall, the OSS agent explained.

Sheehan was given the green light to prepare for the machination. At a secret base in Florida he assembled about two hundred and fifty OSS men and provided them with a flotilla of PT boats, swift eighty-footers loaded with torpedoes and automatic weapons.

This sea armada was to carry newfangled television cameras and fifty thousand pounds of explosives. An airplane flying overhead would direct this tiny fleet by remote control to the targeted tubes.

Before this combined sea and air team could depart for the Pacific, atomic bombs wiped out Hiroshima and Nagasaki.[24]

Odd Interlude on a Train

MAJOR JAMES HAMILL, a graduate of Fordham University with a degree in physics, was summoned to the Pentagon by his boss, Colonel Holger N. "Ludy" Toftoy, chief of the Ordnance Rocket Branch of the Army. The twenty-six-year-old Hamill was told that he had a special mission: Go to New York City and meet seven German scientists who had signed up to perform rocket research for the United States after the collapse of the Third Reich. It was now September 20, 1945.

German rocket genius Wernher von Braun (right) with his "shadow," Major James Hamill. (U.S. Army)

Colonel Toftoy and Major Hamill had worked together a few months earlier in Germany, when, under their direction, the Americans literally stole one hundred huge missiles from the Soviet zone only hours before the Red Army arrived. These rockets were shipped in great secrecy to the White Sands Proving Ground in New Mexico.

After his session with Toftoy, Hamill flew to New York City and looked on as a U.S. Army transport plane touched down at an airport. Emerging was thirty-four-year-old Wernher Magnus Maximillan von Braun, widely regarded as the world's foremost rocket scientist, and six of his associates. They were the vanguard of scores of rocket specialists to follow in the weeks ahead.

Ringing in Hamill's ear was the admonition he had been given by Toftoy: "Jim, I want you to stick with von Braun like glue—twenty-four hours a day!"

There was good reason for this order: the German rocket experts had been brought to the United States under the strictest secrecy. President Harry Truman and other leaders in Washington knew that their services would be crucial in the Cold War that was already raging between the world's only remaining superpowers: the United States and the Soviet Union. The Americans did not want the Soviets to know of the German "brain invasion." And the American people, many of whom had lost loved ones in the war, might react in a hostile manner should word get out that "a bunch of Hitler's scientists" had been brought to the United States.

Major Hamill, in civilian clothes, herded his seven "wards of the Army" (as they were known) onto a train, and the group arrived at Union Station in Washington, D.C., at dawn. Six of the Germans, escorted by Army officers, were taken to the Aberdeen Proving Ground in Maryland. Hamill and von Braun took a Yellow Cab to a leading Washington hotel, where they registered under fictitious names. After they had settled into a two-bedroom suite, a U.S. technical intelligence team began questioning the rocket expert, a procedure that continued off and on for five days.

When the exhaustive interrogation of von Braun was concluded, he and Hamill, now wearing his major's uniform, caught a train for El Paso, Texas, not far from the White Sands installation. At St. Louis, they changed trains, and Hamill learned that the two men were to have sleeping berths in Car O, which was filled with wounded veterans of the U.S. 82nd and 101st Airborne Divisions.

Fearing that an awkward incident might erupt should the wounded GIs learn von Braun's true identity, Hamill arranged for berths in another coach. However, the sleeping accommodations were at opposite ends of the Pullman. So Hamill decided that the two men would pretend that they were not traveling together.

That night the Texas-bound train chugged out of St. Louis's Union Station, and the next morning, after porters had made the berths, Hamill settled in a seat at one end of the coach and conducted long-range surveillance of von Braun, who was involved in an animated conversation with a passenger at the other end.

"Where you from?" von Braun's seatmate asked.

"Switzerland," the rocket genius replied, knowing that the mountainous nation had a large German-speaking population.

The American's eyes lit up. "Switzerland!" he almost shouted. "Why, I've been there many times! What business are you in?"

Usually quite voluble, the German felt that he should say as little as possible. "Steel," he replied.

"What kind of steel?"

"Ball bearings."

Von Braun was uneasy. He knew little about Switzerland and even less about the ball-bearing business. Worse, the other man knew a great deal about the steel business and the ball-bearing industry specifically.

All the while, Major Hamill, at the far end of the coach, was growing steadily more apprehensive, fearful that the customarily talkative German would let slip some clue that the world's foremost rocket expert was in the United States. Hamill could visualize the haunting headlines across the nation: "Prominent Nazi a Guest in the United States."

While von Braun was searching for a peg on which to change the direction of the conversation, the train pulled into Texarkana, on the border of Arkansas and Texas. Much to the scientist's relief, his seatmate got up and said, "Well, here's where I get off."

Rising, von Braun shook hands with the man, just as a nervous Major Hamill walked up and heard the American exclaim: "If it hadn't been for you Swiss, I doubt if we could have beaten those goddamned Germans!"

Hamill struggled to keep from bursting out laughing.[25]

A Soldier's Thirty-Year War

EARLY IN 1945, while the Japanese and the Americans were locked in savage fighting in the Philippines, Army Lieutenant Hiro Onoda stole ashore at night on Lubang in the northern islands. Trained in guerrilla tactics, Onoda's mission was to help a beleaguered Japanese garrison prevent capture of a key airstrip by the Americans.

There was nothing Onoda could do. The defenders were overrun by stronger American forces. The airstrip was seized and most of the Japanese were killed. Lieutenant Onoda, who had been ordered to hold on until reinforcements arrived, escaped into the jungle.

Six months later a Japanese delegation signed a surrender document on the deck of the battleship *Missouri* in Tokyo Bay. The bloody war was over. But not for Hiro Onoda. Newspapers, magazines, and leaflets telling of Japan's capitulation were dropped from airplanes over the thick jungles of Lubang.

Onoda believed that these were American tricks, so he continued to hang on as ordered—for the next thirty years. He lived off the land, and reinforced his resolution each day by reading the *Bushido* code that proclaimed death before dishonor.

Back in Japan, Onoda's loved ones somehow had been made aware that the lieutenant was hiding out on Lubang. Year after year they tried to lure him out, but all their efforts were in vain. In 1975, a young Japanese, Norio Suzuki, hit on a novel scheme to get Onoda to come out of the jungle. Deducing that the refugee would be lonely, he landed on Lubang and pitched a tent as close as possible to where he thought Onoda was holed up. He waited. And waited.

One day Suzuki looked up and saw an apparition, wearing shredded clothing and a long, bushy beard, walking unsteadily toward him. Suzuki was elated. But Onoda refused to violate the Bushido code by "surrendering."

Finally, Onoda's commanding officer of thirty years ago, now a bookseller in Tokyo, was flown to Lubang and read the holdout Emperor Hirohito's 1945 proclamation of surrender. Only then did Onoda agree to capitulate.[26]

Notes and Sources

Part One—A Rocky Road to War

1. **Amazing Encounter at Pier 86**
   Author's archives.
   Leon Turrou, *The Nazi Spy Conspiracy in America* (New York: Books for Libraries, 1949), pp. 150, 153.

2. **A British "Mystery Plane" Vanishes**
   Author's archives.

3. **A One-Man Espionage Apparatus**
   Author's archives.
   Ladislas Farago, *The Game of the Foxes* (New York: McKay, 1971), p. 157.

4. **Recruiting Crossword Puzzle Geniuses**
   Michael Smith, *Station X* (London: Channel Four Books, 1997), pp. 81–82.
   Author's archives.

5. **New York's IRA Hoodwinks Spymaster**
   Author's archives.
   Don Whitehead, *The FBI Story* (New York: Random House, 1956), p. 166.
   Ladislas Farago, *The Game of the Foxes*, p. 511.

6. **Stalking a Soviet Defector**
   Author's archives.
   Walter G. Krivitsky, *In Stalin's Secret Service* (New York: Harper, 1940), pp. 271–273.

7. **Two Spies Roam British Ports**
   Author's archives.

8. **Stealing Secrets by Mail**
   Author's archives.

9. **"Simple Simon" Trips Himself Up**
   Ladislas Farago, *The Game of the Foxes*, p. 261.
   Author's archives.

10. **A Taxi Ignores Theory**
    Author's archives.
    Stephen Budiansky, *Battle of Wits* (New York: The Free Press, 2000), p. 162.
    Anthony Cave Brown, *Bodyguard of Lies* (New York: Harper & Row, 1975), p. 71.

11. **The IRA Bilks the Abwehr**
    Author's archives.

12. **Clash of Two Top Nazis**
    William L. Shirer, *The Rise and Fall of the Third Reich* (New York: Simon & Schuster, 1960), p. 684.

Documents on German Foreign Policy 1918–1945, Messages of Dr. Hans Thomsen, *DGFP*, Series 13 (Washington, D.C.: National Archives).
Author's archives.

13. **Hitler's Pipeline into Washington**
Author's archives.
Messages of Dr. Hans Thomsen, *DGFP*, IX, Series 13 (Washington, D.C.: National Archives).

14. **A Senator Helps a German Spy**
Anthony Cave Brown, *Bodyguard of Lies*, p. 224.
Author's archives.

15. **A Peculiar River Crossing**
Rupert Butler, *The Black Angels* (New York: St. Martin's Press, 1979), p. 45.
Author's archives.

16. **Dame Fate Saves General Rommel**
Author's archives.

17. **Going in Style to a POW Camp**
Author's archives.

18. **Clanging Bells Rock Germany**
Author's archives.

19. **Did Prime Minister's Mistress Influence Surrender?**
André Pertinax, *The Gravediggers of France* (Garden City, N.Y.: Doubleday, 1944), p. 509.
Alistair Horne, *To Lose a Battle* (Boston: Little Brown, 1969), p. 177.
Author's archives.

20. ***Venus de Milo* Fools Germans**
Author's archives.

Part Two—The Allies' Hours of Crises

1. **Mission: "Nazify" a Conquered Nation**
Author's archives.

2. **Curfew for Dutch Dogs and Ducks**
Author's archives.

3. **Wild Schemes for Saving England**
Gerald Pawle, *The Secret War* (New York: Sloane, 1957), pp. 42, 250.
Author's archives.

4. **Curious Duel in British Skies**
Author's archives.

5. **A German Pilot's Unlikely Captor**
Author's archives.

6. **The Royal Navy's Invisible Ship**
Gerald Pawle, *The Secret War*, p. 184.
Author's archives.

7. **Hitler's Plot to Murder Franco**
Hugh Thomas, *The Spanish Civil War* (New York: Harper, 1961), p. 82.

A. Russell Buchanan, *The United States and World War II* (New York: Harper, 1962), p. 151.

Author's archives.

8. **A Cleaning Woman Foils Hitler**
Author's archives.
Don Whitehead, *The FBI Story*, pp. 227–228.
Edwin P. Hoyt, *U-Boats Offshore* (New York: Stein & Day, 1978), p. 73.

9. **The Battle of the Birds**
Author's archives.

10. **Roosevelt in a Shouting Match**
Author's archives.
OSS Report A22884A, "Ireland as a source of information to the Germans" (Washington, D.C.: National Archives).

11. **Democracy in a Battlefield Hospital**
Author's archives.
Ronald H. Bailey, *Partisans and Guerrillas* (Alexandria, Va.: Time-Life Books, 1978), p. 55.

12. **Strange Means for Urgent Warning**
Cordell Hull, *Memoirs* (New York: Harper, 1948), p. 1025.
Author's archives.
Stanley Weintraub, *Long Day's Journey into War* (New York: Dutton, 1991), p. 229.

13. **A Dedicated Blood-Bank Volunteer**
Author's archives.

14. **The Spymaster's Peculiar Scheme**
Author's archives.

15. **A Pursuit of Bugs and Lice**
Bradley F. Smith, *The Shadow Warriors* (New York: Basic Books, 1983), p. 104.
Author's archives.
Don Congdon, ed., *Combat WW II* (New York: Arbor House, 1958), p. 87.

16. **A Cantankerous Torpedo**
Sharon A. Maneki, *The Quiet Heroes* (Fort Meade, Md.: National Security Agency, 1996), p. 204.
Geoffrey S. Ballard, *On Ultra Active Service* (Victoria, B.C.: Privately printed, 1991), p. 148.
Author's archives.

17. **Curious Death of a German Bigwig**
Albert Speer, *Inside the Third Reich* (New York: Macmillan, 1970), pp. 191–192.
Author's archives.

18. **Ernest Hemingway Stalks U-Boats**
Dan van der Vat, *The Atlantic Campaign* (London: Grafton, 1990), p. 347.
Author's archives.

19. **Fluke Saves a British Fleet**
Author's archives.
Samuel Eliot Morison, *U.S. Naval Operations in World War II*, vol. 4 (Boston: Little, Brown, 1962), p. 125.
Ludovic Kennedy, *Pursuit* (London: Collins, 1974), pp. 155–156.

20. **The War's Craziest Wedding Scenario**
Faith Bradford, *Elizabeth J. Somers* (Norwood, Mass.: Plimpton, 1947), p. 31.
Washington Post, November 25, 1942.
David Brinkley, *Washington Goes to War* (New York: Knopf, 1988), p. 117.

21. **Two WACs on a Secret Mission**
David Alvarez, *Secret Messages* (Lawrence: University Press of Kansas, 2000), p. 124.
Author's archives.

22. **Strange Place for Royal Jewels**
Robert H. Alcorn, *No Bugles for Spies* (New York: McKay, 1962), pp. 145–146.
Author's archives.

Part Three — The Tide Starts to Turn

1. **Navajo Code-Talkers Ignite Panic**
Alison Bernstein, *American Indians and World War II* (Norman: University of Oklahoma Press, 1991), p. 56.
Author's archives.
Nathan Aaseng, *Navajo Code Talkers* (New York: Walker, 1992), p. 41.
Colliers, November 1944.

2. **Adolf Hitler Plays Santa Claus**
Files of Canadian General Staff Historical Section, 1939–1946, Ottawa.
Author's archives.

3. **Purple Heart Stripped from Sailor**
Associated Press report, June 1943.

4. **Saga of Top-Secret Maps**
Author's archives.

5. **Eisenhower Aide Helps Trick Germans**
Author's archives.
Anthony Cave Brown, *Bodyguard of Lies*, p. 563.
Harry C. Butcher, *My Three Years with Eisenhower* (New York: Simon & Schuster, 1946), p. 127.

6. **The General's Pants Go AWOL**
Author interview with four-star General Mark W. Clark (Ret.), November 1983.

7. **Mystery of the Vanishing Report**
Author's archives.
Anthony Cave Brown, *Bodyguard of Lies*, p. 260.
Stephen Roskill, *The War at Sea* (London: HMSO, 1954), p. 213.

8. **Hostile Horsemen Chase Airplane**
Author interview with Lieutenant General William P. Yarborough (Ret.), 1994.

9. **A Dead Sergeant Walks Away**
Author's archives.
Danger Forward: The Story of the 1st Infantry Division (Washington, D.C.: Privately printed, 1947), pp. 72, 86.

10. **A Tank Commander's Close Call**
George F. Howe, *Northwest Africa* (Washington, D.C.: Chief of Military History, 1947), p. 112.

11. **Espionage in the Vatican**
R. Harris Smith, *OSS* (New York: Delta, 1972), p. 84.
Author's archives.

12. **OSS Agent's Hidden Bribes**
Author's archives.

13. **An Unlikely Spy Scores Coup**
Author's archives.

14. **Eisenhower Disclosure Stuns Reporters**
Author interview with John H. "Beaver" Thompson, 1994.
Author's archives.

15. **A Horrendous Bombing Error Pays Off**
Wesley Craven and James Cate, eds. *Europe: Torch to Pointblank* (Chicago: University of Chicago Press, 1949), pp. 327–328.
Author's archives.

16. **Freak Encounter in No-Man's-Land**
Author interview with Edwin M. Sayre, 1993.

17. **A Mule-Borne Commander**
Author interview with Willard R. Follmer, 1993.

18. **The Captain Refused to Be Killed**
Author interview with Major Max Shelley (Ret.), 1995.
Author interview with Virgil Carmichael, 1999.

19. **Two GIs Beat Patton to Goal**
Author interview with Colonel Carlos C. Alden (Ret.), 1993.
Author's archives.

20. **"Prescriptions" for the Lady Spy**
Author's archives.

21. **Huge Bonus for a Jungle Spy**
Allison Ind, *Allied Intelligence Bureau* (New York: McKay, 1958), pp. 41–42.
Author's archives.
Charles A. Willoughy, *MacArthur* (New York: McGraw-Hill, 1954), p. 76.

22. **"The Madame" Was a Secret Agent**
Robert H. Alcorn, *No Bugles for Spies*, pp. 97–98.
Author's archives.

23. **A Movie Fan on Bougainville**
William F. Halsey, *Admiral Halsey's Story* (New York: McGraw-Hill, 1947), p. 185.
Author's archives.

24. **A GI Carries His Eyeball**
Author interview with Dr. Robert Akers, 1996.
Author interview with Charles H. Doyle, 1992.

Part Four—Beginning of the End

1. **An Odd Place for Spying**
Author's archives.

2. **Hitler's "Creatures" at Anzio**
Author's archives.

3. **American Spymaster Shocks London**
   Author's archives.
   Robert H. Alcorn, *No Bugles for Spies*, p. 37.

4. **Exciting Races on a Beachhead**
   Author's archives.
   Robert H. Adleman and George Walton, *The Devil's Brigade* (Philadelphia: Chilton, 1996), p. 146.

5. **A Social Visit to the Enemy**
   Author's archives.

6. **The Spy Who Spent the War in Bed**
   Robert H. Alcorn, *No Bugles for Spies*, pp. 102–105.
   Author's archives.

7. **Secret Agent Saved by a Blacksmith**
   Author's archives.

8. **A Bomb Explodes Too Late**
   A. B. Sanford, *Force Mulberry* (New York: Morrow, 1954), p. 117.
   Author's archives.
   Gerald Pawle, *The Secret War*, p. 266.

9. **An Ingenious Escape Artist**
   Ronald H. Bailey, *Prisoners of War* (Arlington, Va.: Time-Life Books, 1980), p. 25.
   Author's archives.

10. **A Prophetic German Cook**
    Author's archives.

11. **Gods Smile on Teddy Roosevelt Jr.**
    Author's archives.

12. **"Don't Worry . . . I'll Shoot You First!"**
    From a speech by Ambassador David K. E. Bruce to a reunion of OSS veterans, Washington, D.C., May 26, 1971. As quoted in the *Washington Star*.

13. **An Enemy Saves "Father Sam"**
    Author interview with Major General Francis L. Sampson (Ret.), 1997.

14. **Firefighters Center of Attention**
    Author's archives.

15. **The "Mess Sergeant" Was a Lady**
    Author's archives.

16. **Massacre in the Wrong Village**
    Author's archives.

17. **A General Turned Fire Chief**
    Author's archives.

18. **The Great Soap Bubble Scheme**
    Gerald Pawle, *The Secret War*, p. 252.
    Author's archives.

19. **A Triumph for Two OSS Men**
    Russell Braddon, *The White Mouse* (New York: Norton, 1956), pp. 210–211.
    Author's archives.

20. **Four Newsmen Bag a German Platoon**
Author interview with John H. "Beaver" Thompson, 1991, *Chicago Tribune*, August 1, 1944.
Author's archives.

21. **German Shoot-Out among Themselves**
Author's archives.
The Invasion of Southern France (Washington, D.C.: U.S. Army, 1948), pp. 128–129.
Jacques Robichon, *Le Debarquement de Provence* (Paris: Laffont, 1962), pp. 67, 70.

22. **Ordeal for Missing Identical Twins**
Author's archives.

23. **Parachute Pack Saves Trooper**
Author interview with Dr. William W. Lumsden, 1991.

24. **Drone Boats Go Berserk**
Author's archives.
Vincent K. Lockhart, *T-Patch to Victory* (Canyon, Tex.: Staked Plains Press, 1981), p. 7.

25. **"Am I Having Hallucinations?"**
Author's archives.

26. **A Doctor Captures a German Hospital**
John W. Warren, *Airborne Missions in the Mediterranean* (Washington, D.C.: Department of the Air Force, 1955), pp. 147–148.
Author's archives.
Author interview with Dr. Judson I. Chalkley, 1992.

27. **A Colonel's Unique "Uniform"**
Author's archives.

Part Five—Allied Road to Victory

1. **Banzai Charge in a POW Camp**
Author's archives.

2. **A Nazi Zealot Obeys His Führer**
Author's archives.

3. **Miracle Saves Woman Spy's Life**
Robert H. Alcorn, *No Bugles for Spies*, pp. 110–111.
Gertrude Legendre, *Sands Ceased to Run* (New York: William-Fredrick, 1947), pp. 98, 112, 242.
Author's archives.
Elizabeth P. McIntosh, *Sisterhood of Spies* (Annapolis: Naval Institute Press, 1998), pp. 136–140.

4. **The War's Unexplained Mystery**
Author's archives.

5. **Dutch Boys Capture Nine Germans**
Author interview with Major General Francis L. Sampson (Ret.), 1996. As a Catholic chaplain in the 101st Airborne Division, he had learned of the episode at the time of the Holland invasion.

6. **Luck Runs Out for the Blue Goose**
   Author's archives.

7. **"Baby Patrol" in No-Man's-Land**
   Author's archives.
   John Devaney, *America Storms the Beaches* (New York: Walker, 1993), p. 126.

8. **Providence Saves a Polish Spy**
   Joseph E. Persico, *Piercing the Reich* (New York: Viking, 1979), pp. 250–252.
   Author's archives.
   William J. Casey, *The Secret War Against Hitler* (Washington, D.C.: Regnery Gateway, 1988), pp. 147, 149.

9. **The Choirboys Plot to Doom Hitler**
   Author's archives.
   R. Harris Smith, *OSS*, p. 222.

10. **"Kidnapping" a Thirty-Ton Tank**
    Author's archives.

11. **A Hero "Resigns" from the Navy**
    Author interview with U.S. Navy Captain Stanley Barnes (Ret.), 1995.
    Author interview with U.S. Navy Commander Edward J. Garvey (Ret.), 1998.

12. **A Jeep Bonanza for "Scarface Otto"**
    Author's archives.

13. **A Peculiar Reception Committee**
    Author's archives.
    New York Times, December 18, 1944.

14. **Hitler Humbles His Generals**
    Author's archives.

15. **History Repeats for German Colonel**
    Author's archives.
    John Toland, *Battle* (New York: Random House, 1959), p. 41.

16. **A Jinxed Town in Belgium**
    John Toland, *Battle*, pp. 212, 240.
    Author's archives.
    Hugh Cole, *The Ardennes* (Washington: Department of the Army, 1952), pp. 327–328.

17. **A Belgian Woman Halts the Panzers**
    Author's archives.

18. **Hex by a Lieutenant's Pal**
    Author interviews with Hoyt R. Livingston and Kenneth R. Shaker, 1993.

19. **A Fluke Halts Eisenhower Trip**
    Author's archives.

20. **A GI "Division" of Thieves**
    Author's archives.

21. **The Miracle of Wiltz**
    John Toland, *Battle*, pp. 330, 341.
    Author's archives.

22. **Unique Distinction for a Survivor**
    Author's archives.
    William F. Halsey, *Admiral Halsey's Story*, p. 240.

23. **Digging Up a Revered German Hero**
Alan Bullock, *Hitler* (New York: Harper, 1962), p. 247.
Author's archives.
Anthony Cave Brown, *Bodyguard of Lies*, p. 167.

24. **An Unlikely Battlefield Hero**
Author's archives.
John Devaney, *America Storms the Beaches*, p. 142.

Part Six—A Shaky World Peace

1. **Amazing Scenario in Manila**
Author's archives.
Bertram W. Wright, *The First Cavalry Division in World War II* (Tokyo: Toppan, 1947),
pp. 193–194.

2. **Death Stalks a Navy Pilot**
William F. Halsey, *Admiral Halsey's Story*, p. 270.
Keith Wheeler, *The Road to Tokyo* (Alexandria, Va.: Time-Life Books, 1979), p. 81.
Author's archives.

3. **Shoot-Out at a Boxcar**
Author interview with Brigadier General George M. Jones (Ret.), 1994.
Author's archives.
Author interview with Lieutenant General John J. Tolson (Ret.), 1993.

4. **MacArthur Recaptures His Home**
Author's archives.
Douglas MacArthur, *Reminiscences* (New York: McGraw-Hill, 1963), p. 214.

5. **Offering Up a Bonfire of Money**
Author's archives.

6. **A Tommy-Gunning Pilot**
Author interview with Colonel Henry W. "Hoot" Gibson (Ret.), wartime commander
of the 462nd Parachute Field Artillery Battalion, 1989.
Author's archives.

7. **Gods Smile on German General**
Author's archives.

8. **A Tail Gunner's Miraculous Survival**
Martin W. Bowman, *Castles in the Air* (Wellingborough, England: Stephens, 1984),
p. 191.
Author's archives.

9. **Curious Incident in a Command Post**
Author interview with Haynes W. Dugan, 1994.

10. **Hoax to Seize a Rhine Bridge**
Conquer: The Story of Ninth Army, Infantry Journal Press, 1947, pp. 237–238.
Author's archives.

11. **Churchill "Consecrates" the Siegfried Line**
John Toland, *The Last 100 Days* (New York: Random House, 1966), p. 209.
Author's archives.

12. **An Airman Dodges Certain Death**
Martin W. Bowman, *Castles in the Air*, p. 121.
Author's archives.

13. **Pilot's Prayer Gets Results**
Gerard M. Devlin, *Silent Wings* (New York: St. Martin's Press, 1985), p. 322.
Author's archives.

14. **Glider Used as a Weapon**
Gerard M. Devlin, *Silent Wings*, p. 324.
Author's archives.

15. **His Masseur Coerces Himmler**
Mark M. Boatner III, *Biographical Dictionary of World War II* (Novato, Ca.: Presidio, 1996), p. 218.
Author's archives.
Alan Bullock, *Hitler* (New York: Harper, 1962), p. 306.

16. **A Surrender-by-Telephone Tactic**
Cornelius Ryan, *The Last Battle* (New York: Simon and Schuster, 1966), p. 291.
Author's archives.

17. **Kidnapping Polish Underground Leaders**
Author's archives.
John Toland, *The Last 100 Days*, p. 315.
Dwight D. Eisenhower, *Crusade in Europe* (Garden City, N.Y.: Doubleday, 1948), p. 396.

18. **El Darbo's Charmed Life**
Author interview with Colonel Carlos C. Alden (Ret.), 1992.
Author's archives.

19. **Air Dogfight with Pistols**
Cornelius Ryan, *The Last Battle*, p. 311.
Author's archives.

20. **Comic Opera in the Bavarian Alps**
Author's archives.

21. **Collaring a Nazi Bigwig**
Author's archives.

22. **Peculiar "Capture" of an SS Colonel**
Author's archives.

23. **Stalin's Son in Strange Mission**
Willi Ley, *Rockets, Missiles, and Men in Space* (New York: Viking, 1968), p. 444.
Anthony Cave, Brown, *Bodyguard of Lies*, p. 364.
Author's archives.

24. **A Scheme to Blow Up Japan**
Author's archives.

25. **Odd Interlude on a Train**
Author interview with Walter Wiesman, member of the German rocket team, Huntsville, Alabama, 1993.
Author's archives.

26. **A Soldier's Thirty-Year War**
The New York Times, July 12, 14, 1975.
Author's archives.

Index